LANGUAGE IN RELIGIOUS PRACTICE

A Sacred Hymn in Primal Darkness

Our real father Ñamandu old Number One
Took a little piece out of his own divinity
And the wisdom contained in his own divinity;
And with his wisdom's power to create
Caused flames and a thin fog to come to be.

> Having made himself stand tall,
> Took the wisdom in his own divinity,
> And with his wisdom's power to create,
> Conceived the origins of human speech;
> Out of the wisdom of his own divinity
> And with his wisdom's power to create,
> Created the principles of human speech
> And made them part of his divinity.
> Before the earth was there
> In the middle of that primal darkness,
> Before he had a sense of where things were,
> Our Number One real father Ñamandu
> Created the basic principles of human speech
> And made them part of his divinity.

Having conceived the origins of human speech to come
Out of the wisdom in his own divinity,
And with his wisdom's power to create
Conceived the principles of human love;
Before the earth was there
In the middle of that primal darkness,
Before he had a sense of where things were,
And with his wisdom's power to create
Created the origins of human love.

> Having created the principles of human speech,
> Having created a small supply of human love
> Out of the wisdom in his own divinity,
> And with his wisdom's power to create
> Out of his loneliness he made a single sacred hymn.
> Before the earth was there
> In the middle of that primal darkness,
> Before he had a sense of where things were
> He made a sacred hymn out of his loneliness.

"A Sacred Hymn in Primal Darkness" is excerpted from the English version by Jerome Rothenberg of a Guaraní poem, here adapted in format and punctuation, given a title, and used by permission. See "A Poem for the Origins of Human Speech" in *Alcheringa* [*Ethnopoetics*], No. 3, Winter 1971, pp. 38-40, based on León Cadogan's Spanish translation in *La Literatura de los Guaraníes,* Mexico: Editorial J. Mortiz, 1965.

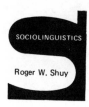

SOCIOLINGUISTICS

Roger W. Shuy

SERIES IN
SOCIOLINGUISTICS

Roger W. Shuy, *Series Editor*
Georgetown University and
Center for Applied Linguistics

The term *sociolinguistics* has been used since approximately the mid-1960s to designate the complex intersection of the fields of language and society. Sociologists have used linguistic data, often referring to the expression, *the sociology of language*, to describe and explain social behavior. Linguists, on the other hand, have tended to make use of social behavior to interpret linguistic variation. Still others have conceived of sociolinguistics in a more practical or applied sense, usually related to social dialects in an educational setting or language teaching. These three perspectives, sociological, linguistic and educational, are all legitimate, for it would be difficult to claim that any one group has an exclusive right to the term. It has become apparent increasingly that those who are interested in the ethnography of speaking, language planning, linguistic variation, the dynamics of language change, language attitudes, pragmatics, multi-lingualism and applied sociolinguistics are all concerned with sociolinguistics in one sense or another. As might be expected in any field, some scholars prefer the more linguistically dominating aspects, some the social or ethnographic, and some the applied or relational. Thus sociolinguistics may be studied in a number of different contexts.

This new series of books will cover a broad spectrum of topics which bear on important and changing issues in language and in society. The significance of social, linguistic, and psychological factors as they relate to the understanding of human speech and writing will be emphasized. In the past most language analyses have not taken these factors into account. The most exciting development of recent linguistic theory and research has been the recognition of the roles of context, variability, the continuum, and cross-disciplinary understanding.

Library of Congress Cataloging in Publication Data
Main entry under title:

Language in religious practice.

(Series in sociolinguistics)
Includes index.
1. Religion and language—Addresses, essays,
lectures. I. Samarin, William J.
BL65.L2L37   200'.1'4   76-17553
ISBN 0-88377-059-8

Series cover design by Lois Jefferson Kordaszewski

NEWBURY HOUSE PUBLISHERS, Inc.

Language Science   Permission to use the
Language Teaching   frontispiece poem is gratefully
Language Learning   acknowledged. See page iii.

68 Middle Road, Rowley, Massachusetts 01969

Printed in the U.S.A.   First printing: November 1976
                                    5   4   3   2   1

Language in Religious Practice

Edited by

William J. Samarin

Professor of Anthropology and Linguistics
University of Toronto

NEWBURY HOUSE PUBLISHERS, Inc. / ROWLEY / MASSACHUSETTS

Acknowledgment

All the chapters in this volume were prepared at the invitation of the Editor, some of them in connection with the session on "Sociolinguistics and Religion" he organized for the Annual Linguistic Round Table at Georgetown University (Washington, D. C., 1972). For their stimulating contributions the Editor is indebted to all who took part in the meeting, but especially to the formal participants: Robert Cromack (State University of New York, Cortland), David Crystal (University of Reading, England), Johannes Fabian (Wesleyan University), Charles A. Ferguson (Stanford University), Dale K. Fitzgerald (University of California, Berkeley), Barbara Kirshenblatt-Gimblett (University of Texas, Austin), Philip L. Ravenhill (New School for Social Research, New York City), Bruce A. Rosenberg (The Pennsylvania State University), D. E. Saliers (Yale Divinity School), Austin J. Shelton (State University College, New Paltz, N. Y.), Dennis Tedlock (Boston University, Massachusetts), and Don Yoder (University of Pennsylvania). The Editor is similarly indebted to the invited participants in the session on "A Sociolinguistic Examination of Religious Behavior" at the Annual Meeting of the Society for the Scientific Study of Religion (Chicago, 1971): Edward Dimock (University of Chicago), Johannes Fabian (Northwestern University), Donald Larson (Bethel College, Minneapolis), and Marvin Meyers (Wheaton College, Illinois). The Editor takes personal responsibility for the way in which this collection is organized and for the chapter summaries.

Contents

Language
in
Religious
Practice

Introduction

1   The Language of Religion

William J. Samarin

During her long imprisonment, Mary Queen of Scots began to contemplate the possibility of death. She wrote to the Pope asking if her sins would be forgiven if, at the moment of death, she could only repeat the words *Jesu, Maria* in her heart rather than saying them aloud.

Students of religion will see in this concern an example of the Christian's view of death and afterlife. Catholics, while commending the believer's faith, may, however, argue over what precisely was required at this crucial moment without a confessor and the last rites. Protestants can cite this case to illustrate the Pope's authority over a Catholic. A sociolinguist sees something entirely different. He sees the way in which language is used in the performance of a religious act. Mary wanted to be certain that she would be doing the right thing, saying the proper words in the required manner. For the theologian this would be an act of faith; for the sociolinguist an act of speaking. The theologian sees in it an expression of a system of belief; the sociolinguist a realization of patterns of language use. Mary was taking for granted the priority of audible speech.

Sociolinguistics, the study of language in relation to social realities, examines religion only because it is another domain of human behavior where language is an important component. Its primary allegiance is to linguistics, the science of language. Within this discipline it has its own goals and methodologies. But because it is *socio*-linguistics, it draws from and contributes to a wide range of studies. The papers in this volume illustrate the interdisciplinary implications of this field.

It will be useful to summarize what is meant by a sociolinguistic examination of religion, for when we talk about "the language of religion" or "language in religious practice," we mean something quite different from what philosophers and theologians mean by these expressions.

Sociolinguistics

The way people use language is our concern. (Speech, instead of language, might be a more appropriate term if it were not for the fact that every means of linguistic expression must be examined, the written no less than the spoken.) Linguistics deals with the complex system of rules (the grammar) that permits a set of speakers abiding by the rules to verbally interact with each other. In contrast, sociolinguistics studies the ways speakers select products of their grammar (one might call them texts or discourse) according to social variables. Sociolinguistics is concerned therefore with choices or decisions that speakers make (a) where the linguistic code (or grammar) permits and (b) where these choices have cultural significance.

It is axiomatic to our approach that speakers of all languages, according to the patterns of their respective speech communities, have many ways of speaking that require selection, according to what—in a given setting—may be obligatory or more appropriate. (The *meaning* of any choice is, of course, a separate problem.) Even in a monolingual community there are different ways of talking. If there is a *formal* manner distinct from an *informal,* it differs, for example, in vocabulary, sentence structure, and diction. There are frequently other options as well: different dialects (rural vs. urban, working class vs. middle class) or different languages. In a broad sense, any of these ways of talking can be called a *language*; and if it is consistently used with religion, it would be appropriate to call it the *religious language.*

The linguistic repertoire of a community is only one of its sociolinguistic dimensions. Another set of variables is represented by the genres of discourse: conversation, narrative, prayer, divination, or sermon for instance. These have linguistic features, as some of the papers in this volume illustrate, that submit to careful analysis and description.

In another sense, then, a *religious language* is the product of the intersection of language variables of different sorts within this one domain of human experience. It is this localization of ways of using language in a given sphere of social action that attracts sociolinguistic attention, for we expect to find here, as elsewhere, linguistic means responding to social motivation and having cultural meaning.

The *motives* for linguistic choices stem from such factors as place, time, topic of discourse, participants (role of speaker, nature and size of audience), or nature of the speech act. One needs only to think of different sorts of Protestant prayers to begin to understand how these variables intersect with each other to produce such prayer events as invocations, blessings, and meal-time prayers.

For *meaning* we need only find a recognition of what is deemed appropriate. It may be acceptable in a given Protestant church to use contemporary pronouns while praying in Sunday school, but the main worship service requires the use of *thee* and *thou.* For every speech community, whether it be a whole denomination on a national scale or the congregation of one church in this denomination, there are taken-for-granted expectations for the way language will be used and for what purposes: at ritualized worship services, weddings, funerals, or hospital visits by the clergy, for example.

If sociolinguistics brings a new perspective to religious studies, as indeed it does, we should expect to learn more about the nature of religious practice: how it is structured and how it relates to other aspects of a given culture; and we should surely refine our generalizations about universal religious practices. This is not a premature hope, for we already have a promise in this direction in this present collection that deals with Christianity, Judaism, Hinduism, and three different traditional or folk religions; with praying, preaching, and the reading of religious texts; with private and public events; with social relations in religious settings; with history and change.

Sociolinguistic studies of religion seek to determine the way in which language is exploited for religious ends. We start with no different assumptions. For us religion is no unique domain of experience; we do not begin our examination of religious language *expecting* to find here what we might not find elsewhere. Whatever validity we might claim for religious propositions, we insist on the inescapable fact of the thoroughly human, therefore common and accessible, mediation of religious experience.

There are theologians in the Christian tradition who accept the human mediation of religious faith through language but who also claim that language serves religious ends. They go even further to insist that language is transformed or is adapted to the expression of religious propositions. Religious language is therefore unique; it is more than ordinary language serving a religious purpose. Then they take the product and make it a tool, using language not only as a hermeneutical device for the explication of religious assertions but even as a means to defend their validity. Language is crucial in contemporary theological discussion. (There must be scores of books on religious language or *God-talk.*) One such linguistic philosopher even claims that the crisis in Roman Catholic thinking, if not in all Christendom, is really a linguistic one.

Sociolinguistics may have some bearing on religious language as philosophically understood. For the time being, however, our goals are modest. We aim for a kind of ethnography of religious language; and although we do not begin with the a priori notion of the uniqueness of religious linguistic usage, we should be happy if we were to discover it.

This uniqueness or domain specificity of language in religion would be found in any number of points where sociolinguistic variables intersect. In the following pages we discuss some of the functions, ends, or goals that language serves in religion, the various kinds of linguistic resources that are exploited, and some of the social processes that characterize the use of language.

Religious ends

Whatever the term *religion* might comprehend, language serves in a number of ways to set it apart from the profane or nonreligious. This specialization might be expected with practices that occur only within this domain (as with prayers), but a religious event elicits appropriate speech even when the separate parts are neutral (like announcements in a church service). Within a single religion there may be different levels of perception or experience. At the one extreme are found the numinous or mystical, like the use of the sacred syllable *ōm* in Hinduism (Christian),[1] Piyyut hymns with esoteric vocabulary in Judaism (Rabin), and "holy words" in an African independent church (Turner 1967).

Religious communities, defined simply as groups adhering to a given set of beliefs and practices, also are set apart linguistically. The fact that language is used as an ethnic boundary marker, symbolic of social oneness, is not itself in any way surprising, but we need to give attention to the way in which language is used to reinforce the social identity: Arabic is the sacred language of all Muslims; the Chamula language is part of the Fourth (and best) Creation; the Amish insist that if their children are taught in English the Amish way of life will disappear. Language is either looked at in very pragmatic terms or it is made integral to the ideology of the community. In either case this leads to legitimating linguistic theories (like those of contemporary theology just mentioned) that need to be studied for their own sake.

The range of linguistic resources used in social marking is broad but still relatively limited. The least interesting perhaps are instances of language differences inherited from migration, conquest, and the like. Thus, the immigrant Molokan and Doukhabor sectarians of the United States and Canada continue to use Russian in all of their religious events in spite of the fact that in the Molokan case an urban environment leads to intense and intimate interaction with the dominant language. More interesting are cases where linguistic differences are asserted in unilingual settings. The Ashkenazi-Sephardi differences with respect to the pronunciation of Hebrew is not really an example, because these differences are the result of the geographical separation of these communities in the past. This is just a case of dialect speakers finding themselves living together. A better field for study would be the linguistic usage of Israeli youth who have been indoctrinated in Modern Israeli and have experimented with new synagogue liturgies. What we seek to know is how people establish a new social identity.

The assertion of a new social identity can, of course, be accomplished by adopting an entirely different language as the religious one. Pidgin Sango is the Protestant language of the Central African Republic even where there is no need for it, as in unilingual villages. But social change can lead to new feelings of identity that revive interest in the native language. (This happened with those ethnic groups in the Cameroun Presbyterian church that had used Bulu as lingua franca and as religious language.) On the other hand, the "new" language may be an old one that is disguised or one that is drastically altered. Argots or "secret languages"—where intelligibility, perhaps minimal, is possible—are often of the first type. Of the second type are pseudolanguages. Cargo cults in the Papua-New Guinea area have arisen with "new languages" that are hardly more than a mish-mash of words from non-native languages (Worsley 1957).

New "languages" in a different sense, more accurately argots, arise in a new movement as the effect of the new ideology. The emergence of Spiritualist churches in the last century, for example, led to an argot where words as common as *see* and *feel* have special meanings (Zaretsky 1972).

In the present discussion the word "language" is an ambiguous one, for it refers both to form and function in the dynamics of interaction. It should be made clear that in religion, as in other human experience, the replacement of one language by another need not be complete either for form or for function. The practitioners of a religion require only that the "language" fulfill its immediate function. A Spiritualist minister must certainly give the impression of talking English even though her ambiguous messages only provide suggestions to a seeker for getting its meaning. There is less need for satisfying intellectual requirements in a Rhodesian spirit-cult rite (Blakney 1969), with Pentecostal glossolalia (Samarin 1972a), or in a Ceylonese healing ritual (Tambiah 1968).

The need, of course, is determined by the given religious phenomenon, and it is a product of several factors. For example, "identifying one's social identity" can include conversion experiences and initiation rites, but it can occur without them. Becoming a member of the neo-Pentecostal movement, for example, necessitates the learning of its argot as in Spiritualist churches. A person is not incorporated into such social units as a prayer fellowship, church congregation, or weekend retreat simply because he assents to the group's belief, but also because he can *talk* about it. From one point of view, therefore, Pentecostal talk is more important than glossolalia in this movement. Yet glossolalia is the linguistic evidence, traditional Pentecostal doctrine claims, of the new religious experience. De facto socialization into the movement is through the argot; the symbol of the new social reality is glossolalia. The convert to Pentecostalism therefore acquires two "new" languages.

An argot is undoubtedly learned when one becomes a member of the Jamaa movement in Zaire (Fabian 1971), for there are many Swahili words whose meanings are peculiar to the movement. But full membership, which is formal and explicit, is achieved by going through four stages of initiation, each characterized by a specific kind of speech event and reflecting kinds or qualities of personal relationships established during this process. (*Jamaa* means *family* in Swahili.)

Time is only one of the factors that determines the nature of the language of initiation. Where neophytes are brought into cult membership during a relatively brief training period, the acquisition of a real foreign language is virtually impossible, but disguised forms of languages and pidgins are more accessible. Easier yet are pseudolanguages. Glossolalia is such an effective initiation symbol. It marks the precise moment when a seeker at a revival meeting gets "the experience." (Many people like to remember the precise day and hour when this happened.)

It would be a mistake to think that language serves religious ends without being influenced by or venturing into the profane world. We thus find language being used to support structure and privileged position. In Spiritualist churches the four ranks in leadership are characterized by the right to use certain argot terms, each rank using terms from those available to the lower one(s), but not vice versa. The minister is alone at the top, and she can discipline the colleague who violates the rule. Igbo go to shrine priests to have prayers said to certain capricious gods, but these priests are descendants from former conquerors who still have political power in the villages (Shelton). Members of a Kewa cult in New Guinea use their argot to extort food from unwary fellow villagers (Franklin, Ms.). This is possible, because the argot consists of words and expressions that replace standard Kewa words that, on the initiative of the cult, have become taboo: for example, *ipa agi,* literally "water mother" for *nogo* (girl). The villager who mistakenly violates the taboo is required to atone with a payment of pigs or pearl shells.

Linguistic means

It is a sociolinguistic premise that speech is adapted to culturally relevant functions. In a description of the linguistic means at the disposal of religion we are concerned with the parts of language that are exploited and the products of the exploitation.[2] Substitutes for native language have already been mentioned: a switch from English to Hebrew or an argot or a pseudolanguage. But even without these more or less drastic departures from normal speech, special varieties of native language can be built with available resources or with an admixture from other languages. The result is a register or style. There is, for example, a testimony-giving style among traditional Pentecostals (such as the Assemblies of God) that consists of rapid delivery at a flat and higher-than-usual level of pitch. Cutting across different genres of discourse such as sermons, prayers, and testimonies is the practice of breaking speech up into rhythmic units, sometimes punctuated by verbal ejaculations or grunts. (On sermons see Rosenberg 1970 and Samarin 1972b.) Many other examples of styles that are peculiar to certain kinds of religious acts are found in the following chapters (especially Crystal, Tedlock, and Christian).

The general picture for religion, then, is similar to that for other domains of experience. Religion may not be unique in its inventory of linguistic resources, but it may be with respect to their predominance. That which in other domains is infrequent may in religion be frequent. This would seem to be the case with the use of anomalous utterances of the *mumbo-jumbo* and *abracadabra* type. (Here too the form-function relationship cannot be ignored. Remember that what is linguistically "normal" in the cognitive-denotative sense may in its magical use be meaningless. Examples are to be found in the repetitive verbalization of names, words, or sentences. The adherent of a "high" religion may thus be the religious brother of an adherent of a "low" religion in a specific use of language, if not in the form used.)

Perhaps, however, there is a higher-level typology of which the use of anomalous speech is just one instance. It appears that in religion greater liberty is taken to satisfy the esthetic appreciation for the substance of language. The average man does not have an opportunity to speak in metered units, but he can do this when he prays or repeats a spell. This happens in extemporaneous Pentecostal prayers (since Pentecostals are hardly given to liturgical ones), but satisfying sounds (the alliteration is deliberate in this nonreligious essay) are also provided in the corpus of religious texts.

Repetitive patterns are pointed out explicitly in this volume with respect to Igbo, Christian, and Chamula prayers (Shelton, Ferguson, Gossen) that are part of the tradition of these religions. Yet even these texts must be seen as the products of deep-seated motivations. Even where texts were originally produced with little or no intent to be esthetically pleasing, they are interpreted (in the elocutionary sense) so that they are prosodically pleasing. When people defend the King James Version of the Bible, for example, they frequently cite its "majestic rhythm." Since there is no inherent rhythm to this 17-Century translation, these tradition-alists are really defending the style of reading with which they have become familiar. Obviously, any version, even the one in Basic English, could have its own majestic style. What is true of Christian Scriptures is also true for Judaism and Hinduism (see Rabin and Christian).

Linguistic adaptation to religious needs is not limited to the selection of linguistic resources for the creation of special varieties of language. It also leads to special kinds of discourse. The "language" of religion—the means whereby religion expresses itself—therefore consists of genres like song, recitations, prayer, and magical or divinational formulae. Here the domain specificity of religious language may be seen, perhaps more clearly than anywhere else. One does not address or petition the gods in the same way that one addresses chiefs and kings (unless the chiefs and kings are theocratic figures!). As linguists, we are concerned with the structures of these genres insofar as they are the product of "grammatical" discourse rules (Ferguson) and as sociolinguists we are concerned with their function in speech events (Gossen).

The linguistic means of religion, whether extemporaneous or traditional, are expressed in either oral or written form. It makes a difference for religious behavior if the society is literate or preliterate and, in the latter case, if it is in contact with literacy. Of particular interest to sociolinguistics is the way in which the language of the sacred writings affects later forms of language. (For the influence Sanskrit and Hebrew have had see Christian and Rabin in this volume.) In the case of the Church of the Lord, an "independent" Christian movement in West Africa, foreign orthographies may be responsible for the spelling of "holy words": for example, what is pronounced something like Kokamula is written Kieokkammullal with a predilection for extra letters and long words (Turner 1967).

Social processes

The realization of speech ends is a social process, and the linguistic products that effect this realization are social phenomena. These facts have not been ignored in the foregoing discussion. Now we should turn our attention to some facets of the social nature of the interrelationship between ends and means.

Sociolinguistic competence.

This refers to one's ability to use language—the language product is constructed according to the rules, and it meets the requirements of the setting. The identification of genres of discourse presupposes a structure that is characteristic for each. In a given community it is therefore possible for a person to fail in his linguistic performance, if only by not achieving the ideal. Several papers in this volume touch on the rule-governed nature of the speaker's task, for we must know for each religion—or some given part of it—what it means to be sociolinguistically competent in it.

In our eagerness to describe rules, however, we must not ignore the fact that people force rules to yield. Both form and function are involved. Although prayers in many religions are set by tradition and are augmented or varied with great conservatism, the Protestant "free" prayer, being extemporary, is susceptible to great variation and exploitation. It is indeed possible for a prayer to approach the nature of a sermon. (This is a personal impression supported by casual observations of many Protestants.) On one occasion I heard a preacher admit that in the morning service the congregation heard one announcement included in the prayer, since he forgot to make it with the other announcements! He made his point more explicit by saying that the announcement had bounced back from heaven like something from a satellite. In such examples, it should be evident, the intended purpose of a speech act is also affected. An example of a change in function only is the use of a body of scripture for oracular or magical purposes.

What kinds of rules are more subject to strain and what are the social phenomena that accompany particular changes or periods of change? These are questions fundamental to sociolinguistics in general, but we do not now have good answers. Yet it should be observed, for example, that the Reformation seems to have led to only a few innovations in language use. On the other hand, dream interpretation as part of religious behavior in the Jamaa movement (mentioned above) is probably an innovation when seen in the context of African Roman Catholicism where this movement is found.

The domain of religion reminds us that we must study the acquisition of sociolinguistic competence for all domains in a given society. An adult who "becomes religious" after a lifetime of irreligiosity or one who leaves one religious community for another has to learn a new kind of behavior. Language—as we have already seen—is often a very important part of this process. In any case, there are drastic differences between what adherents of different religions are required to know and how—and at what age—they go about acquiring this knowledge. (See, for example, Christian 1971.) Judaism places very great value on a knowledge of religious writings; memorization is important in Eastern religions; but Christian clerics, at least in our day, usually read the liturgy. In most fundamentalist churches one is supposed to bring his Bible to church and follow the sermon by looking up all the text citations, of which there can be quite a few. In some churches, generally lower-class ones, the preacher makes it a practice to let volunteers in the congregation read as soon as they find the place. One can very well imagine both the contribution this practice makes to group cohesion and also the opportunities it provides for competition.

This last example, like so many others, illustrates the way the ability to behave in an appropriate manner can be used to symbolize what it means to be an adherent of a given religious community and to regulate behavior within it. In some Protestant groups one learns to pray aloud in public—something that every "good Christian" is supposed to be able to do—so as to express solidarity of the group. With this function praying aloud can be described as a ritual act, equivalent to attending church, but whose social meaning has greater forcefulness and clarity.

Metalinguistics.

This, for our present purposes, refers to beliefs and attitudes about language. Religion may be the source or determiner of a society's metalinguistic notions, but in any case the expression of religion—sometimes its very conceptualization— is influenced by the way people think about language.

If language is viewed as having a supernatural origin or in some way being part of the divine essence, everyday speech or speech on certain occasions is affected. Both among the Dogon of West Africa and in Hinduism language figured in the creation of the world (Calame-Griaule 1965; Christian). We all know about the *logos* of St. John's gospel, but we have no information about how this concept was related to social behavior. Well documented ethnographic observations would lead us to be careful about assuming certain kinds of behavior on the basis of certain kinds of beliefs. Evangelical Protestants assert as part of their creed that the Bible in the original language was wholly and verbally inspired by God: that every word is precisely the one God wanted. (They are not alone among those who have inspired texts.) Yet the linguistic and philosophical implications have never been adequately worked out. In evangelicalism's fundamentalist sector there is a strain of antirationalism: human language is but an imperfect instrument that God over-rides in his power; for Pentecostals human language is even carnal whereas glossolalia is spiritual. A similar attitude appeared among early Quakers (Bauman 1970).

In religion perhaps one finds the most explicit expression of belief in the power of language as a force in its own right. Among the Chamula "heated words" during a ritual are like incense (Gossen); in Spiritualist churches certain words "do" what they "say," so one avoids words like sickness and death (Zaretsky 1972); in Hinduism certain verses are repeated for their efficacy (Christian); African Muslims wear verbal charms and Tibetans use prayer wheels for the same purpose. Ethnographic literature provides abundant documentation of this aspect of linguistic belief and practice.

The study of sacred texts has led to extensive grammatical and lexicographical work, and linguistic science is indebted to religion for this legacy, but the linguistic history of religion is, as one might expect, uneven in quality. The ancient grammar of Sanskrit attributed to Panini is acclaimed by modern linguists for the quality of its generalizations, its elegance, and its economy. Long before the Renaissance—when Greek and Hebrew began to be studied assiduously— Muslim scholars had already arrived at a highly enlightened understanding of Arabic. The ecumenicity of scholarship in the west had its influence at that time on Jewish studies of Hebrew. It is these ancient Jewish attitudes towards grammatical studies, as Rabin points out in this volume, that explain in part the present state of Hebrew: the Sephardi had a great respect for the study of grammar, but the Ashkenazi frowned on it. Native linguistic notions, however, certainly had a prejudicial effect on the study of sacred texts. One that has pervaded (in many seminaries) and dominated Catholic and Protestant thought is belief in the deterministic nature of Hebrew and Greek: because one is static and the other dynamic, they led to different views of life. Theologians thus discovered and accounted for different theologies in Judaic and Christian religions. (Barr 1961 debunks this notion; Penn 1972 traces its history in secular thought.)

Linguistic notions, on the other hand, can be used to explicate or defend belief and to provide a model for the belief system. The history of theological argumentation is replete with illustrations of linguistic use, such as the repetition of *kai* (and) in Matthew 28:19 ("in the name of the Father and of the Son and of the Holy Spirit") which is said to prove that baptism must consist of three separate immersions in sequence. Much more sophisticated is Augustine's use of the relationship between the form of a sentence and its meaning in explaining eternity (Burke 1970: 142). The chapters by Gossen, Tedlock, Christian, and Long in this volume provide other examples of the way language beliefs and attitudes affect religious behavior.

Since language attitudes can affect any aspect of a community's linguistic resource, the use of different languages also will be affected. Such use is not necessarily uniform throughout the community or in the whole domain of religion. Religion is a domain that either inhibits or elicits the use of a second language. The Telugu, like Indians generally, borrow extensively from Sanskrit, but some styles more than others (Christian). Molokans now living in the United States speak Russian or English with a great admixture of the other in settings that might be called casual or intimate. In religious settings only Russian is used and that in a form free of English loans except for an occasional culture-specific item. On the other hand, Haitian Protestants require a great deal of Standard French in their Creole on formal religious occasions, and they might be happier with a sermon entirely in French even if it were incomprehensible (Orjala 1970).

Another way of looking at the process of language selection is in terms of the event rather than text. Thus, in the synagogue sabbath service conducted for the most part in English, certain parts are restricted to Hebrew, and different parts of a Ceylonese healing rite (Tambiah 1968) take different languages or mixtures of languages, reflecting the hierarchical positions of gods and demons.

NOTES

1. References are to other chapters in this book unless a date of publication is given.

2. Although we do not ignore the study of the systematic use of silence and noise (for example, Jackson 1968), we are especially interested in the beliefs about language that lead to or rationalize a society's practices, for example, the Quaker advocacy of silence and economy in the use of speech (see Bauman 1970 and discussion below).

REFERENCES

Barr, James, 1961, *The Semantics of Biblical Language*. Oxford University Press.
Bauman, Richard, 1970, "Aspects of 17th century Quaker rhetoric." *Quarterly Journal of Speech* 56: 67-74.
———, in press, "Quaker folk-linguistics and folklore." In *Folklore: Performance and Communication*, ed. by Kenneth S. Goldstein and Dan Ben-Amos. The Hague: Mouton.
Blakney, Charles P., 1969, "Chipunha, a Rhodesian cult." *Practical Anthropology* 16: 98-108.
Burke, Kenneth, 1970, *The Rhetoric of Religion*. Berkeley and Los Angeles: University of California Press.
Calame-Griaule, Geneviève, 1965, *Ethnologie et Langage: La Parole Chez les Dogon*. Paris: Éditions Gallimard.
Christian, Jane M., 1971, "Style and dialect selection by Hindi-Bhojpuri speaking children." In *Proceedings of the Conference on Child Language, 1971*, ed. by Theodore Anderson. Chicago: International Association of Applied Linguistics.
Fabian, Johannes, 1971, *Jamaa: a Charismatic Movement in Katanga*. Evanston: Northwestern University Press.
Franklin, Karl J., "A Kewa religious argot." (Manuscript)
Jackson, Anthony, 1968, "Sound and ritual." *Man* 3: 293-299.
Orjala, Paul, 1970, *The Dialects of Haiti*. Hartford Seminary Foundation, unpublished Ph.D. dissertation.
Penn, Julia M., 1972, *Linguistic Relativity versus Innate Ideas: the Origins of the Sapir-Whorf Hypothesis in German Thought*. (Janua linguarum, series minor, 120.) The Hague: Mouton.
Rosenberg, Bruce A., 1970, *The Art of the American Folk Preacher*. New York: Oxford University Press.
Samarin, W. J., 1972a, *Tongues of Men and Angels: the Religious Language of Pentecostalism*. New York: The Macmillan Co.
———, 1972b, Review of Rosenberg 1970. *Folklore Forum* [Bloomington, Indiana] 5(3): 106-111.
———, 1973, "Protestant preachers in the prophetic line." *International Yearbook for the Sociology of Religion* 8: 243-257.
Tambiah, S. J., 1968, "The magical power of words." *Man* 3: 175-208.
Turner, H. W., 1967, *African Independent Church. Vol. 2: The Life and Faith of the Church of the Lord (Aladura)*. Oxford: Clarendon Press.
Worsley, Peter, 1957, *The Trumpet Shall Sound: a Study of "Cargo" Cults in Melanesia*. London: MacGibbon and Kee.
Zaretsky, Irving I., 1972, "The language of Spiritualist churches." In *Culture and Cognition: Rules, Maps, and Plans*, ed. by James P. Spradley. San Francisco: Chandler Publishing Co., 355-396.

PART I

Performance

Three approaches to the description of verbal behavior are contrasted in this section. Crystal (Nonsegmental phonology in religious modalities) *argues that religious speech, like other categories that have sociolinguistic reality, are characterized by phonological features that have entered rarely in grammatical descriptions. He thereby challenges the linguistic approaches that concentrate on syntax or lexicon. Four kinds of speech from the same religious tradition are seen to differ from nonreligious speech and from each other with respect to nonsegmental features. Speech form is handled in different ways in Parts II and III and prosodic features in particular are treated by Tedlock and Christian.*

Ravenhill (Religious utterances and the theory of speech acts) *exploits a schema developed within the tradition of philosophical concern with language. However, unlike most of the contemporary philosophical-theological discussion of the nature of religious assertions (such as "I believe in God"), this paper analyzes a set of rituals described originally by the anthropologist Malinowski. Like his anthropologist and linguist colleagues, Ravenhill seeks to establish rules that would account for speech acts. Rules come up again for discussion in papers by Ferguson, with respect to the production of a certain genre of religious discourse, and by Christian, with respect to the governing of appropriate verbal activity in given settings.*

Gossen (Language as ritual substance) *exploits the possibilities of an "ethnography of speech" approach by identifying the various categories of speech perceived by the Chamula of Mexico. Brought to the analysis of a set of annual change-of-office ceremonies, these techniques reveal a unity of belief concerning the nature of the universe. Speech, like nonlinguistic material, turns out to be part of the total "language" that expresses Chamula myth.* Editor

2 Nonsegmental Phonology in Religious Modalities

David Crystal

In order to clarify the relevance of the study of religious language to sociolinguistic theory and practice, it seems necessary to make a preliminary, broad identification of those foci of attention which are conditioning our ideas about priorities in contemporary sociolinguistic thinking. As perspective for what follows, then, I wish to isolate three current emphases, which I loosely label empirical, methodological, and theoretical.

By an empirical task within sociolinguistics, I mean the establishment of a detailed formal description of systematic covariation between linguistic features (of whatever kind) and social context.

By a methodological task, I mean the establishment of explicit criteria and techniques which will enable us to assess the factual validity of our observations about covariation and provide a basis for comparative analysis and research consistency.

By a theoretical task, I mean the establishment of as general explanatory principles as possible to account for the range and kind of covariation observed in terms of some sociolinguistic model of patterns, categories, rules, and the like. If the study of religious language is to be fruitful, it should be able to contribute to the advancement of any or all of these tasks. I feel that a threefold contribution of this kind is perfectly possible; and will indicate one area of religious linguistic studies in which this might be done.

I will concentrate on the empirical, for this seems to me to be the area in which the most urgent claims for sociolinguists' attention lie. Current literature displays ample theoretical speculation, and some well-developed methodological routines; but there are precious few facts. Hypotheses abound; but few have been adequately tested.

The paucity of facts is best reflected by the limited answers we can give to the question "What exactly constitutes the linguistic distinctiveness of the sociolinguistic category X?"—where X refers to any of the usually recognized range of social functions (ethnic, regional, class, professional, purposive, etc.). Putting this another way, one might ask, "What features in the physical form of an act of communication lead us to identify (to a stated degree of certainty) that act as a token of a particular sociolinguistic type?" Apart from a very few detailed surveys, this question cannot be answered for most sociolinguistic contexts, even in English. Doubtless this dearth of evidence makes so much of our present-day output seem like theorizing rather than theory; for there are some very important types of linguistic evidence which so far have been little investigated. Indeed, in the case of nonsegmental phonology, discussed below, the evidence sometimes has been ruled out as irrelevant on a priori "general" grounds.

If one holds the view, still widely maintained by structuralist-inclined linguists, that paralinguistic features and related features are not "language proper," then one will be unlikely to introduce them as parameters on which to plot sociolinguistic distinctiveness. Many studies have ignored them as a result. A critical examination, however, of the grounds on which the "language properness" concept was originally set up might lead one to disregard this premise and pay attention instead to the potentially highly significant use paralinguistic features have in constituting the sociolinguistic identity of a spoken text.[1]

The model of language presupposed by this discussion, in broadest outline, sets up three levels, or components: phonological, syntactic, and semantic. (This latter subsumes both lexicon and semantic discourse relations.) Clearly, a sociolinguistically distinctive use of language might make use of features which could be analyzed in terms of any or all of these levels. We are all familiar with papers that deal with the "syntactic" analysis of, say, scientific English, or the distinctive "lexis" of class-variation in English. The research literature, however, displays a remarkable concentration on the syntactic level alone. Apart from the recent work into segmental phonological matters (Labov and others) and a few scattered studies of lexis, the general feeling seems to be that most of the sociolinguistic distinctiveness of spoken language is syntactic in character. This feeling almost certainly derives from recent preoccupations with syntactic models of analysis. If one is told to investigate the sociolinguistic distinctiveness of a text, but given only a syntactic "knife and fork" to do it with, then naturally one's overall conclusions are going to be syntactic in character. I want now to argue that, in fact, the basis of most sociolinguistic distinctiveness in speech is phonological in character and nonsegmental phonological in particular.

By *nonsegmental,* I am referring to sets of mutually defining phonological features which have an essentially variable relationship to the segmental/verbal items of an utterance, as opposed to those features (vowels, consonants, syllabic structure) which have a direct and identifying relationship. Nonsegmental features contrast auditorily in pitch, loudness, duration, or silence, and they expound meanings of an attitudinal, grammatical, or social kind. I have argued elsewhere that these features are best viewed as being organized into prosodic systems of pitch-direction, pitch-range, loudness, tempo, rhythmicality, and pause. Intonation, in this view, is seen not as a single system of contours or levels, but as a complex of features from different nonsegmental systems, primarily pitch-range, pitch-direction, and loudness. Nonprosodic variability is referred to as *paralinguistic,* and subsumes such features as labialization, nasalization, and types of supraglottal tension.

My hypothesis, then, is that the distinctiveness of a spoken variety of language lies primarily in its use of prosodic and paralinguistic features. (A parallel hypothesis, arguing for the graphological distinctiveness of written texts in terms of lay-out, type-contrasts, etc. might also be made.) As evidence, I shall look at the nonsegmental properties of certain categories of religious language, illustrated from English.

There are a number of reasons why religious language makes an excellent area for testing sociolinguistic hypotheses.

Firstly, it presents a well-institutionalized area of sociolinguistic experience. Because of its formalized dependence on linguistic traditions (certain texts of old viewed as sacred or dogmatic) and the regular and frequent repetition of linguistic situations, it should be possible to make representative samples of usage much more easily than in many other areas of sociolinguistic behavior and to describe the "facts" of the variety relatively quickly. Indeed, the chimerical notion of an "exhaustive" analysis may, in such a restricted linguistic area, turn out to be a real possibility.

Secondly, although institutionalized, religious language is by no means homogeneous. It displays a number of well-recognized categories of linguistic variation: sermons, litanies, prophecies, etc. Accordingly, it permits an investigation of the classic theoretical question, "Are the following usage samples tokens of the same type (i.e., do they belong to the same variety) or are they not?" Putting the question another way, "Can all these samples be generated by the same set of rules, or not?" It must not be forgotten that the social conventions operating to produce this category of sociolinguistic behavior impose severe limitations upon the length of texts and the range of variability of the language they contain. With these data interesting questions about the generalizability of rules, the economy of descriptions, and the like, may be more likely to receive a satisfactory answer than in the case of many other sociolinguistic categories. There is less material, quantitatively and qualitatively speaking, to be accounted for.

Thirdly, and very clearly in the case of English, the features of religious language are by no means restricted to the analysis of religious behavior.

While the basis of religious language obviously lies in the specific practices of particular groups, the *effect* of religious language transcends this, affecting the community as a whole. Religious linguistic effects enter into other areas of sociolinguistic experience and give rise to questions requiring more general explanations. One sees this most clearly in the regular use of religious language features in literature; but it is also apparent in the various kinds of humor within a culture, especially satire and joke telling. There is, in a phrase, a "national consciousness" about the features (or at least, the most important features) of religious language, and this is far more marked than in the case of other linguistic varieties.

There are at least three reasons for this. To begin with, there is the length of the historical traditions of religious practice, stemming from the common Christianity of English-speaking cultures, which manifests itself in such matters as obligatory Bible instruction in state schools. Religious linguistic behavior is regularly taught, albeit not always practiced. Second, religious language has had a peculiarly pervasive influence on the development of the literary language and indeed the language as a whole (see Brook's 1964 study of the Book of Common Prayer from this point of view). Thirdly, the high degree of personal relevance of the language's purpose and the domesticity of much of its subject matter, makes it much more likely to enter into everyday life than, say, the forms of legal language, which display a comparable historical tradition. As a result, there is a clear stereotype of religious language in the community as a whole, part of the linguistic equipment of believers and nonbelievers alike. This seems to be far more marked than in the case of any other variety, and would seem to constitute an additional reason for investigating the properties of religious language.

Religious modalities

All sociolinguistic investigation commences by assuming on intuitive grounds that a particular category of language-situational covariation exists. The subsequent analysis is then intended to verify this intuition (or perhaps, more strictly, to falsify it). In the case of religious language, general intuition of the categories operating within this area would lead one to recognize several distinct "genres," or *modalities* (to use the term I have used in previous work): for instance, sermons, litanies, Biblical readings, blessings, invocations, spontaneous expressions of various types, individual and group prayer.

I shall restrict myself here to four modalities which were intuitively identified in a Catholic church in England over a period of two weeks—the only ones regularly used (excluding the confessional, where the participants showed marked reluctance to permit a tape recorder!). They were unison prayer, individually read liturgical prayer, Biblical reading, and sermon.

One hour of each category was recorded, transcribed, and analyzed. I should like to emphasize that each sample was given a rating for "typicality" and "success." A number of participants were asked to say whether they felt that the samples were "abnormal" or "poor" in any respect, these labels not being further defined. Only utterances about which there was a consensus of "normality" were included in the final samples.

The reason for this procedure should be clear. There is little point in trying to discern general linguistic patterns if one's selection of data may be misleading, as when a sermon is felt to be too informal or too intellectual by the congregation. Some safeguards of this kind are prerequisite for satisfactory sociolinguistic generalizations, but they are rarely reported in the literature, and they often seem to be ignored. Analysts seem to make the invalid assumption that any selection of data (e.g., of scientific or journalistic or religious language) is bound to be satisfactory merely because it has been used.

Briefly, four points emerged in this investigation.

(1) Vocabulary was of little diagnostic significance. The range of vocabulary in the hour samples overlapped considerably between the different modalities. On the basis of a straight frequency count of items, or of item-combinations (collocations), it would be impossible to make valid predictions of a type-token kind with any great accuracy.

(2) Nor was syntax particularly helpful. The main syntactic features of religious language of this kind I have outlined elsewhere (see Crystal and Davy 1969, Ch. 6), and classified in terms of sentence type, sentence connection, clause structure, group structure (noun-phrase, verb-phrase), and word structure. Many features emerge at each "rank" in the analysis: for instance, the use of extensive vocative structures, archaic verb morphology, and other well-known characteristics. The point is that all of the important features of syntax and morphology are to be found in all modalities. Frequency and distribution of syntactic patterns display few important differences across the samples; and the differences which do emerge are not those which one would intuitively consider to be the defining characteristics of religious language. The syntactic parallelism of litanies would presumably be exceptional, but analogous sequences may be found in other modalities too, as in many Old Testament Biblical passages and in sermons. (Metrical phrasing is noticed in certain types of sermon, Rosenberg 1970.) In such cases phonological distinctiveness still obtains.

(3) Segmental phonology for all three speakers involved was identical on all recorded occasions. All used varieties of Received Pronunciation, and the vowel/consonant systems displayed no significant variations of a regional, class, or temporal character. There were certainly no grounds for discriminating between the modalities here.

(4) The nonsegmental phonology remains, and this, it emerged, was fundamentally different within each sample. The main differentiating characteristics of the four modalities are summarized in the following paragraphs.

Unison prayer.

This modality has the text available as a cue. Each punctuation group is a prosodic unit, but it is a prosodic unit of a rather different kind from the tone unit (or primary contour) found in all other varieties of spoken English. It requires only two obligatory prosodic features: a most emphatic syllable, and stress conforming to the distribution of lexical words within the unit. The introduction of variation in nuclear tone type (e.g., rising, falling-rising tones) or in pitch range (e.g., high-falling or low-falling) is optional, and usually not present. Any participant in a congregation may, if he wishes, articulate his words with as much feeling as possible, introducing a wide range of pitch patterns; but as far as the total, cumulative, auditory effect is concerned, such effort is unnecessary, and few speakers bother. A congregation—or any speakers in unison—has very much one voice. When a group speaks in unison, differences in the phonology of individual articulation become blurred and the outside listener is left with a "single voice" impression, consisting solely of variations in emphasis. The pitch level on the whole is low and monotone, though towards the end of a longer stretch of utterance than normal there may be a noticeable descending movement. This is absolutely predictable at the very end of a prayer, where the "Amen" (and often the words immediately preceding it) is given a marked drop in pitch. But otherwise pitch contrasts are regularly reduced to zero, leaving monotone and rhythmicality as the defining characteristics of unison liturgical prayer.

Individual liturgical prayer.

Whether spontaneous or cued by a text, this is marked particularly by a narrowness of pitch range, which affects all types of nuclear tone; level tones are more frequent than in other modalities of speech by individuals; there is a gradual descent of pitch towards the end of the prayer (as above), and a strong tendency to keep tone units short and isochronous. Of particular importance is the absence of the usual range of prosodic and paralinguistic variations (in speed, loudness, rhythm, tension), and the avoidance of any prosodic variability that might be construed as idiosyncratic. There is also the related point that this is one of the few cases where one is allowed to speak with little or no significant kinesic accompaniment. We find a minimum of facial expression and bodily gesture in this modality, a marked contrast with sermons.

Biblical reading.

The important point to note about this modality is the expected effect of the written language on the individual recitation, which obtains whether the person actually follows the text as he reads, or whether he has learned it by heart either in advance, or from some oral tradition. The regularity of the speed and rhythm, the tendency of intonation to follow the punctuation, the predictable occurrence and length of pauses, the avoidance of prosodic and paralinguistic features to express extremes of attitude or characterization (even where the narrative might justify them), the use of lengthy tone units and pitch-range "paragraphs" to impose structural organization upon the text (as the prosodic organization of radio news reading)–these are the main features which place this modality at considerable remove from individual prayers and sermons.

Sermons.

Whether learned, much-rehearsed, or spontaneous, sermons display prosodic and paralinguistic variation (see Crystal and Davy 1969: 227ff). At times the variability is so marked that the utterance takes on some of the characteristics normally associated with a different communicative medium, song or chant (Rosenberg 1970; Marks, manuscript). Different degrees of prosodic expressiveness exist; but even the most "reserved" kind of sermon analyzed presents a considerable prosodic range. The point needs no laboring.

Even from these sketchy generalizations, it should be clear that nonsegmental features are easily able to demarcate the four modalities. There is very little overlap in terms of either selection or frequency of use. One might display a similar nonsegmental distinctiveness within other modalities also, such as the litany, or the confessional interchange and the point has been noted in the analysis of other rituals and other traditions. One would point also to the centrality of metrical and pausal systems in Rosenberg's analysis of the qualities of certain kinds of spontaneous sermon (1970); or Fitzgerald's (1970) listing of twelve outstanding characteristics of prophetic speech in Gã, nine of which fall within my definition of prosodic and paralinguistic features; or Goodman (1969), who pays particular attention to intonation and related features in her analysis of glossolalia.

There now seems to be an increasing body of evidence to support the view that nonsegmental factors are crucial in identifying the distinctiveness of religious modalities;[2] but as far as I know there has been no attempt to formulate any corresponding general hypothesis as an explanatory principle of widespread applicability, and points of methodological and theoretical importance have not been made. I conclude, then, with a mention of three more general points, one theoretical, one methodological, and one "rhetorical."

General observations

First, the range of nonsegmental variation manifested in the above modalities would seem to be better accounted for by postulating a concept of prosodic "code switching" rather than attempting to bring in the nonlinguistic background that accompanies these samples. In each modality, the speaker tends to adopt a fresh "articulatory setting" (cf. Honikman 1964 and the "voice-set" concept of Trager 1958). One can see this, for example, in the larynx-raised articulation of a preacher, or the laxness and low pitch range of the unison speaker, or the variations in the tone unit length which ultimately relate to breath group and emotional role.[3] It would seem difficult to handle all these modality differences within a single description of nonsegmental phonology. The system seems radically different in each case. But to what extent is it theoretically acceptable to set up a "multiglossia" situation solely for one linguistic level? Diglossia situations as usually outlined normally assume that the linguistic distinctiveness operates throughout the whole of the language system, which is very far from being the case here.

The basic methodological point is to ensure that analysis of nonsegmental variability does not continue to be ignored or minimized in sociolinguistic investigations of speech. Its explanatory power seems to be considerable. Religious language makes the point clearly, in my view, but such analysis could also be shown to apply to other categories of speech (as is argued in Crystal and Davy 1969). To accept such claims, though, it is important to remember that nonsegmental variation subsumes far more than traditional models of intonation, stress and juncture would lead one to suspect. If one approaches the prosodic analysis of sociolinguistic variation using the simplistic model of four pitches, stresses and junctures, for instance, one will not get very far. Most of the interesting distinctions utilize a far wider range of nonsegmental contrasts, and an appropriately complex model must be used to demonstrate this.

In addition, there is the methodologically central question of ensuring that some psycholinguistic verification is provided for our sociolinguistic analyses—dealing with such matters as the perception of sociolinguistic distinctiveness, the rating of descriptive labels, and so on, but this goes beyond the bounds of the present chapter.

Finally, there is the rhetorical point that research of the present kind indicates the interdependence of sociolinguistics with other aspects of linguistics very clearly. In the process of selecting samples, obtaining popular reactions to them, evaluating intuitions, investigating perceptions and determining how to label what we perceive, we are much in need of the expertise of psycholinguistics, as already mentioned. In the objective statement of text similarities, we may need the help of statistical linguistics, with its suggestions for multivariate analysis, improved techniques of significance testing, and the like. In our search for descriptive generalizations, we need to use the concepts developed by fields such as literary criticism (especially in work on metrics, oral literature, etc.) and musicology. And of course there is the ultimate reliance on a metalanguage the validity of which general linguistic theory must ultimately assess. It is fashionable to talk of sociolinguistics as if it were a separate field, and attempt to define its boundaries. But its success is crucially dependent on progress in related fields, and attempting to isolate it too far can ultimately only be stultifying.

NOTES

1. A detailed critique of these positions may be found in Crystal 1969 (Ch. 4) and Crystal 1974.

2. And of course for other sociolinguistic categories too. See, Von Raffler Engel (1971) and Von Raffler Engel and Sigelman (1971) concerning the prosodic distinctiveness of black and white children.

3. This point has been made also in the context of urban dialect studies (Trudgill 1974), and is discussed in relation to social categories in general by Crystal (1971).

REFERENCES

Brook, S., 1965, *The Language of the Book of Common Prayer.* London: Deutsch.

Crystal, D., 1969, *Prosodic Systems and Intonation in English.* London: Cambridge University Press.

———, 1971, "Prosodic and paralinguistic correlates of social categories." In *Social Anthropology and Language,* ed. by E. Ardener. London: Tavistock, 185-206.

———, 1974, "Paralanguage." In *Current Trends in Linguistics, Vol. XII: Linguistics and Adjacent Arts and Sciences.* The Hague: Mouton and Co.

Crystal, D. and D. Davy, 1969, *Investigating English Style.* London: Longmans; Bloomington, Indiana: Indiana University Press.

Fitzgerald, D. K., 1970, "Prophetic speech in Gã spirit mediumship." Working Paper 20, Language-Behavior Research Laboratory, University of California, Berkeley.

Goodman, F. D., 1969, "Phonetic analysis of glossolalia in four cultural settings." *Journal for the Scientific Study of Religion* 8: 227-239.

Honikman, B., 1964, "Articulatory settings." In *In Honor of Daniel Jones,* ed. by D. Abercrombie et al. London: Longmans, 73-84.

Marks, M., manuscript, "Afro-American gospel music." (Personal communication).

Rosenberg, B. A., 1970, "The formulaic quality of spontaneous sermons." *Journal of American Folklore* 83: 3-20.

Trager, G. L., 1958, "Paralanguage: a first approximation." *Studies in Linguistics* 13: 1-12.

Trudgill, P., 1974, *The Social Differentiation of English in Norwich.* London: Cambridge University Press.

Von Raffler Engel, W., 1971, "Intonational and vowel correlates in contrasting dialects." Paper given at the Seventh International Congress of Phonetic Sciences, Montreal.

Von Raffler Engel, W. and C. K. Sigelman, 1971, "Rhythm, narration, and description in the speech of Black and White school children." *Language Sciences* 18: 9-14.

3 Religious Utterances and the Theory of Speech Acts

Philip L. Ravenhill

As a study in sociolinguistics, this essay is intended to have relevance for both linguistics and social anthropology. The inherent danger in any so-called hyphenated discipline, as I see it, is that the questions or the answers posited may emphasize one discipline at the expense of the other to which it is yoked. For example, there is danger applying a model indigenous to one discipline mechanically and unquestioningly to the data of another.

It is my purpose here to examine in some detail a theory generated within philosophy and nourished within linguistics as it relates to some of the phenomena to be found within anthropology. Hopefully such a quest will not only be illuminative within anthropology, but also the anthropological application will provoke implications for the theory. Thus we may see that there is a relevance for the theory beyond the confines of philosophy or linguistics and yet show how the problems confronted in our use of anthropological data in turn feed back on a positive critique of the original theory.

Kinds of speech acts

The philospher J. L. Austin, in attempting to deal with various types of speech utterances, posited a distinction between performative and constative utterances. (Constative is derived from the French *constatif,* meaning something like "statement.") Constative utterances, he held, were declarative and thus capable of being true or false, whereas performative utterances performed actions and could

26

only be "happy" or "unhappy" (Austin 1963: 22f; 1962: passim). For example, "he named the ship . . ." and "I name the ship . . ." are contrastive speech acts in that the former predicates an action of a subject (and is thus testable only for infelicity). This performative-constative distinction, as John Searle notes, is "supposed to be a distinction between utterances which are sayings and utterances which are doings" (1968: 405), but the antithesis does not bear up under closer scrutiny and Austin goes on to attempt a broader theory of speech acts.

In *How to Do Things with Words* Austin proceeds from the performative-constative distinction to a more specific definition of three types of speech acts: (1) the *locutionary* act—the performance of an act *of* saying something; (2) the *illocutionary* act—the performance of an act *in* saying something; and (3) the *perlocutionary* act—the performance of an act *by* saying something (1962: 91ff). Thus a locutionary act may be viewed as uttering a sentence with a particular *force,* and a perlocutionary act as uttering a sentence with a particular *effect* (ibid.).

John Searle, in his exploration and expansion of Austin's theory, rejects for a variety of seemingly valid reasons the locutionary-illocutionary distinction in favor of a distinction between propositional acts and illocutionary acts (1968: passim; 1969: 23). Thus the utterance "I state such-and-such" contains both a propositional and an illocutionary act; the proposition can be true or false whereas the illocution cannot (Searle 1968: 424). Under the general term "speech acts" Searle then puts forward the following:

(1) utterance acts—uttering words (morphemes, sentences)

(2) propositional acts[1]—referring and predicating

(3) illocutionary acts—stating, questioning, commanding, etc.

To which is added Austin's notion of:

(4) perlocutionary acts—the consequences or effects of illocutionary acts upon the actions, thoughts, beliefs of the hearers. For example, my asserting (the illocutionary act) may convince or persuade the hearer (the perlocutionary act) (Searle 1969: 23-25).

After noting that the regularities of language usage are best explained by recognizing that "the speakers of a language are engaging in a rule-governed form of intentional behavior," Searle then proceeds to a "full-dress" analysis of the illocutionary act (ibid: 53).[2] There are, he asserts, certain necessary and sufficient conditions for the illocutionary act to be successfully and nondefectively performed in the utterance of a particular sentence. These conditions he formulates as a series of propositions—each proposition being a necessary condition and the total set of propositions being the sufficient condition. From these conditions is extracted a set of rules for illocutionary acts (ibid: 54-71). These rules may be stated in general terms:

(1) propositional content rule—specifies the necessary propositional content.

(2) preparatory rule(s)—specifies the necessary preparatory conditions.

(3) sincerity rule—specifies the attitude of the speaker to the propositional content.

(4) essential rule—specifies what the act is to count as.

[In Searle's usage, the sentence "X *counts as* Y in context C" can be paraphrased as "X *is to be considered as* Y in context C." See, for example, page 49: "The rules specify that under certain conditions an utterance of "Hello" counts as (i.e., is to be considered as, P.R.) a greeting of the hearer by the speaker." For a further understanding of Searle's usage of this term see pages 48, 49, 52, 66-67.] Of these rules the fourth is the most important for Searle's theory because of two factors: first, only rule four is one of those constitutive rules which "constitute (and regulate) an activity the existence of which is logically dependent on the rules" (ibid: 34); and second, in general it is the essential condition which determines the others (ibid: 69). The rules can be illustrated by examining them in relation to a specific type of illocutionary act, such as assertion. Regarding a speaker S and a hearer H, the rules for asserting are thus (Searle 1969: 62-71):

(1) propositional content rule—any proposition *p*.

(2) preparatory rules—[a] S has evidence (reasons, etc.) for the truth of *p*. [b] It is not obvious to both S and H that H knows (does not need to be reminded of) *p*.

(3) sincerity rule—S believes *p*.

(4) essential rule—counts as an undertaking to the effect that *p* represents an actual state of affairs.

The broad outlines of this theory may now be summarized: first, there are four types of speech acts: utterance, propositional, illocutionary, and perlocutionary; second, to engage nondefectively in illocutionary acts certain necessary and sufficient conditions must be met; third, from these conditions may be explicated certain rules: propositional, preparatory, sincerity, and essential; and four, by these rules various types of illocutionary acts can be analyzed and contrasted.

Let us now proceed to an examination of the utility of this theory in sociolinguistic analysis. I intend to examine the theory in relation to the specific data of religious ritual, to see what problems arise in this practical application of the theory, to see if the theory needs adjusting, and finally to see the general benefits of this theoretical point of view.

Magical formulas analyzed

Anthropology has long recognized the importance of the study of language and speech, although many anthropologists have done little more than perform that act of recognition. Of those who have gone beyond the recognition and have theorized about language and/or speech there would appear to be a distinction between those who emphasize the semantic component of language and those who emphasize the social function of speech. I do not propose to assign seminal figures to one or the other camp, but rather to point out that, generally speaking, each of these emphases has been carried out at the detriment of the other. Malinowski, of course, attempted to do both; he theorized about meaning in language (1923), and yet also stressed the importance of speech as social action.

It is not my intention either to review or criticize Malinowski's theories but rather to utilize the data in his two-volume work, *Coral Gardens and Their Magic*, particularly that of Volume Two, *The Language of Magic and Gardening*. This work is a particularly suitable source for speech examples because of the wealth of detail it contains and because of the fact that some of Malinowski's emphases presage some of Austin's notions. For example, Austin's concepts of illocutionary and perlocutionary acts are hinted at by Malinowski when he says: "Take utterances such as statements . . . requests . . . challenges . . . ; each of these is a definite act which produces effects . . . and the function of these is obviously defined by these effects" (1935b: 48-49). Furthermore his plea for the study of language within the actual context of usage is echoed by Austin: "The total speech act in the total speech situation is the only actual phenomenon which, in the last resort, we are engaged in elucidating" (1962: 147). Malinowski's account of the speech of Trobriand gardening ritual is rich in detail, because it presents each ritual speech in relation to:

(1) its sociological context—how the words reach and affect the community;

(2) its ritual context—the manual procedure accompanying the speech;

(3) its "dogmatic context"—the beliefs surrounding the act of speech; and

(4) its linguistic content.

The ritual from which I would like to draw examples is the Trobriand Grand Inaugural Rite, the rite which inaugurates the gardening season and the alternating cycle of ritual followed by technical activity (cf. Malinowski 1935a: 95f; 1935b: 253f). Specifically I shall utilize the first two magical formulas (in Malinowski's words) which comprise (a) the offering of food to the ancestors, and (b) the charming of the axes to be used in gardening.

The first two formulas have as their function the specific task of inaugurating the first attack on the garden, the cutting of the scrub, and more generally the gardening season's work as a whole. The main actor in the ritual is the "magician" appointed by the chief; indeed he is the only speaker. The hearers, however, are numerous, ranging from the pantheon of ancestors, to specific ancestors, to recently deceased kin, to various kinds of insects and bugs. Rather than give a line-by-line examination of the parts of the ritual, I shall first give a broad outline, or approximation, of some types of illocutionary acts to be found therein and then examine the problems which arise in the application of the theory.

The magician, alone in his hut, utters the two formulas in succession; the oblation to the ancestors sets the scene for the charming of the axes which are to be used in the next day's activities. Three types of illocutionary acts found in the ritual are as follows.

Invocation.

I posit invocation as a type of speech act related to the act of greeting (as specified by Searle) in that there are certain rules in common. Both acts have no propositional content rule and thus no sincerity condition (since the sincerity rule specifies the attitude of the speaker to the propositional content). Both share the essential rule that the act is to count as the courteous recognition of the hearer by the speaker. The acts differ, however, in the preparatory rules. Whereas Searle states that the preparatory rule for greeting is that S has just encountered (or been introduced to) H, I posit for invocation two rules:

(1) H is in a position to hear S, and

(2) H is superior to S.

Rule One covers religious situations in which H is (believed to be) present but invisible, and in which the encountering of H by S is not physical. Rule Two specifies the relative positions of S and H; thus the recognition is of a superior by an inferior. In Formula One, oblation to the ancestors, invocations are addressed to three different hearers:

(1) the ancestral spirits generally—"old men, our ancestors";

(2) the magician's father—"Yowan, my father"; and

(3) the originators of the ritual—"O Vitika, O Iyavata, fountain head of our myth and magic."

In invocation the positions of S and H may be made explicit. For example, the successive invocations of this formula make explicit a series of related oppositions: ancestors vs. living, father vs. son, and originators vs. receivers of tradition. The net effect of these invocations is to "allow" the requests and assertions which follow as well as to place the ancestors in a position of witnessing all of the ritual and illocutionary acts which are to follow.

Consecration.

Formula Two, the charming of the axes, is a speech act with the illocutionary force of consecration, that is, a speech act which sets aside a person or an object as a channel for divine (or ancestral) attributes such as power. Consecration is posited as a member of the exercitive class of related speech acts as defined by Austin: "exercitives are the exercising of power, rights, or influence" (1962: 150), and an "exercitive is . . . a decision that something is to be so, as distinct from a judgment that it is so: it is advocacy that it should be so, as opposed to an estimate that it is so . . . " (ibid: 154). Consecration is an act of enablement which in this ritual "positions" the axes so that they may be effective tools in the subsequent gardening activities. Consecration thus makes liturgical objects out of technological objects. We may attempt to specify the rules for consecration as follows:

(1) propositional content rule—future event or state E;

(2) preparatory rules—(a) S has reason to believe E will occur and in C's interest (where C equals the community), (b) it is not obvious to both S and C that E would occur in the normal course of events, (c) S is in a position of authority over the object O;

(3) sincerity rule—S believes E should be so; and

(4) essential rule—counts as an undertaking that E is to represent an actual state of affairs, namely that O is a liturgical object having a specific purpose and effectiveness.

Exorcism.

Exorcism may be thought of as similar to consecration in that it also has a "positioning" function: it attempts to send the garden pests where they belong. The rules for exorcism must be amended, however, to take into account a hearer (an addressee) as well as the witnessing community. The preparatory rules thus need to include the fact that S believes E is not in H's interest, and also that S is in a position of authority over a potentially active and responsive hearer H, rather than an object. One might think it more correct to say that S desires a future act of H instead of a future event of E, but on reflection one sees that it is a particular state that is desired—the state of bug-free gardening.

In addition to these three specifically religious types of speech acts the ritual also includes such illocutions as assertion, request, and command. All manifest the same rules as those put forward by Searle in his discussion of types of illocutionary acts (1969: 66-67). An examination of the rules makes possible the explications of all the illocutions. The theory of speech acts thus provides a point of view for preliminary discussion of some dimensions of speech within the context of ritual.

Our attempt is not an exhaustive analysis, but we have been able to use the speech-act framework to examine various topics, such as the point or purpose of the acts, the relative positions of the actors, the differences in propositional content, the different ways in which the propositions relate to the actors' interests, and the preparatory conditions necessary for the acts. Furthermore, by applying the theory we come to realize its importance. The theory is important because it allows us to distinguish between the propositional and illocutionary acts and also to explicate the necessary and sufficient conditions for the performance of an illocution. Instead of more closely scrutinizing the Trobriand material alone, I would like to go on to examine the problems which arise in the application of the theory to any acts of speech *in situ.*

Problems with the theory

A number of difficulties arise in the attempt to apply Searle's theory of speech acts to data from another culture, especially when such data have been collected by a fieldworker with a necessarily different theoretical viewpoint. A basic problem lies in the reconstruction of the data for purposes other than that for which they were intended. There may be various lacunae and various emphases that need to be interpolated and de-accentuated respectively. In such reconstruction one is limited to the data which the investigator chose to include since his excluded data are irretrievable; and one is denied the option of asking new questions of the informants.

For an analysis of speech acts it is important to investigate native intuitions in order to explicate the conditions necessary and sufficient for the successful performance of a particular illocutionary act. One could ask questions like: What did he mean? What did he do? What did the utterance count as? While not explicating all of the conditions, these or similar questions would put us well on the way to a successful analysis. Using the data collected by another fieldworker limits us to etic approximations, but we must proceed to emic analyses since speech acts are conventionalized and rule-governed.[3]

A related question is the isomorphism or non-isomorphism of the illocutionary acts found in various linguistic and/or cultural groups. Searle remarks that there are "several different continua of illocutionary force, and the fact that the illocutionary verbs of English stop at certain points on these various continua and not at others is, in a sense, accidental" (1969: 70). We might suppose, therefore, that some illocutionary acts will be approximately the same no matter what the language (e.g., questioning, requesting, ordering) while others may be idiosyncratic or idiomatic. In attempting the cross-cultural analysis of speech acts we must therefore look at the conventions of such acts in terms of the social or linguistic community under investigation.

The most difficult problem confronting a performative analysis of speech acts is the problem of interpretation. How do we know what a particular utterance is to count as, especially if the illocutionary verb is not specified? In such a nonexplicit sentence we are aware of a possible illocutionary *force ambiguity*: the utterances may count as either illocutionary act A or illocutionary act B. The utterance is intended to have a single force, but which one? In addition to this problem of force disambiguation, there is the notion of *force multiplicity* as pronounced by Fraser in his criticism of the contention that a sentence has one and only one underlying performative verb which specifies its force (1971a: 3ff). Force multiplicity refers to sentences having a composite of two or more forces: instead of the "either/or" of ambiguity there is the "both/and" of multiplicity. There is, however, another notion of force equivocalness with which Fraser does not deal. This notion may be characterized as *force dimensionality* and refers to a situation in which the speaker intends a single utterance to have two different illocutionary forces, a singular force A for hearer H_1 and a singular force B for hearer H_2. An example of such an utterance is given by Searle:

> ... suppose at a party a wife says "It's really quite late." That utterance may be at one level a statement of fact; to her interlocutor, who has just remarked on how early it was, it may be (and be intended as) an objection; to her husband it may be (and be intended as) a suggestion or even a request ("let's go home") as well as a warning ("You'll feel rotten in the morning if we don't") (1969: 70-71).

Force dimensionality can only occur in the context of two or more hearers, and each illocutionary force of the utterance must satisfy its own specific rules in order to be successful and nondefective. It appears that this type of force dimensionality would most likely be limited to sentences in which the sentence meaning underdetermines the sentence force, as opposed to sentences with a performative verb in which the sentence meaning makes explicit the sentence force (cf. Fraser 1971b: 47, 50). Even in sentences with explicit performatives, however, a type of force dimensionality may appear when an utterance addressed for a specific purpose to a specific individual is intended by the speaker to be *over*heard by overhearer OH. There may thus be a difference in intention between the act of S promising *p* to H when they are alone and when they are in the presence of others. This type of force dimensionality is readily understood in the legal context of witnessing, where the added presence of OH has a legalizing effect.

In the context of religious ritual a speaker, such as a priest, may intend to address the gods, request favors, promise actions, or assert divine authority, and also intend the congregation to know that such actions have been performed and that the overhearers are now permitted or prohibited certain undertakings in consequence. The priest may make known two types of knowledge: the knowledge of the propositions and the knowledge of the illocutions. In the Trobriands, people overhearing the ritual of the various stages of gardening know that order is achieved, or that the ancestors are invoked, and therefore certain technical activities must follow.[4]

In analyzing and interpreting the speech acts found in ritual we must take into account all these notions of force ambiguity, force multiplicity, and force dimensionality. The problem of force ambiguity may perhaps be resolved by a careful hermeneutics specifying the various criteria to be weighed for a correct disambiguation—such criteria as sociological context, ritual context, dogmatic context, and linguistic analysis (cf. Malinowski, 1935b: 249-250). The notion of force multiplicity allows us to investigate the possible compositeness of illocutions in single utterances. Our earlier interpretation of invocation thus can be clarified by viewing it as both greeting and assertion. It not only courteously recognizes the ancestors but also reasserts a relationship having attendant obligations; it is a composite utterance. The notion of force dimensionality makes it possible for us to examine the intended perlocutionary effect on the hearer(s) and also the intended sequential illocutionary effect on the overhearer(s). (On illocutionary effect, see below.)

Utterances in discourse

In both the philosophical and linguistic use of the theory of performative analysis the basic unit of study is felt to be the single utterance or sentence (Searle 1969: 16; Fraser 1971b: 1-2), but when it comes to an examination of the practical utility of the theory in dealing with anthropological data, it soon becomes apparent that we cannot limit ourselves to such artificially isolated minimal units. Two problems force themselves on our attention: first, the question of the interrelations existing between successive speech acts; second, the question of whether successive speech acts constitute larger units which also must be analyzed.

The first question is important in relation to the interpretation or disambiguation of the illocutionary forces of sentences which do not contain explicit performative verbs. Speech acts must be analyzed in terms of the total context, because the context, be it verbal or nonverbal, may make clear what force is intended. This is especially true in relation to ritual which is, after all, conventionalized behavior. The conventionalized behavior may be the explicator of the illocutionary force. There is no a priori reason to assume that meaning and force are isomorphic with the syntactic boundaries of the sentence. The essential condition of any illocutionary act (i.e., what the act counts as) may be made clear by a gesture, or the essential condition may be made explicit by the preceding or following utterances. It should be obvious that our quest is more than the examination of single utterances. It must be the examination of illocutionary acts within the total context, including the context of discourse.

As to the other question of whether single utterances can combine into other, larger, illocutions with their own rules, I would like to answer tentatively in the affirmative. We can easily imagine that a type of religious illocution such as exorcism or consecration could be composed of various other illocutions such as invocation, assertion, request, command. In fact this is exactly what we find in Formula Two of the Trobriand gardening ritual recorded by Malinowski. If we attempt to analyze the individual component utterances as equivalent in terms of importance, we run into difficulty. If instead we look at the whole of Formula Two as being one speech act with a multiple force, namely, consecration and exorcism, then we can weigh the importance of the constituent sentences.

It is obvious from Malinowski's record that the total formula functions primarily as a consecration. As proof of this we need only to look at the objects over which the formula is repeated on separate occasions—the axes, torches, digging sticks, and adzes, or what Malinowski characterizes as "liturgical objects" (1935b: 258). The fact that every illocution in the whole formula is aimed directly at these objects (breathed on them, as it were) further shows the functioning of a single unit. Thus even the act of exorcism which takes up a major part of the formula, and which uses explicit performative verbs, is ancillary to the act of consecration. To examine the intention of single utterances we must examine the relation of their intentions to the intentions of the larger illocution.

Acts in context

In examining the speech of religion the question of the relation between the illocutionary act and the perlocutionary act assumes significance, because some illocutions have a direct tie to perlocutions. As Searle says: "Some illocutionary verbs are definable in terms of the intended perlocutionary effect, some not. Thus requesting is, as a matter of the essential condition, an attempt to get a hearer to do something, but promising is not essentially tied to such efforts or responses from the hearer" (1969: 71). Before discussing the nature of the relation which holds between the illocutionary act and the perlocutionary act, we need to make clear the difference between an illocutionary effect and a perlocutionary effect.

Every illocutionary act has an intended illocutionary effect. In an utterance T, S "intends to produce an illocutionary effect IE in the hearer H by means of getting H to recognize S's intention to produce IE" (Searle 1969: 47). That is to say, S wants H to understand that he, S, is uttering a conventional speech act so that H may know what the utterance counts as. This illocutionary effect is not a response to S's utterance but rather an understanding of it. All illocutionary verbs thus have intended illocutionary effects. Additionally, however, some (such as requests) may have an intended perlocutionary effect—they may attempt to achieve a certain response from H.

Now in ritual it would appear *prima facie* that most illocutions are similar to requesting in that they are performed to get something done, and should therefore be definable in terms of the intended perlocutionary acts. Thus we can see an essential tie between illocutions such as command, consecrate, and exorcise, and their attempted perlocutions.[5] But what of the illocutionary acts of invocation and assertion which cannot be thus defined? Exactly why is an act of assertion performed? Searle's specification of the essential rule of assertion is that it "counts as an undertaking to the effect that p [the propositional content] represents an actual state of affairs [and does not] seem to be essentially tied to attempting to convince" (1969: 66). It is not, however, sufficient to say only that assertion *qua* assertion has no intended perlocutionary effect. We must examine the correlation it may have with following utterances. In the Trobriand ritual there are a number of assertions which have to do with the relation between the speaker and the hearer. Some of these are the assertions bound up with invocations, as previously mentioned, but others are assertions connected with commands. For example, in the second formula the following is addressed to the garden blight, the bugs: "Thou art my sister. Begone! Be ashamed of me! Avoid me!" (Malinowski 1935a: 98). This assertion of a brother-sister relationship, a relationship strongly tabooed, adds weight to the subsequent commands. It is as though the magician were saying, "Because of the nature of our relationship, do this . . ." or "This is our relation, therefore . . ." Thus, whereas the assertion alone has no intended perlocutionary effect, it does have a specific relation to the preparatory rules of utterance following in that it makes explicit the relative positions of S and H. In this case it asserts authority. Once again is demonstrated the need to examine all speech acts in relation to context.

Having looked in a very tentative way at the theory of speech acts within the context of ritual we may now go on to discuss the possible benefit of the approach in sociolinguistics generally.

Content and effect

My attraction to the theory of speech acts, as originated by Austin and amended by Searle and others, is based upon:

(1) the hypothesis that speaking a language is engaging in a rule-governed form of behavior;

(2) the argument that an adequate study of speech acts is a theory of *langue*; and

(3) the placing of heavy reliance upon the intuitions of the native speaker (Searle 1969: 14-15).

I see the above points as beneficial as well as intuitively satisfying.

In making explicit the rules underlying various acts of speech, especially the illocutionary, we are provided both with a framework for comparing types of utterances and also with a method for abstracting various levels, or aspects, from single utterances. The distinction made between the propositional act and the illocutionary act is extremely important; it allows us to examine the propositional content of specific sentences in relation to the intended illocutionary effect. Now we can analyze sentences in terms of their intended use *and* meaning, instead of looking at use versus meaning. The abstraction of the two levels of propositional and illocutionary is, in fact, a warning against studying one to the exclusion of the other. As Austin warns, "It is the total speech act in the total situation . . . which . . . we are engaged in elucidating" (1962: 147).

By way of looking at the benefits derived from a study of illocutions (including their propositional content), let us inspect some of the dimensions which come to light in the explication of various underlying rules. What different levels of distinction are made in and by the conditions and rules for illocutionary acts? Searle answers (1969: 70):

> *First* and most important, there is the point or purpose of the act (the difference, for example, between a statement and a question); *second,* the relative positions of S and H (the difference between a request and an order); *third,* the degree of commitment undertaken (the difference between a mere expression of intention and a promise); *fourth,* the difference in propositional content (the difference between predictions and reports); *fifth,* the difference in the way the proposition relates to the interest of S and H (the difference between boasts and laments, between warnings and predictions); *sixth,* the different possible expressed psychological states (the difference between a promise, which is an expression of intention, and a statement, which is an expression of belief); *seventh,* the different ways in which an utterance relates to the rest of the conversation (the difference between simply replying to what someone has said and objecting to what he has said).

Of course, some of these points have to be amended to include the existence of an overhearer OH as well as possible plural hearers, and we must remember the problems of force multiplicity and force dimensionality. But given speaker S, hearers H_1 and H_2, and overhearer OH, the theory presents in an integrated way many significant components of speech acts. Furthermore, it shows that these components may combine into different illocutionary verbs at specific points on different continua of illocutionary force—a significant point for those concerned with cross-cultural analysis.

The domain of religious behavior can provide examples to illuminate some of the benefits of the theory. In their introduction to *African Systems of Thought,* Fortes and Dieterlen mention the fact that there seem to be two broadly contrasted approaches to the description and analysis of African religious systems, one approach emphasizing the peoples' total body of knowledge and belief about the cosmos, and the other linking the body of knowledge and belief to the actualities of the peoples' social organization (1965: 3-4). The former is an attempt, as it were, to relate cosmology to sociology; the emphases in both are upon total bodies of knowledge.

I would like to claim that the theory of speech acts can give us an approach which mediates between cosmology and sociology via an analysis of the speech acts of practical religion. Instead of abstracting the theology which inheres in the speech of the magician, priest, or other religious virtuosi, we can examine the significance of the speech acts for the other participants. For example, what is the significance of religious speech if delivered in a foreign language understood only by the priest (xenoglossia, not glossolalia)? If we emphasize the importance of the propositional content, we must say the people don't understand, but if we assume that the people do know what illocutionary act is being performed (i.e., what the act counts as), then we begin to see the light. The importance of an act of exorcism may lie not in the propositional content of the priest's words, but rather in the fact that the community witnesses a particular illocution which counts as a specific action, say of cleansing or creating order. The same might be said of the oft-mentioned problem of the untranslatable and archaic words found in religious rituals. Might they not be indicators of illocutionary force?

Given this view of illocutions, a natural question arises as to the comparability or equivalence of religious illocutionary acts with "normal" illocutionary acts. Are some religious illocutions the same as those found in nonreligious discourses; are some unique or different; are some analogous and related?

Among the Limba of Sierra Leone, Ruth Finnegan informs us, there is at least one illocution which is the same whether found in religious context or not (1969: 550).

> ... the normal word for "to pray" (*theteke*) is exactly the same as the word for "plead." Furthermore, it is used in a precisely analogous way. Even if the audience addressed (the dead) is necessarily somewhat different, in other respects when a Limba prays he is performing just the same kind of act as when a man entreats a chief: he is making a formal acknowledgment of his inferiority and dependence and/or a request for aid or forgiveness; at the same time he is expecting that the one(s) addressed will recognize their side of the relationship, "accept" the plea and answer it; and he is also asserting a continuing relationship between speaker and audience, living and dead. The token gift that accompanies a plea performs the same function whether it is to the dead (the "sacrifice") or to the living; it helps to "make the words heavy"; but the act consists in the words not in the gift.

The importance of this equivalence is that it demonstrates how artificial the distinction between sacred and profane may be. In the realm of pleading it makes no difference to the Limba whether the addressee is alive or dead—exactly the same conditions are in effect for either. I am not claiming that there is no disjunction between "sacred" and "profane" in every instance of Limba life. There may well be occasions which seek to recognize or emphasize this disjunction (e.g., burial rituals), but the above activity would not seem to be one of them. As to illocutions which are only religious, we can imagine that one might be the act of consecration.

The advantage of the emphasis on illocutionary acts is that it forces us to see speech as rule governed and only making sense because of the institutional conventions, and it allows us to see what dimensions are used by native participants themselves.

NOTES

1. It should be noted that propositional acts cannot occur alone, i.e., there cannot be any utterance of prediction or reference without an illocutionary act, such as assertion (Searle 1969: 25).

2. For a detailed discussion regarding rules see Searle, sections 2.5 and 2.7, pages 33-42, and pages 50-53 respectively. Note especially his use of the notions of constitutive rules and institutional facts.

3. Compare Pike on etic and emic descriptions (1966: 153f) with Searle on rule-governed behavior and institutional facts (1969: 33-42, 50-53). Searle's point of view stresses the actor's knowledge, albeit unconscious or preconscious, but seeks to make explicit rules rather than structural units.

4. It would seem that many religious rituals, whether "primitive" or our own, have this auxiliary effect of ordering time. Cf. Leach 1961: 132-136.

5. Perhaps there are illocutions of "magic" in which the speech is held to be a stimulus-response type of communication and thus naturalistic rather than institutional. Cf. Searle 1969: 71.

REFERENCES

Austin, J. L., 1962, *How to Do Things with Words.* Cambridge: Cambridge University Press.
–––, 1963, "Performative-constative." In *Philosophy and Ordinary Language,* ed. by Charles E. Caton. Urbana: University of Illinois Press, 22-54.
Finnegan, Ruth, 1969, "How to do things with words: performative utterances among the Limba of Sierra Leone." *Man* 4: 537-552.
Fraser, Bruce. 1971a, "An examination of the performative analysis." Unpublished manuscript.
–––, 1971b, "Sentences and illocutionary forces." Unpublished manuscript.
International African Seminar, 1965, *African Systems of Thought.* (Studies presented and discussed at the third International African Seminar, Salisbury, 1960.) Prefaced by Meyer Fortes and G. Dieterlen. London, New York: Oxford University Press for the International African Institute.
Leach, Edmund, 1961, *Rethinking Anthropology.* New York: Humanities Press.
Malinowski, Bronislaw, 1923, "The problem of meaning in primitive languages." In *The Meaning of Meaning,* ed. by C. K. Ogden and I. A. Richards. London: Kegan Paul, 451-510.
–––, 1935a, *Coral Gardens and Their Magic.* Volume I, *Soil-Tilling and Agricultural Rites in the Trobriand Islands.* New York: American.
–––, 1935b, *Coral Gardens and Their Magic,* Volume II, *The Language of Magic and Gardening.* New York: American.

Pike, Kenneth L., 1966, "Etic and emic standpoints for the description of behavior." In *Communication and Culture*, ed. by Alfred G. Smith. New York: Holt, Rinehart and Winston, 152-163. Reprinted from K. L. Pike, *Language in Relation to a Unified Theory of the Structure of Human Behavior.* The Hague: Mouton and Co.

Searle, John, 1968, "Austin on locutionary and illocutionary acts." *Philosophical Review* 77: 405-424.

–––, 1969, *Speech Acts: An Essay in the Philosophy of Language.* Cambridge: Cambridge University Press.

4 Language as Ritual Substance

Gary H. Gossen

Field research for this paper was carried out over sixteen months with financial support from the National Institutes of Mental Health and the National Science Foundation. I am grateful to them for making my field work possible. I was a participant in the Harvard Chiapas Project, a long-range research effort in the Central Chiapas Highlands of southern Mexico, under the direction of Evon Z. Vogt of Harvard University. His support and encouragement throughout my research are gratefully acknowledged. The ideas in this paper took shape both in the field and afterward. I thank Victoria Bricker, James Fox, Michelle Rosaldo, and M. S. Edmonson for several discussions which helped me greatly in organizing my thoughts on Chamula ritual language. I also thank Shelly Errington and Thomas Rohlen for their critical reading of earlier drafts of this paper.

With his usual insight and succinctness Edmund Leach wrote many years ago that "myth regarded as a statement in words 'says' the same thing as a ritual regarded as a statement in action" (1954: 13-14). In other words, they are two codes which ultimately carry the same message. Recently he has added ritual language to the set of metaphorical equivalents which must be considered together in decoding the meaning of ritual action. He puts this quite simply: "in ritual, the verbal part and the behavioral part are not separable" (1966: 408).

Victor Turner's major contributions to the study of ritual symbolism have generally affirmed Leach's position and greatly extended it to consider the message of ritual action as "quintessential custom," or the crystalline essence of social life (1968: 23). The elementary units of Turner's and Leach's holistic approaches to ritual action are symbols. Both however emphasize that the symbol which is mobilized for the ritual stage is of a special nature. It is multivocal, to use Turner's term. This implies that it has many meanings at once, each of which represents an important sense or referent of the symbol (1967: 50). Leach also has emphasized the special qualities of the "language" of ritual, pointing out that it is enormously condensed, redundant and characterized by a "great variety of alternative meanings in the same category sets" (1966: 408). Ritual action consists, then, of a complex mesh of critical information rendered in several different codes at once. Some of these codes are linguistic, others nonlinguistic.

I wish to consider here one such code—formal language—in Chamula ritual behavior. More specifically, I will deal with Chamula formal language as a ritual symbol—one of several which must be present for proper interaction with the supernatural world. The discussion will follow Victor Turner's useful classification of fields or levels of meaning in ritual symbolism (1967: 50-51). The first section deals with "exegetical meaning," that is, what the Chamulas say about formal language. The second section involves my observations about what Chamulas do with formal language—a level of interpretation which Turner has called the "operational meaning." The third section considers the "positional meaning" of ritual language; that is, how it fits into the whole of Chamula life and ritual symbolism.

Throughout, I shall be concerned as much with the *non*linguistic as with the linguistic features of Chamula ritual language. The reason for such concern is that formal language, to Chamulas, is like any other important ritual substance. Indeed, it shares important structural patterns with other substances such as fire, incense, tobacco, rum, and maize gruel—which are not linguistic at all except in a special metaphorical sense. This essay, therefore, considers language as a ritual substance which shares messages with the actions and other ritual substances present in the same setting. In these shared ritual messages—stated in different codes—we may hope to find some crystals of essential information about the Chamula cosmos and social universe.

The Chamula community

Chamula is a conservative Maya community (Tzotzil-speaking) of about 40,000 which lies in the cool oak- and pine-forested Chiapas Highlands of southern Mexico. The Chamulas live virilocally in more than one hundred scattered hamlets which belong to three barrios. These *barrios* converge on a ceremonial center which serves as the focus for religious and political life. All Chamulas engage to a greater or lesser extent in swidden agriculture, with emphasis on maize, beans, squash, and cabbage in that order of importance. Population pressure forces many men to work outside the *municipio* as day laborers; others stay and engage in cottage industries. Chamulas are governed by a civil hierarchy which is partly traditional and partly prescribed by Mexican law. A religious hierarchy consisting of sixty-one major positions supervises ceremonial activities and cults to the saints and also coordinates its ritual activities with those of the civil hierarchy. Political authority on the local level lies in the hands of past cargoholders and heads of segments of patrilineages. Religious authority in the hamlets is exercised by shamans, past religious cargoholders, and by elder males in the patrilineages. (For more detail on general Chamula ethnography see Pozas 1959, 1962, and Gossen, 1974a).

Chamula religion and cosmology form a complex syncretistic system which is the product of 16th-Century Spanish Catholicism and pre-Columbian Maya cults to nature deities, particularly to the sun (now the same as Christ), the moon (now the same as the Virgin Mary), water spirits, and earth lords. The other saints, including the patron saint of Chamula, San Juan, are kinsmen of the sun (the son of the moon). Chamulas also believe in individual animal soul companions which share certain aspects of people's spiritual and physical destinies.

Basic to Chamula religion is the belief that they live in the center of the universe. They view their home *municipio* as the only true safe and virtuous place on the earth. As geographical distance increases, danger lurks more threateningly. The edges of the earth are populated by demons, strange human beings, and huge wild animals. From there one can see the terrifying spectacle of the sun and moon deities plunging into and emerging from the seas every day in their respective vertical circuits around the island universe. Not only does the sun deity delimit the spatial extent of the universe, but he also determines the temporal units (days and solar years) by the duration and position of his path. It was the sun who established order on the earth. He did this in progressive stages, separately creating the first three worlds and then destroying them, for people behaved improperly.

Chamulas say that behavior equivalent to that of the people in the first three creations may still be found at the edges of the universe and, occasionally, among bad Chamulas. It is only the Fourth Creation which has been successful. This is a moral world which Chamulas must constantly strive to defend from bad behavior and evil people. Language, particularly the oral tradition, is a crucial tool for the defense, continuity, and ritual maintenance of the Fourth Creation.

Exegetical meaning: language within a taxonomy of verbal behavior

Chamula views of formal language can best be introduced within the framework of their taxonomy of verbal behavior. I have described a complete Chamula taxonomy of *k'op* (language) elsewhere (Gossen 1971 and 1974a) and will sketch it here only briefly. It is necessary, however, to place formal language in a larger scheme for the simple reason that neither its structure, content, nor style is truly unique to it. It is part of a generic, stylistic, and behavioral totality. This larger scheme must be described before considering a particular part.

A bewildering number of processes, abstractions, and things can be glossed as *k'op*, which refers to nearly all forms of verbal behavior, including formal language. The word *k'op* can mean: word, language, argument, war, subject, topic, problem, dispute, court case, or traditional verbal lore. Chamulas believe that correct use of language (i.e., the Chamula dialect of Tzotzil) distinguishes them not only from nonhumans, but also from their distant ancestors and from other contemporary Indian groups and Spanish-speaking groups. According to Chamula narrative accounts, no one could speak in the distant past. That was one of the reasons why the sun-creator destroyed the experimental people of the First and Second Creations. The more recent people learned to speak Spanish and then everyone understood one another. Later the nations and *municipios* were divided, because they began quarreling. The sun deity changed languages so that people would learn to live together peacefully in small groups.

Chamulas came out well in the long run, for their language was the best of all. They refer to Tzotzil as *baȼ'i k'op* or "true language." Language, then, came to be the distinguishing trait of social groups. It is for this reason, among others, that Chamulas care very much about language and recognize many classes of verbal behavior.

The first break in their folk taxonomy of *k'op* distinguishes three general classes. The first and least formal is "ordinary language" (*lo'il k'op*). It is restricted in use only by the dictates of everyday social situations and grammaticality and/or intelligibility of the utterance. It is believed to be totally idiosyncratic and without noteworthiness in style, form and content; it is everyday speech.

The second class of verbal behavior is called "language for people whose hearts are heated" (*k'op sventa šk'išhnah yo'nton yu'un li kirsanoe*). The heat metaphor implies the presence of an excited, emotional attitude on the part of the speaker. The "heated heart" marks the beginning of a continuum of redundancy and parallelism in style which is present in all of the genres of the Chamula oral tradition, particularly so in the formal language under discussion. However, this intermediate level contains only those genres—"children's improvised songs," "children's improvised games," "court speech," "angry or bad speech," and "political oratory"—whose contexts and style are constant. Their *content* is not constant. As a Chamula exegesis of this class states it: "It comes from the heart of each person." This means that constraints of where one says it and how one says it are present. Constraints of content are not present. It is only with the joint presence of predictable content and prescribed formal features (i.e., style) in genres which are associated with specific behavioral settings that we reach the third general class of verbal behavior, "pure words" or "pure language" (*puru k'op*).

Within "pure words" the criterion of time association is the most important one in distinguishing the secular forms ("recent words," or *ač' k'op,* associated with the present, Fourth Creation) from those which have greater ritual and etiological significance ("ancient words" or *'antivo k'op*). "Recent words" include narratives of the Fourth Creation, games and a large group of humorous genres called "frivolous language." These generally assume the present social order and defend it informally. In the opinion of informants, these genres were first given in and are associated with cosmic time like the present. Furthermore, the spatial associations and secular behavioral settings of these genres are close to home.

"Ancient words," on the other hand, were first given in and refer to events of the three creations which preceded the present one. They deal more or less formally with the social order. With the exception of "true ancient narratives," which may be told any time the information in them is necessary, all of the genres of "ancient words" are associated with ritual settings. In addition to "true ancient narratives," "ancient words" include: "language for rendering holy," "prayer" and "song." The language of these four forms is our concern.

Very important to the symbolic value of the formal genres is their style. I have discussed elsewhere (Gossen 1974b) the scheme of Chamula folk criticism of linguistic style. This scheme uses "heat of the heart" as an attitude or mood variable which is reflected in the degree of formalism and redundancy in speech performance. For example, ordinary discourse is not "heated." It is cold in this evaluation scheme, because it does not have constraints of form, content, and context.

As one moves in a continuum from ordinary discourse to the fixed genres of Chamula oral tradition in "pure words," progressively more heat of the heart is required for good performance. In "ancient words" this metaphorical heat reaches its peak intensity. The heightened heat is readily apparent even to a listener who does not know Tzotzil. The cadence is more marked, the voice modulates from higher to lower levels of pitch with great regularity, and one realizes that the whole mood of the utterance differs to a striking degree from the "colder," more secular forms. The most notable difference is that the heated heart speaks in pairs and multiples of pairs, and, nearly always, with a great deal of message redundancy. Dyadic construction is the stylistic hallmark and elementary unit of composition of formal Tzotzil.[1] It is these dyadic units which are taught, in correct sequences appropriate for different contexts, by ritual advisors. This dual construction has several forms, all of which may be called metaphorical couplets. Those most frequently found in "ancient words" are *bound* and invariable and are characterized by grammatical and semantic parallelism. For example, the following couplet enters into hundreds of combinations in "song," "prayer," "language for rendering holy," and sometimes in "true ancient narrative." It usually remains intact or bound wherever it is found:

 lital ta yolon avok
  I have come before your feet,

 lital ta yolon ak'ob
  I have come before your hands.

Another kind of metaphorical couplet, which is much more typical of the narrative than of the ritual genres, is based only upon semantic parallelism. It is more inclined to vary slightly from performance to performance than the bound couplet just discussed. The semantic couplet restates the same information in a slightly different way, repeating in order to emphasize important information, but not necessarily in parallel syntax. Following is a typical example from a "true ancient narrative" about the creation of the earth:

puru ša la banamil kom ta ?ora
Now only the land remained, nothing more.

pero puru la stenleh
Only the open plains, nothing more.

Both of these forms of couplet may be *stacked* one after the other to create highly redundant passages. Often this stacking is stylistically obligatory, as in "song." On other occasions, particularly so in "true ancient narrative" and sometimes in "prayer" and "language for rendering holy," one may add couplets for emphasis, stacking them to the desired intensity. This technique, which I call metaphorical stacking, enables performers to extend texts and give embellishments to them within proper stylistic bounds. It also calls attention to the fact that the information which is so treated is crucial information. In this way redundancy adds clarity to highly condensed statements which deal with important ritual symbols.

The couplet is thus the most common frame in which the multivocality of "ancient words" is expressed. Someone—usually a ritual official—who speaks well in couplets is said to "speak with a heated heart." Heat, then, is the most comprehensive metaphor used in reference to the redundant formal style of "ancient words." It is no accident that the primary referent for this scheme of criticism is the Sun/Christ deity, who set up all temporal and spatial order in the first place. On the Chamula exegetical level, it can be said in summary that the following qualities characterize the language that accompanies and explains ritual action:

(1) heat,
(2) distant time-space associations,
(3) communication with or about supernaturals, and
(4) metaphorical stacking in couplet units.

I should emphasize, finally, that all of these qualities are present at once in any performance of "ancient words."

Operational meaning

So far, I have attempted to follow cues which are suggested by Chamula classification and criticism of "ancient words." We have seen that language, particularly formal language, is considered not only a crucial medium for the maintenance of the social order, but also an important symbol of cosmic heat which must be present in the ritual setting and in reference to it. I now want to consider what Turner has called the "operational level of meaning." Interpreting this, I believe he means that we should observe what people actually do with "ancient words" in concrete social transactions. As basis for brief and systematic discussion, I would like to give a concrete textual example from each of the four genres of "ancient words." For interpretation of each text fragment, I shall take into account the context of performance as well as the level of exegetical meaning, already discussed above.

1. *baȼ'i antivo k'op* "true ancient narrative." Like all genres of "ancient words," "true ancient narrative" reports or refers to events of the first three creations, and like most narratives of this type is etiological and explanatory. It states in one code—which is only implicit in the ritual setting—that which other genres of "ancient words" state in slightly different codes which are explicitly present in the ritual setting. Ultimately, however, we shall see that the four formal genres are "saying" the same thing. Related to the role of "true ancient narrative" in stating the coming of the present order is a greater message redundancy in couplets than one finds in "true recent narrative." Items of assumed knowledge about the nature of order require more metaphorical stacking for emphasis than the threats to order which are reported in "true recent narrative." An example of this pattern follows. It is a fragment from a narrative about the first appearance of "Our Father Sun" in the sky, victorious over his enemies. This is an important myth which nearly every Chamula knows, for it reports the very beginning of temporal and spatial order in the First Creation.[2]

Although the narrative refers to the symbol of greatest religious significance (our Father Sun), it was nevertheless told in what might be called a secular setting. The eliciting circumstances are typical. It was told as a clarification or explanation of something that came up in everyday life. The formal mood appeared only as the sacred content was revealed. Shun Méndez Tzotzek, the middle-aged Chamula informant who told me the following narrative, heard it for the first time when he was working on a coffee plantation in the Pacific lowlands. He and a Chamula friend saw a Guatemalan worker at breakfast one morning while drinking their coffee. He was an old man, and his strange red-and-purple striped clothes were ragged. Furthermore, he did not understand either Tzotzil, Tzeltal, or Spanish— which are the languages Chamulas hear with the most frequency. Thus, the old man came from completely outside the social universe of Shun and his friend. Guatemala is believed to lie at the very edge of the earth, along with the United States and Mexico City. He was literally a being from the edge of the earth—where time past still exists according to Chamula cosmology (see Gossen 1974a). Shun and his friend were deeply suspicious of him because he reminded them of the demons and Jews that killed Our Father Sun. As Shun tells the anecdote, he had never before seen a Guatemalan. This fact, together with the bundle of negative associations conjured up by the sight of the poor old man prompted Shun's friend to tell his long narrative of how Our Father Sun conquered the forces of evil in the First Creation to bring heat and light for the first time to the earth.

1. *ʔora la ʔiȼobsbaik li hurioetike*
    Then the Jews gathered together;
    la sk'elik to livroe
    They looked at the book.

2. *?ato la hyilik*
    Then they saw it;
    ta ša ¢akal la ?un
    There it was written;

3. *ti ta šak' sk'ak'al ti htotik*
    That Our Father Sun would give heat;
    ti k'alal muy ta vinahel
    That he would do thus when he rose to the sky.

4. *pero mu tuk'uk vinahel muy batel*
    But he did not go straight to the sky;
    ba?yel yal batel ta ?olontik čib k'ak'al
    First he went to the underworld for two days.

5. *ta yošibal to k'ak'al sut talel ti hotike*
    On the third day Our Father Sun returned;
    čib la k'ak'al yat yo?nton ti hurioetike
    For two days the Jews had dreaded it.

6. *?i k'alal lok' talel ti htotik ta yošibal k'ak'al*
    And when Our Father Sun came up on the third day,
    ?ok'ik la ti hurioetike
    The Jews cried out.

7. *pero ta vinahel ša la ta šanav*
    For he was already traveling in the sky
    k'alal sut talele ta yošibal k'ak'al
    When he returned on the third day.

8. *ti hurioetike ¢obolik ša*
    The Jews were already gathered together;
    ta smala ya?i k'usi ti š̃čam
    They were waiting to find out how they would die.

9. *?ato la ya?i ti hurioetike*
    Then the Jews felt it;
    k'išin hutuk ti htotike
    Our Father Sun heated up a little bit.

10. *ta ša la sk'ak'ub k'alal ta banamil*
    There was already heat upon the land;
    ?i k'alal ¢o¢ k'ak'ub ti banamile
    Then the heat was stronger upon the land.

11. *čam la ti hurioetike ta luhuneb so?oš ?ora*
    The Jews began getting sick when it was only ten o'clock in the morning;
    čam ti hurioetike k'alal k'ot ta ?olol vinahel ti htotike
    They finally perished when Our Father Sun reached the center of the sky.

This fragment is composed entirely of semantic couplets. It breaks clearly into closely related *stacks* of couplets, each of which is highly redundant. The first, couplets 1 through 3, tells that Our Father Sun, though he had been killed, was destined to bring order and light that the "Jews" would be defeated. The second section, couplets 4 through 11, simply chronicles with great repetition the first emergence of the triumphant sun deity. Each couplet gives an aspect of this fact, but actually presents no "new" information. The couplet structure thus serves as a medium for expressing the multivocality of Our Father Sun as a sacred symbol. We are told not only that his coming was predestined, but that he would be the antithesis of evil (enemy of the "Jews" and demons); the marker of cyclical time (origin of days); the marker of cosmic space (underworld, sky and earth differentiated for the first time), the source of heat energy—in sum, the most comprehensive symbol of order.

The narrator is able to underscore the importance of this passage by stacking his couplets to make the message overwhelmingly apparent. Our Father Sun does indeed do and represent for Chamulas all that the passage says. Yet this assumed knowledge is so fundamental that when it is stated, it must be done in a heated, redundant style which complements its importance. Shun told me that he became more afraid of the old Guatemalan after hearing this "true ancient narrative" of the First Creation. He and his friend felt threatened by the old man, who was a threat also to the world in which they lived. The Guatemalan was like the "Jews" in the narrative.

The passage illustrates that Chamula formal narrative style is not merely a vehicle for language but also that the style carries complementary information on its own. Furthermore, nonlinguistic information, much of it mundane—such as the original performance setting of the fragment cited—must be known in order to appreciate Chamula formal language at the operational level. It perhaps goes without saying that basic categories of cosmology and sociology are also prerequisites for understanding the meaning of "ancient words" as they are used in the narrative.

2. *k'op ta šak' rioš* "language for rendering holy" or "ritual speech." This genre includes all ritual language which is not directed to supernaturals and which is not in narrative form. All adult Chamulas must know some kinds of "language for rendering holy"; religious and political specialists know many kinds for their respective tasks. This genre is used by ritual officials and laymen to carry on transactions among themselves on the elevated plane of the ritual setting. It is constantly present in Chamula life from drinking ceremonies to installation of new ritual officials to bride-petitioning rites. Since it always accompanies ritual transactions, its content is as varied as these settings. "Language for rendering holy" (with some exceptions, such as drinking toasts) is entirely built of bound formal couplets, which are the irreducible components of all "ancient words" except narrative.

"Language for rendering holy" is actively involved in the ritual process, whereas "true ancient narrative" is only implicit in ritual action as background information. The words spoken as "language for rendering holy" are supposed to please the deities although they are not addressed directly to them. It is their capacity to express and generate heat which makes them so important as a kind of sacred substance in the ritual setting. Again, it should be remembered that all of the genres of "ancient words" share with other major ritual symbols the qualities of heightened heat, redundancy, and multivocality. One of the factors is that all good supernaturals, including the Sun/Christ deity and the saints, consume essences. This practice contrasts with that of humans, who consume solids. The gods' requirement for essences is one of the reasons that formal speech, music, candles, incense, tobacco, rum, fireworks, flowers, and aromatic leaves—usually all of these together—must be present in the ritual setting. They all emit heat, smoke, aroma, or sound. These essences disperse and travel easily and ultimately reach the gods and serve as their food. They also help men to transcend the temporal and spatial bounds of the mundane world. Men may participate in the religious experience by consuming, producing, or simply being in the presence of the gods' substances. Formal language is one of these substances.

The following example of "language for rendering holy" comes from a community-wide ceremony which takes place on December 30 and 31 and January 1. It is part of the change-of-office rituals in which new cargoholders receive the blessing of the outgoing cargoholders and finally take the oath of office in the ceremonial center. The ritual activity during this period is intense, for all civil cargoholders (there are over sixty) and many religious cargoholders enter and leave office at this time. Household altars and patio shrines of all outgoing and incoming officials are decorated with pine, laurel, and spectacular lowland bromeliads. Each cargoholder sponsors, with the assistance of personally recruited musicians playing harp, guitar, and rattles, a full two-day sequence of ritual meals and drinking ceremonies. "Language for rendering holy" is constantly present at each focus of activity.

The text fragment below comes from the beginning of the first day of this ceremony. The outgoing Alcalde for Barrio San Juan and his assistants have just arrived, after a long early morning walk, at the house of the First Alcalde's replacement for the following year. There has already been much ritual drinking and singing. Assistants finally announce their arrival by setting off hand cannons and skyrockets, but the inductee does not come out of his house. He simply stands in the open door, listening to the *h[?]ak'riošetik* (those who give the blessing). They stand in the patio in a line parallel to the front of the house. The outgoing official stands in the middle of the group and leads the blessing:

1. *mi teyot htot.*
    Are you there, Father?
   mi teyot hme?.
    Are you there, Mother?

2. *č'ul bankilal kurus,*
    Holy senior cross,
   č'ul bankilal vašton.
    Holy senior staff.

3. *ʔul ta bahel ʔabek'tal,*
    May your body emerge,
    ʔul ta bahel ʔatakipal.
    May your flesh emerge.

4. *čak k'u ča ʔal ʔuninal rioš,*
    Like unto the young god,
    čak k'u ča ʔal ʔuninal hesus,
    Like unto the young Jesus,

5. *heč vok',*
    As he burst forth,
    heč ʔayan,
    As he was born,

6. *ta ʔabek'tal,*
    So with your body,
    ta ʔatakipale
    So with your flesh.

7. *heč noplih ʔo,*
    So it was considered,
    heč t'uhlih ʔo.
    So it was chosen.

8. *ta ʔabek'tal,*
    Your body,
    ta ʔatakipal,
    Your flesh,

9. *ta ʔarma rioš,*
    At the armory of God,
    ta ʔarma hesukristo.
    At the armory of Jesus Christ.

10. *ta hel tos,*
    At the changing of tasks,
    ta hel mok,
    At the crossing of the wall,

11. *ti stomele,*
    At the oath-taking,
    ti sbičel,
    At the assumption.

12. *ti č'ul bankilal kurus,*
    Of the holy senior cross,
    ti č'ul bankilal vašton
    Of the holy senior staff,

13. *ti sčabi bel yolon yok,*
    That which is cared for at the feet,

ti sčabi bel yolon sk'ob,
That which is watched over beneath the hands,

14.   *ti muk'ul san huan,*
Of Great San Juan,
ti muk'ul patron.
Of the Great Patron.

15.   *ti hbeh ša me viƒ,*
There upon the mountain,
ti hbeh ša me sƒeleh.
There upon the hill.

16.   *htatik ta ʔak'oponel,*
We seek your sacred words,
htakik ta ʔatiʔinel,
We seek your blessed speech.

It is clear that the metaphors employed in the blessing refer not only to the new cargoholder's change in status, but also to his task of helping the Sun/Christ deity. He is actually likened to the "young god . . . the young Jesus. As he burst forth . . . As he was born." This states that the cargoholder will have the responsibility of helping the sun to maintain social, temporal, and spatial order. It is particularly appropriate at this time in the ritual year, for Christmas has just come and gone, along with the winter solstice. Christmas is, of course, associated with the ritual rebirth of the sun as well as with the birth of Christ. Therefore, we see again that the multivocal aspects of the sun are being invoked in the medium of stacked metaphorical couplets. The code, however, is different from the "true ancient narrative." It does not give the background, as in "narrative," nor is it addressed as praise, or supplication to the deities, as in "song" and "prayer." Rather, it imbues the ritual personnel who will maintain civil order with sacred authority. No Chamula symbol could be more appropriate for this purpose than the Sun/Christ himself who gave men social and cosmic order in the first place. Within the passage cited are mentioned several other symbols which stand for the authority of Our Father Sun: San Juan, the sacred mountain, the sacred words, the armory of God, the holy senior cross. In predictable, redundant fashion all these are associated with Sun/Christ *as well as* with the new Alcalde. His sacred mandate cannot be misunderstood; nor can the complexity of his new job be denied. The blessing given in "language for rendering holy" pours a kind of cosmic heat upon him. And much of this essence lies in the setting, style, and cadence of the language as well as in the words of the blessing themselves.

3. *resal* "prayer." This genre is still another code present in the ritual setting. Its language is explicitly addressed to supernaturals. Like "language for rendering holy" it consists wholly of formal, bound couplets. I have never heard a prayer composed of smaller elements. The reason for this, Chamulas say, is that supernaturals will not listen to ordinary speech. All prayer settings are also ritual settings and nearly always include at least one or a combination of the familiar

ritual substances: candles, rum, tobacco, incense, flowers, aromatic plants, music, fireworks, and other "ancient words." All laymen know some prayers, and specialists know many more. Length of prayers is highly variable, but in general greater length is associated with more important ritual transactions. A shaman's prayer for a curing ceremony will nearly always be longer than an ordinary prayer of salutation to the saints which the laymen offer in the church.

The fragment which I have chosen as an example comes again from a change-of-office ritual, that of the prestigious Mayordomo of San Juan. The three-day ritual takes place between December 22 and December 24, and, like the Alcalde cargo discussed immediately above, acquires some of its symbolic strength from the fact that it falls near the time of the winter solstice and Christmas.

The incoming Mayordomo's entourage of assistants comes to his house in his hamlet at dawn on December 22. After a morning of drinking liquor and partaking of a ritual meal, the whole party begins the procession to the Chamula ceremonial center, amid singing, cannon blasts, and skyrocket explosions. All of the assistants carry ritual objects from the Mayordomo's household in bundles on their backs. They literally move him to his new house and new role.

At about two o'clock in the afternoon, they arrive at the incoming Mayordomo's house in the Center, which he has previously made arrangements to rent. When they arrive at the patio of the new house, they go to the patio cross-shrine which the Mayordomo's flower gatherers have previously decorated with pine, laurel, and other plants. An assistant places a lighted censer before the patio shrine, and the whole party, together with ritual adviser and incoming Mayordomo leading, begins to pray for the success of their coming year of service to San Juan, the patron saint of Chamula. They look straight at the shrine with eyes open, as is the custom with all prayers that I have witnessed. The recitation of prayers resembles that of a chant, and may be related to Roman Catholic praying styles. This fragment is from the beginning of the prayer. The prayer makers cross themselves, make proper salutations to Our Father Sun and then proceed:

1. *misirikočyo, kahval.*
   Have mercy, My Lord.

2. *muk'ul san huan.*
   Great San Juan.
   muk'ul patron.
   Great Patron.

3. *k'u yepal čital ta yolon ?avok,*
   How much I come before your feet,
   k'u yepal čital ta yolon ?ak'ob.
   How much I come before your hands.

4. *šči?uk hnup,*
   With my spouse,

šči²uk hči²il.
  With my companion.

5. *šči²uk ²avob.*
      With your guitar,
    šči²uk ²asot.
      With your gourd rattle.

6. *šči²uk ²avah, ²ulovil.*
      With your servant, the gruel maker.
    šči²uk ²avah, ȼayovil.
      With your servant, the cook.

7. *šči²uk ²atuk',*
      With your shotguns,
    šči²uk ²akanyon.
      With your cannons.

8. *ta ȼobol ma ²avalab,*
      Your children are gathered together,
    ta ȼobol ma ²anič'nab,
      Your offspring are gathered together.

9. *ta ²ayilele;*
      For you to see;
    ta ²ak'elele.
      For you to witness.

10. *muk'ul san huan,*
      Great San Juan,
    muk'ul patron.
      Great Patron.

11. *ta ša me ša²oč ta kok.*
      Now you are to be delivered at my feet.
    ta ša me ša²oč ta hk'ob.
      Now you are to be entrusted to my hands.

12. *Ho²on ša me ²avač' mosovun;*
      Now I am your new servant;
    Ho²on ša me ²avač' ki²ara ²un.
      Now I am your new attendant.

13. *čahtotin ²o;*
      I shall be as father to you;
    čahme²in ²o.
      I shall be as mother to you.

14. *ti hun ²avil*
      For one year
    ti hun k'ak'al.
      The same as for each day.

15. *muk'ul san huan,*
    Great San Juan,
    muk'ul patron.
    Great Patron.

16. *štun ʔo hbeh pom.*
    There is incense for you.
    štun ʔo hbeh č'aʔil.
    There is smoke for you.

17. *čahpet;*
    I shall lift you:
    čahkuč.
    I shall carry you.

18. *ti hun ʔavile*
    For one year
    ti hun k'ak'ale
    The same as for each day.

The members of the Mayordomo's party conclude many dozens of couplets after the last one given in the sample fragment. At this time, they cross themselves, taking temporary leave of the deities. The incoming Mayordomo remains at the altar for more prayer while cannoneers begin to shoot fireworks which mark their arrival in the Ceremonial Center. The women and assistants begin placing the goods in and around the house for the next two days of ritual, in which the new Mayordomo will formally assume the burden of serving San Juan for one year.

This is an interesting text to examine for time-space coding of style and meaning. Once again, we see that "ancient words" are multivocal in that they imply a great deal more than they say explicitly. The heat and the ritual mood are intense. Thus, much more than a mnemonic device, the repetitive dyadic style is itself a reflection of the cyclical cosmic order which is always implicit and sometimes explicit in the ritual setting. Just as redundancy was necessary (in the several creations) to bring man to his present state of order, it is likewise necessary in symbolic restatements of the conditions of that order. This applies to ritual action and symbolism as well as to the language used to execute the ritual and to talk about it. Thus, it seems plausible that the two- to four-part parallel structure in "prayer" recapitulates in style the polysegmental temporal and spatial realities of its content. In this way, stylistic redundancy may be seen as an aspect of the cyclical temporal order which Our Father the Sun created.

These stylistic and symbolic dimensions can be observed together in a passage of the "prayer" just cited (couplets 12 through 17). This passage begins with the couplet "Now I am your new servant/Now I am your new attendant," which is said in an impassioned chanted rhythm, with the chanters facing the pine bough-laden shrine. Incense burners pour out the aromatic smoke to the open sky, harps and guitars are played, and sky rockets and cannons burst in the air. The ritual setting breaks the spatial and temporal barrier between men and gods. The past becomes present; the dwelling place of the gods becomes the same as the sacred space in which the officials carry out their tasks. The incense mentioned in the "prayer," like the formal language used to deliver the "prayer," is one of the media—one of the essences—that unite the space of men and the space of gods and make them one for the ritual setting.

Note also that the incoming cargoholder promises to carry the burden of the saint. This he will quite literally do when he carries the litter of the saint in processions in the sacred space of the church atrium. This concept of carrying the burden of time and deity for a yearly cycle is not unlike the "year bearer" concept of Maya antiquity (see Bricker 1966). The cargoholder metaphorically promises to accept the burden of cyclical time ("I shall embrace you/I shall carry you"), a task which he will share with the deity for his year in office "as for each day."

The incense, which the Mayordomo must burn each day, not only will tie the servant to his sacred patron, but also will serve as food for San Juan and impart holiness to his servant. The cargoholder, through his identification with the maintenance of the cosmic order, carries the presence of virtuous men into the most distant reaches of time and space. As he announces in the "prayer," in all humility, he will serve as "father" and "mother" to San Juan. He thereby ties himself metaphorically to the First and Second Creations and to the lineages of Our Father Sun as well as to the sacred (and threatening) space of the edge of the universe.

We see, therefore, that "prayer" is still another code of the "heated heart" which transcends mundane time and space. It says the same thing as ritual action and the other "ancient words," ritual symbols and cosmological principles with which it shares the ritual stage. Its semantic complexity and sacred power lie in the fact that it implies all of this at once.

4. *k'ehoh* "song." "Song" may be seen as the opposite end of a continuum of formalism and redundancy beginning with "ordinary language." (See Gossen 1974a for the full continuum of style.) Again, the truly heated heart is speaking. "Song" has all of the formal stylistic attributes of "prayer" and "ritual speech," plus musical form and instrumental accompaniment (harp, guitar, and rattle). It is language so hot that it becomes, as it were, an essence, like the smoke of tobacco or incense. Indeed, the "audible essence" can be heard at great distances, more so than any of the other forms of "ancient words."

"Song" is present at nearly all Chamula public rituals and at most private ones. Few major Chamula ritual performances take place without musicians. Their task is not only to accompany the singing of the ritual officials, but also to remember the sequence of the "songs," with the appropriate words and actions, so that they can "prompt" the officials if necessary when they become very intoxicated.

"Song" is like "prayer" in that it is addressed directly to supernaturals. In addition to praise and supplication, however, it reports to the deities the progress of ritual action which is being held on their behalf. "Song" behaves as an extreme statement of redundant metaphorical heat, for the musical form and heavily stacked couplet structure together make it possible to repeat them ad infinitum until the ritual events they accompany have concluded. Directed to the sun deity and his kinsmen (the saints), they are the pure essence of linguistic heat. Furthermore, the instruments are said to sing with heated hearts, just as people do.

It can be seen, therefore, that "song" is another code which gives essentially the same message that other "ancient words" and ritual actions give in slightly different form. Again, it should be noted that all of these codes are typically performed together, not separately.

An example comes from a fragment of a "song" for the change-of-office ritual for the Mayordomo Santo. This is sung during the preparation of the sweet maize gruel which will be given by the Mayordomo as part of a ritual meal on December 23, the second day of the ceremonies. The gruel is prepared in giant ceramic pots and is served hot. It symbolizes the heavenly rain of San Juan (and the sun) which comes down to earth as the warm rays of heat from the sky. Drinking the substance imparts heat and an aspect of divinity to the consumer. The Mayordomo and his ritual adviser sing the following song (to the accompaniment of rattles, which they play, and of the harp and guitar, which their musicians play) as the gruel is being prepared. Note the four-part parallel structure and complex metaphorical stacking.

1. *ta ša me šyal ta Hoʔ,*
     Now it is surely descending as rain,
     la ʔač'ul šohobale bi.
     Your blessed radiance.

2. *ta ša me šyal ta Hoʔ,*
     Now it is surely descending as rain,
     la ʔač'ul nak'obale bi,
     Your blessed shadow,

    muk'ul patron.
     Great Patron.

    la la li la lai la ʔo
    la la li la lai la
    la li la lai la ʔo
    la la li la lai la

3. *ta ša me šyal ta Hoʔ,*
     Now it is surely descending as rain,
     la ʔač'ul kompirale bi.
     Your blessed ritual meal.

4. *ta ša me šyal ta Hoʔ,*
     Now it is surely descending as rain,

la ʔač'ul korason bi
  Your blessed heart,

muk'ul patron.
  Great Patron.

la la li la lai la ʔo
la la li la lai la
la la li la lai la ʔo
la la li la lai la

The gruel is expressed metaphorically in five different ways: as rain, radiance, shadow, ritual meal, and heart—all of San Juan, who is the sun's kinsman. The metaphors share the quality of heat and heavenly origin (heat is heavenly rain; regular rain comes from caves in the mountains). The metaphors also establish a tie between the ritual setting and the limits of the cosmos. The symbol of rain also ties the event to the establishment of the cyclical ordering of time in the beginning, for the people of the First Creation (those who made stewing meat of their children) were destroyed by a rain of boiling water sent by the Sun-Creator. Better people were created to replace them.

The Mayordomo, as a Chamula, is a descendant of these better people. Furthermore, he is participating in his cargo role as a maintainer of order. He expresses this, among many other ways, by serving a ritual meal of sweet maize gruel. It is relevant that the Sun-Creator originally cut the first ear of maize from his own groin to provide the staple food for his children. Furthermore, human semen, the life-giving symbol par excellence, is called "gruel" (*ʔul*) in men's speech. Not only are semen and gruel similar in appearance, but also are believed from first premises to have similar anatomical origin. It can therefore be seen that the hot rain from heaven and all of its extensions symbolize the life-force itself. The "song" expresses metaphorically that the Mayordomo is embarking on a reaffirmation of order, a concept which is so general that time, space, reproduction and sustenance are all implied at once, and are not easily separated.

Positional meaning

I have emphasized that all four genres of "ancient words" are either implicitly or explicitly present at the same time in ritual action. They clearly "say"—in different codes—virtually the same thing as one another *and* the same thing as the cosmological principles which underlie them.[3] Furthermore, the linguistic aspects of their polysemic messages are not only part of their complex function as ritual substances. Their monotonous cadence, general redundancy, and variable density of metaphorical stacking—built almost entirely of metaphorical couplets—are themselves symbols of cyclical heat, a sacred principle of great importance in Chamula thought. Heat derives ultimately from Our Father Sun, Our Mother Moon, and their kinsmen, the saints. Together, these supernaturals created and now maintain the social and cosmic order, including such elementary facts of everyday life as day and night, the agricultural cycle, and the spatial categories and boundaries of the universe. To Chamulas, the human life itself is a metaphorical cycle of heat—beginning with the cold of childhood and ideally ending in the mature heat of old age. It is therefore not surprising that a striking number of the actions and other symbols which are present in any Chamula ritual setting attempt to replicate or create patterns which resonate with the solar cycle. "Ancient words" from the heated heart are part of this effort. Linguistic and nonlinguistic aspects of them work together to state the virtually countless ways in which men are dependent upon the temporal and spatial order given by the Sun/Christ deity and his kinsmen. They also state man's role to this effect is maintenance of ideal order—quintessential custom—in the microcosm of ritual space. However, I must emphasize that "ancient words" do not act alone in this space.

Lest I find myself so taken by the Chamula concept of redundancy that I repeat what I have to say needlessly, I should like to proceed further in the field of positional meaning to demonstrate how "ancient words" share the ritual stage with other ritual substances—or codes—which carry the same information. In other words, what do "ancient words" share with other sets and substances in the ritual microcosm?

In another paper (1972), I have attempted to demonstrate that the preponderant patterns of spatial symbolism in Chamula ritual action—such as counterclockwise motion, preference for the right hand, emphasis upon height, initial movement into the northeast quadrant of ritual circuit, climax of festivals at noon, position of personnel at ritual tables—all assume a conceptual eastern horizon as a point of orientation. Such primacy in their cosmological symbolism is offered as a key which ties all of these patterns together and makes them internally consistent and intelligible. It is further implied that spatial units—such as the sun's orbit—which are replicated in the ritual microcosm also stand for the fundamental temporal cycles of the natural world—day and night, the agricultural cycle, and the solar year. Hence, space and time become a single primordial concept. I am convinced that the language of the ritual stage is but another code for this same time-space unity which has Our Father Sun as its primary—though not its only—referent. It is my argument that "ancient words"—linguistic and nonlinguistic aspects—are but another way of expressing the polysemy of divine heat or "celestial rain," as the Chamula song puts it.

I noted above that "ancient words" share with many other ritual substances the quality of transformation from solid to essence, for the latter is the only medium which is believed to reach the supernatural world. In both a real and metaphorical sense, heat is the abstraction which unifies the *essential* qualities of attitude and substance which are necessary for ritual transactions. Rum liquor, for example, comes from raw brown sugar made in the tropical lowlands and is consumed by personnel in rank order at all stages in a ritual sequence, causing intoxication and "heat of the heart." According to the narrative which explains the origin of rum, it was created by Our Father Sun and San Juan from the juice of flowers in the First Creation. They found that it was good and had a party. It was so pleasant that they decided it should be used whenever their "children" talked to them and got together in their honor. I cite the narrative not only to show the ultimate association of rum with the sun deity, but also to illustrate its association with flowers, which, with pine boughs and other leaves (known metaphorically as flowers in prayers), are nearly always present on the ritual stage. Their aroma or essence is believed to be pleasing to the deities. Aromatic pine needles and pine boughs in particular are associated with the "living tree" on which the Sun/Christ was killed, later to ascend to the sky. Pine is therefore a kind of anticipation of, or precondition for, the sun's presence and, by extension, a symbolic precondition for almost any ritual transaction.

In similar fashion, candles, tobacco, fireworks, and incense—all typically present in a ritual setting—are transformed by fire into heated essence (i.e., sound or smell) which is highly mobile. Similarly, the human body transcends its present time and space limitations by producing "ancient words" with a heated heart. In this form, they reach the deities. All of these substances impart their divine heat to those humans who consume or produce them and even to those who are merely in their presence. Although space does not allow full discussion of the role of each of these sacred substances in Chamula ritual, I hope that sufficient data have been presented to show that these ritual symbols belong to the same set of codes as "ancient words" and ritual action. All of these codes possess something approaching an equivalence relationship with one another. They do not merely support one another, but rather, they make up a chorus of many voices on the ritual stage which sing together of the ideal and complex order of Our Father Sun's universe.

NOTES

1. The parallel couplet is, of course, a very common trait of formal language in many parts of the world. Not only in the Indo-European languages (Jakobson 1966 and Lord 1958), but also in many of the other major linguistic families, dyadic construction is typical of the "high forms" of many individual languages (Edmonson 1971b: 83-84, 96-98, 104-105, 119-120; Fox 1971; and Reichard 1944). There is also every reason to believe that dyadic construction characterized the formal language of the Ancient Maya as well (Edmonson 1971a and Thompson 1960: 61-63).

2. This fragment is taken from a much longer text recited by Shun Méndez Tzotzek. The term "Jews" (*hurioetike*) in the text does not refer to a living group of persons as far as the Chamula are concerned. These beings are negative supernaturals which were associated with other forces hostile to the Sun/Christ deity in the first three creations. The term *hurio* is from the Spanish *judio,* "Jew," which no doubt was introduced in the 16th Century.

3. Examples above were chosen to emphasize the unity of message with passages relating to "Our Father Sun." In nearly all other texts of the four genres of "ancient words" the same principle—same message, different code—applies, but is greatly complicated by the fact that other deities and personages of the first three creations share certain of the Sun/Christ's qualities, but not others. For example, female saints and "Our Mother Moon" (the Virgin Mary) are also associated with heat, but it is with "nocturnal heat," heat of the underworld and the directions west and south. This implies variation in the ritual activity and verbal references which correspond to female deities (see Gossen 1972). However, the unity of the several codes referring to the same sacred symbol is not affected by this transformation.

REFERENCES

Bricker, Victoria R., 1966, "El hombre, la carga y el camino: antiguos conceptos mayas sobre el tiempo y espacia y el sistema zinacanteco de cargos." In *Los Zinacantecos,* ed. by E. Z. Vogt. México, D. F.: Instituto Nacional Indigenista.

Edmonson, M. S., 1971a, *The Book of Counsel: the Popol Vuh of the Quiché Maya of Guatemala.* (The Middle American Research Institute, Publication 35.) New Orleans: Tulane University Press.

———, 1971b, *Lore: an Introduction to the Science of Lore and Literature.* New York: Holt, Rinehart and Winston.

Fox, James J., 1971, "Semantic parallelism in Rotinese ritual language." *Bijdragen tot de Taal-, Land-, en Volkenkunde* 127: 215-255.

Gossen, Gary H., 1971, "Chamula genres of verbal behavior." In *Towards New Perspectives in Folklore,* ed. by A. Paredes and R. Bauman, 145-167. (*Journal of American Folklore,* Vol. 84.)

———, 1972, "Temporal and spatial equivalents in Chamula ritual symbolism." In *Reader in Comparative Religion: an Anthropological Approach,* ed. by W. Lessa and E. Z. Vogt, 3rd ed. New York: Harper and Row.

———, 1974a, *Chamulas in the World of the Sun: Time and Space in a Maya Oral Tradition.* Cambridge: Harvard University Press.

———, 1974b, "To speak with a heated heart: Chamula canons of style and good performance." In *Explorations in the Ethnography of Speaking,* ed. by R. Bauman and J. Sherzer. London and New York: Cambridge University Press, 389-416.

Jakobson, Roman, 1966, "Grammatical parallelism and its Russian facet." *Language* 42: 398-429.

Leach, Edmund R., 1954, *Political Systems of Highland Burma.* Cambridge: Harvard University Press.

———, 1966, "Ritualization in man in relation to conceptual and social development." *Philosophical Transactions of the Royal Society of London,* Series B, No. 772, Vol. 251, pp. 403-408. Reprinted in *Reader in Comparative Religion* (3rd ed.), ed. by W. Lessa and E. Z. Vogt (New York: Harper and Row).

Lord, Albert, 1958, *The Singer of Tales.* Cambridge: Harvard University Press.

Pozas, A., Ricardo, 1959, *Chamula: un Pueblo Indio de los Altos de Chiapas.* (Memorias del Instituto, No. 8.) México, D. F.: Instituto Nacional Indigenista.

———, 1962, *Juan the Chamula: an Ethnological Re-creation of the Life of a Mexican Indian.* Berkeley and Los Angeles: University of California Press.

Reichard, Gladys A., 1944, *Prayer: the Compulsive Word.* (Monographs of the American Ethnological Society, No. 7.) Reprinted by University of Washington Press (Seattle).

Thompson, J. E. S., 1960, *Maya Hieroglyphic Writing: an Introduction.* Norman: University of Oklahoma Press.

Turner, Victor, 1967, "Ritual symbolism, morality and social structure among the Ndembu." In *The Forest of Symbols,* by V. Turner. Ithaca: Cornell University Press, 48-58.

———, 1968, *The Drums of Affliction.* Oxford: Clarendon Press and the International African Institute.

PART II

Form

The topic of Part I, Performance, was the meaning *of a speech event: what is* said *by the performance of magical rites, religious ceremonies, and the preaching of sermons.* In this part are gathered analyses of the product *of speech acts: discourse. With but one possible exception the papers deal with what might broadly be called prayer.*

Shelton (Controlling capricious gods) *describes the formal features of a set of prayers used by shrine priests among northern borderland Igbo in addressing gods with whom "formal relations" are not established and whose behavior is therefore not "predictable." The fact that these prayers are absent in the rest of Igboland whereas the belief in capricious gods is everywhere present reveals the unique position of the priests, descendants of the Igala who once conquered these people.*

The delivery of Zuni prayers is demonstrated by Tedlock (From prayer to reprimand) *to vary considerably in spite of the numerous restrictions that govern both their transmission from one practitioner to another and their use, allowing a person to "interpret" his memorized prayers by varying the gradient features of prosody. Moreover, in spite of the uniqueness of prayers in form, content, and use, their delivery is comparable to certain forms of nonreligious speech. Prosody is again brought up for discussion by Christian in Part III of this volume.*

Whereas the preceding two chapters concern themselves with oral traditions, Long (Divination as model for literary form in Ancient Israel) *and Ferguson deal with literate societies. Long, without speculating about the advent of writing in an oral society, seeks to demonstrate the way in which the linguistic "schema" of the divinational event might have been incorporated into very different genres of discourse: prophecy and narrative. Although this is "reconstructed sociolinguistics," it illustrates at once the methodology of form criticism, much of it practiced on Hebrew and Christian Scriptures, and the wealth of material that awaits those who have specialized in nonliterate societies. (Working in the same scholarly tradition, Rabin in Part III writes about speech registers at the time the* Psalms *were recorded.)*

The prayers that Ferguson (The collect as a form of discourse) *analyzes are literary products, at least as far back as we can go in the Christian tradition (not to deny that there may be recurrent structural patterns in prayers from different religions, whether literate or not). Although, like Long, Ferguson attempts to account for the form of a type of discourse, the approach is that of "formal linguistics." Accepting the rule-based nature of speech, restricted in linguistic theory for the most part to the production of sentences, he finds rules that will account for the genre as a whole. In this case also the rules are not language specific, for the collect is written in Latin, English, and other languages; and they transcend the boundaries that distinguish various expressions of Christianity. In dealing with the history of this form of prayer, Ferguson's paper is a link to Part III that is devoted to Tradition.* Editor

5 Controlling Capricious Gods

Austin J. Shelton

The sociolinguistic analysis of a people's prayers can usefully supplement functionalist, structuralist, and other analyses of their religion, for the content and style of prayer not only reflects the belief system and rituals of the religion but reinforces those beliefs, requires those activities, and acts as a means of control over divinities and other forces. This paper is a study of one cluster of prayers and verbal formulae among the northern borderland Igbo of Nigeria. On one hand, these are special indices to religious belief in the existence of unpredictable beings, and they function as verbal means of assuring the ritual participants and the people that capricious attack may be averted. On the other hand, they are means to regularly reinforce belief in chance events which cannot be permitted to occur, and in capricious gods whose powers must be channeled to ensure the stability necessary for successful agrarian life and social order. By their very recitation the formulae also support the position of the priestly mediator as an agent not only of religious but of social control.

The value of stability

The Igbo place high value upon social order and stability of expectations for their survival and success as farmers, and their sedentary livelihood has conditioned them to value peace of mind and to dislike unanticipated excitement. Such cultural features as the extremely high incidence of proverbs result from, yet reinforce, the valuing of custom and the status quo (see Shelton 1969). Although as typical farmers Igbo engage in many land disputes, these are settled mostly by inter-village negotiations. Traditionally, Igbo seldom sought glory through feuding or warfare, but achieved status and derived prestige from the acquisition of nonhereditary titles obtained mainly through hard work and accumulation of wealth. The standard picture, then, is of a rather sober, practical, industrious people.

As in other oral-aural customary societies, among Igbo the ordered life is valued highest, so religion involves explanation, prediction, and control of all forces which affect one's life. Igbo dislike uninvolvement or detachment from events, especially from matters concerning their own fate, preferring participating in and as much control over their destiny as possible (see Holas 1968: 263). In northern Igbo language the same word, *ébénébé* is used to render "upset" or "somersault" as well as "great misfortune," indicating that any sudden turnabout (except in children's games, of course) is terrible. Related etymologically is the low-toned *èbènèbè* meaning "pity," one result of "great misfortune." Obviously a sudden turning, what is unpredictable, is believed to result often in disaster. Further, *òdachígìrí* is a sudden happening, and is related by slightly more distant etymology to *ódàchí,* which refers to an "obstacle." Similarly, "suddenness" and "accident" are rendered by the same term, *ntúmádí,* for what occurs "suddenly" is unpredictable and unanticipated and usually "upsets" normalcy, resulting in "misfortune" and "accident," and acting as an "obstacle" to right order. Thus the unpredictable is irrational and its results are usually bad (even in story telling and esthetics) from the northern Igbo point of view.

In the Igbo pantheon the "familiar spirits," earth and sky gods as well as ancestors, are predictable. Every Igbo knows what his proper relations with them must be, and he understands the penalties for violating these proprieties. Village morality is thus assured, so if troubles occur they can easily be ascribed to a given household spirit who has retaliated against someone for violating customary morality. For example, if a person is struck down by the dread "swelling disease" (*anasarca*), it is because he has committed an abomination against the earth. Other wrongs have similarly predictable punishments or, viewed otherwise, unfortunate events have similarly common and understandable causes. As Bohannan has said of the Tiv, "any act which disturbs the smooth course of social life—war, theft, witchcraft, quarrels—'spoils the country'; peace, restitution, successful arbitration 'repair' it" (1958: 41-42). Such human-caused disruptions can be made right by normal human means, and in general, as Ezeanya has argued of the Igbo, God, minor divinities, and ancestors are primarily promoters of order and stability in human society (1967; see also Shelton 1968).

Unfortunately for the northern Igbo, some of their gods (and powers of secret societies as well, such as the *Òmábẹ*) are unpredictable and dangerous. These are called by various names, depending upon dialects and local usage: *Agwù* (Caprice), *ájóchù* (Witch), *Àjòchù* (Night Spirit), *Ajómmò* (Evil Spirits), *Ákáloghóli* (Troublemaker), *Álusi* (Dangerous Thing), *Ékwèńsú* (Bringer of Evil), or *Mmúófià*

(Bush Spirit). Arinze says that "they are capricious to the extreme, and delight in torturing the innocent . . . The pagans summarize the activities of these evil spirits by saying that they bring a man *elisi elisi, ekesi ekesi* (lit. 'never finish eating, never finish dividing,' i.e., unending trouble)" (1970: 23, 56). Each borderland village has a localized *álụsi* spirit in charge of a priest descended from the Igala or Idoma people who in the past conquered this area of Igboland, so that no village is free of such troublesome spirits.

Thwarting caprice by verbal means

Unlike the ancestors, the earth goddess, or the sky gods, evil spiritual forces go forth and "seek offerings" by bringing misfortunes upon people. Surprise is important in their method, for it is especially difficult to cope with beings who upon a whim may visit elephantiasis of the scrotum upon a man or the abomination of twins upon a poor woman, neither of whom may have done the least wrong. To the Igbo this is a dreadful state of affairs. Caprice must be avoided, yet by ordinary means it cannot be avoided, so recourse must be had to ritual and magic, both of which are in control chiefly of the Igala priests. To stave off surprise visitations by troublemakers of any sort, the Igbo and the shrine priests resort especially to certain verbal formulae accompanying customary ritual. The major ritual is *ịchụ àjà* (to drive off evil), with the object of removing fear, securing well being, and appeasing malevolent spirits (Basden 1938: 58). The more common verbal techniques directed at thwarting caprice include avoidance by indirection, avoidance by redirection, and patterned invocations. Each of these, further, serves other functions than reflecting belief or believed ritual: each helps to create the basis for its own belief, and satisfies other social needs common to borderland Igbo. (Compare Samarin, 1972.)

Avoidance by indirection.

This is indirection and circumlocution in verbal reference to dangerous powers. One might ask: Is it possible to "avoid" chance occurrences? If one truly believes in chance, it seems that the answer must be negative. But the Igbo, while admitting of the possibility of chance, effectively keep it from operating by insisting that all events have an intentional cause, which may only be the whim of a god and ordinarily may be unknown to the human victim (Shelton 1968). Accordingly, one must avoid calling undue attention of unpredictable spirits to oneself. Such prudence is manifested most obviously by general avoidance of sacred precincts controlled by nonfamiliar and aggressive spirits, and in speech by the use of circumlocution, a technique common to many human groups.

Common among northern Igbo in referring to a god is the use of indirect expression: *Ọ̀bụ̀ ịkọm'éhà*: "The One Whose Name Is Not Spoken" (from *ịkọmà* "to speak out"). At the root of such indirection is the belief that words have power to affect more concrete events; so if one names a god, the latter might think it has been summoned. Such reference to a god by an actual name can be offensive to the deity, whose self-esteem is so great that it will not tolerate reference to it by weak mortals. Naming a god or a power, when not arousing its conscious anger, has the power of activating it, of "bringing it to life," and like the *djinn* let out of the magic bottle it immediately looks around to see who has awakened it. This can be dangerous to the person because of the possibility of spiritual contagion: if a spiritual force gets too close to a person, he is in danger, whether or not that force actually wills harm to him. Indirection also reinforces the belief that such beings are hostile (unlike Earth, the High God, or the ancestors) and emphasizes the need for priestly mediators, as I have argued in *The Igbo-Igala Borderland* (Shelton 1971). Furthermore, indirection implies that even gods can be fooled by humans who behave reasonably, for although people understand that the referent is a god, the god apparently does not—it is actually only by more specific language devices—e.g., its name, its titles, and the like.

Perhaps the most common circumlocutory formulae are those included in prayers to ancestors and gods by which deliberate vagueness or generalization of reference is employed by the celebrant to avoid giving offense to spiritual powers by failing to include some of them in the invocation. These are:

Ńdí ńwèànẹ	Owners of Earth
Ónyè ńwèànẹ	Owner of Earth
Ézẹ̀ ànẹ	Chief of the Earth
Ńdí bìnǎ ígwé	Sky-Dwellers
Ńdí bìnǎ ànẹ̀	Earth-Dwellers
Ńdí ńnọ̀nà áfìfa	Forest-Dwellers
Ụ́mụ̀ ànẹ̀	Children of Earth
Ḿmụ́ọ̀ níne	All Spirits

These formulae occur with varying frequency. Some, such as "Chief of the Earth" and "Owner of Earth," are regularly used as synonyms for the particular deity being worshipped, when they occur in worship directed to an individual deity. Yet even these are used in prayers directed to whole groups such as ancestors. In notes to such a usage in a northern Igbo ancestral prayer, I indicated that "Chief of the Earth" probably referred to the Earth Mother, *Ànẹ̀*: "...but prudence dictates caution, so it is worded generally in case *Ànẹ̀* overnight may have been replaced by some more powerful deity" (Shelton 1971: 109). "Owner of Earth," possibly referring to a specific *álụsi* spirit, yet deliberately worded in this vague way, was used eight times in a thirty-three verse prayer to that spirit, constituting almost twenty-five percent of the referents. A total of only fifteen beings and forces were invoked in that prayer, and the *álụsi*, *Ntiye*, was specifically invoked by name. *Ḿmụ́ọ̀ níne* (All Spirits) was used twice. (See Shelton 1971: 169-172.)

The formula "Owners of Earth" is also frequently used in conjunction with other circumlocutions. For example, in one twenty-six verse ancestral prayer in which fourteen more or less specific forces or ancestors were invoked in a total of sixteen verses, "Owners of Earth" was used five times and there was one reference to each of the following: "Chief of the Sky" (*Ézẹ́ígwé*), "Owner of Earth," "Sky-Dwellers," and "Earth-Dwellers" (Shelton 1971: 114-116). Thus more than one third of this prayer, following the pattern of prayers in this genre, was deliberately ambiguous in its referents, admittedly a high percentage, although in similar ancestral prayers in the northern Igbo borderland I found no prayers without such referents, the usual range of such referents averaging between fifteen percent and twenty-five percent. These verbal techniques further emphasize to the people the potential innumerability of divine forces, thereby strengthening the role of the priest/mediator who somehow can control such forces. Moreover, the formulae help to strengthen the political role of Igala-descended shrine priests as agents of village control while at the same time they affirm the role of the clan elders as interclan leaders and mediators between the people and their ancestors.

Avoidance by redirection.

This is swearing and oathing as ritual redirection of aggressive forces. Swearing is a verbal technique used to ensure order in life by keeping in check potentially destructive forces. Unlike indirection, which is passive avoidance, swearing and oathing are verbal actions whereby one asserts innocence of a deed at the risk of punishment not only for having committed it but for perjury as well, which may more deliberately offend a god. Ritual swearing paradoxically is an arousing of attention to oneself by the formal denial of involvement in events which could later call unanticipated attention to oneself, and is intended to redirect the force of gods away from the oath-maker.

The most common structure of conditional oath formulae is that of balanced segments, one idea expressed as the conditional, the next as its result, although like most Igbo prayers (and unlike Igbo proverbs, for instance) these are free texts whose form is only relatively fixed by custom (see Vansina 1965: 56). The following preliminary oath on *ọ̀fọ́*, the ritual staff of authority, exemplifies this sort of structure, using internal and final tonal and syllabic rhyme to emphasize the balance of segments and to increase the "word-power" of the oath:

Ònyé ọ̀bụ,	*yá bụrụ ya.*
Whoever it is,	let it be him.
Ònyé ọ̀bụhụ,	*yá ábụla ya.*
Whoever it is not,	let it not be him.

In other words: "Let the guilty be known as guilty; let the innocent be known as innocent" (Ezeanya 1967: 5). Structurally these formulae are reminiscent of the Songhay praise-name prayers to Haoussakoy, one of the Tôuru spirits, for the complementarity of dualities which such structures symbolize is common across West Africa:

Celui qui néglige, on le paye en négligence.
Celui qui fait le mal, on le paye en mal (Rouche 1960: 104).

In either case the oath, while reflecting a belief in divine justice, reaffirms the necessity of right judgment among people in society and, moreover, reinforces the role of the priest or the elder headman as the person dispensing justice.

Similarly structured formulae are the curses which commonly form part of prayers to ancestors and gods. Arinze includes such set curses in a typical morning prayer among northern Igbo:

Ònyé sị ànị bèm pùè átá . . .
Whoever says my compound should grow spear grass . . .
ǹké bèyà pùè éló!
may his compound grow fungus!
Ònyé sị m̀ nwuá . . .
Whoever says I must die . . .
nyá bụlụ ọ̀kụ̀kọ̀ ùzọ́ n'ákpué ụ́lá!
let him go into sleep before the chickens! (Arinze 1970: 26)

Another example is the common proverb included as a closing-formula conditional curse in many Igbo prayers:

Ègbé bèlù, Ùgọ́ belù . . .
May Hawk perch, may Eagle perch . . .
            [Unstated]
Ònyé sị íbé yà, 'Ébená!', ǹkù kàpụ̀ yà!
Whoever says the perch is his alone, "Do not perch! ," may his wing fall off!

This emphasizes democracy and human tolerance, as well as the necessary reciprocity between gods or ancestors and the living, suggesting the hope that gods may not permit their vast power to get the better of them and become dangerous to people (Uchendu 1964: 30). The structure itself stresses reciprocity, aside from the content—thus, while the expression manifests a stylistic balance and apposition which reflects the belief, the balance and apposition reinforce the believed content, for the very pattern of a speech in an oral-aural culture is a major means used in remembering it. In this instance, tonal and syllabic rhyme are used as mnemonic devices and for emphasis of the structure.

Patterned invocatory formulae.

The most direct preventive against divine capriciousness is the combined sacrificial offering and the following prayers, which are patterned like many such formulae so that they are easily remembered and verbally effective:

Ákálogheli m̀mụ́ọ̀,	Troublemaking Spirits,
Ákálogheli m̀mádù:	Troublemaking Persons:
lìzùénù;	eat, all of you;
kezùénù;	divide things up, all of you;
mèyàlúnù;	whatever you do, all of you;
dìrịlínù;	stay away, all of you;
wèpúnù ákà ébéà únù jì.	take away from here all of you whatever you have (Arinze 1970: 57).

The following prayer-curse is regularly included in ancestral prayers among several clans in the northern Igbo borderland as a means of redirecting power:

Kwọ, únù, kwọsị ókĩr̃ŏ!
Wash, all of you, wash down upon all of our enemies!
Ákwọ, kwọsịnàmọ̀ nà nwúnyè mừ nà ụ́mùmừ!
Wash, don't wash down upon me or my wife or my children!

A very common formula, and perhaps most widespread insofar as it occurs in prayer directed to almost all classes of beings among the northern Igbo, is a closing formula invoking the spirit to prevent "chance" occurrences. For example, during the installation of one's personal altar to the High God and Personal God, *Chí,* one closes with:

Chĩm, zọ̀'m̃!
My God, stand up for me!
Chĩm, ékwena kà ífè 'mèmù!
My God, let no things happen to me!

In the annual festival to the powers of the ancestors, northern Igbo close with:

Bíkó, zọ̀gịdè ányị̀!
Please, stand up for us!
Ékwene ífè ọ̀bụ́là kà'mà ányị̀!
Do not let unexpected things happen to us!

During the annual visitation of the powerful men's secret society known as *Ọ̀mábẹ,* which is controlled by the *álụsi* priests, the elder and leader of the group welcomes the spirit of the *ọ̀mábẹ* and tells it that the society's members have brought all the sacrificial offerings which they had promised it during its previous visit, and he closes his prayers with:

Bíkó ékwene ífè ọ̀bụ́nà'mè ányị̀!
Please do not let unexpected things happen to us!

What is most remarkable about this is that it is the *Ọ̀mábẹ* society itself which, except for *álụsi* spirits, causes most "unexpected things" to happen in the northern Igbo villages. The formula functions clearly, then, not actually as a plea or a supplication at all, but as a reminder to all the men and boys gathered for the ceremony that their welfare and the welfare of the entire village is subject to virtually uncontrollable forces which ultimately are mediated by the Igala-descended *álụsi* priest.

Priests and social control

How do the foregoing prayers and formulae affect the religious ritual of which they are part or the belief system which they reflect? Northern Igbo borderland history necessitates some of this prayer style of the village priests and elders, and the function of prayers is influenced both by their phonological and by their syntactical features and content. Their structure and content signal their specific functions in ritual, and in these very important circumstances convey and reinforce social values. But certain morphological and phonological features supplement this role—e.g., the repeated *ékwene ífè ọ̀búlà* (Let not things unexpected . . .) is not only a supplication, but repeated as it is, it takes on an invocatory function, Igbo arguing that proper recitation of the phrase amidst other prayers helps to cause gods either to behave predictably or, more often, not to become capriciously aroused. This occurs also with other formulae within set prayers, such as the repeated "Owner of Earth" or the tonal and syllabic-rhymed litany of imperative verbs directed at evil spirits (see above, p. 68):

lìzùénù
kezùénu
mèyàlúnù
dịṛịlínù
wèpúnù.

These formulae are often special speech forms, although not classified as such by Igbo and not so consistently patterned as the speech of divination, which also serves in controlling caprice (see Shelton 1965).

As effective as the form of invocatory formulae may be, the worshippers (as distinct from the specialist priests) are interested primarily in their content, and their repetition serves purposes both religious and political. The prayers and formulae result from man's belief in the supremacy of certain spiritual forces considered as nonfamiliar. Although ancestors and gods have wide powers over humans and can make certain demands, humans in turn exercise a sort of parallel control—that is to say, it is only the living people who can furnish ancestors and gods with the sacrifices which those beings desire and require, and under some circumstances people will even threaten the spirits with refusal to make sacred offerings. This, of course, is seldom the case with those really capricious troublemakers among the gods, yet even with many of them the principle of reciprocity operates: normally, so long as they are "fed" and so long as the formulae in prayers are regularly recited, they are believed to restrain themselves, to be "controlled." in this sense, like the *kpele* prayers and rituals of the Gã people of Ghana (Kilson 1970: 49), the formulae and the ritual of which they are part act as system-maintaining rites.

Compounding the religious situation in the northern Igbo borderland, however, is the fact that the major social control agents are descendants of alien Igala and Okpoto conquerors, who are the priests of the capricious village spirits called *álụsi.* It is to their benefit to maintain belief in the combined power and capriciousness of the beings whom they serve, for by such means they are able to force the villagers to make regular offerings to those spirits and to maintain a respectful relationship with the shrine priest himself, who as the only holder of an inherited title in each of the villages sits on all the important political councils. In this manner, the prayers not only reflect the belief system and reassure worshippers that capriciousness will be averted, therby guaranteeing the peace of mind valued by the people, but they also create (or re-create) the very situation which they ostensibly solve.

Prayers to ancestors and gods would be complete without use of the techniques employed in the borderland villages to avert presumed capricious attack. Indeed, in nuclear Igboland, and in the prayers of most West African peoples, although peace of mind may be desired as a good, one does not encounter such formulae, or if they occur they are infrequent. But in the Igbo-Agala borderland prayers, they are commonplace. They reinforce customary belief in chance events and capricious attack by hostile gods, they re-create felt needs for safety and freedom from fear, they act to reassure the worshippers, and they function to maintain the shrine priests in their positions of power over the communities in which they live.

REFERENCES

Arinze, Francis A., 1970, *Sacrifice in Ibo Religion*. Ibadan: Ibadan University Press.

Basden, George T., 1938, *Niger Ibos*. London: Seeley Service.

Bohannan, Laura, 1958, "Political aspects of Tiv social organization." In *Tribes Without Rulers*, ed. by John Middleton and David Tait. London: Routledge and K. Paul, 33-66.

Ezeanya, S. N., 1967, "Oaths in the traditional religion of West Africa." *West African Religion*, No. 7 (April), 1-10.

Holas, Bohumil, 1968, "Le dogma, l'action liturgique, et le sacrifice." In *Les Dieux d'Afrique Noire*. Paris: P. Geuthner, 257-268.

Kilson, Marion, 1970, "Taxonomy and form in Gã ritual." *Journal of Religion in Africa* 3: 45-66.

Rouch, Jean, 1960, *La Religion et la Magie Songhay*. Paris: Presses Universitaires de France.

Samarin, William J., 1972, "Language in religion and the study of religion." *Linguistica Biblica*, December, pp. 18-29.

Shelton, Austin J., 1965, "The meaning and method of *afa*-divination among the northern Nsukka Igbo." *American Anthropologist* 57: 1441-1455.

———, 1968, "Causality in African thought: Igbo and others." *Practical Anthropology* 15: 157-169.

———, 1969, "The articulation of traditional and modern Igbo literature." *The Conch* 1 (1), 30-52.

———, 1971, *The Igbo-Igala Borderland: Religion and Social Control in Indigenous African Colonialism*. Albany: State University of New York Press.

Uchendu, Victor C., 1964, "The status implications of Igbo religious beliefs." *The Nigerian Field* 29 (1): 27-37.

Vansina, Jan, 1965, *Oral Tradition*. Chicago: Aldine.

6 From Prayer to Reprimand

Dennis Tedlock

The speaker of Zuni has two means of radically removing what he says from the plane of everyday Zuni phonology. On the one hand, he may *ʔána kʔéyatoʔu* (raise it right up); on the other, he may *yam ʔíkʔe·nan·àk·a péyeʔa* (say it with his heart).[1] In "raising it right up," the speaker gives strong stress and high pitch to syllables that would otherwise be weak and low. In "saying it with his heart," he speaks without speaking, thinking the words through in his heart instead of saying them with his vocal organs.[2] Either way, the resultant sound pattern is directly opposed to the normal pattern, in the one case by inversion and in the other by negation.

The phonemes of Zuni, as described by Newman (1965: 13-15), include two stresses (strong and weak) and three pitch levels.[3] In the everyday patterns which are the concern of a grammar, the first syllable of a word of two or more syllables takes the strong stress (´), as in *pénan·e* (word). Sometimes a clause-initial monosyllabic word also takes the strong stress, as in *hóp to ʔá·ne* (Where are you going?). In words of four or more syllables there is sometimes a secondary (and subphonemic) stress (`) on the penult or antepenult, as in *tómtonàn·e* (log drum). All other syllables take the weak stress (unmarked here).

In the everyday patterns of Zuni pitch, the sentence or independent clause begins with a middle pitch (2), sometimes sags to a low pitch (1), and then, on the final word, if it is polysyllabic (which it usually is), rises to a high pitch (3) on the first syllable and drops steeply to a low pitch (1) on the last:

2   1 3   1
lǎ·kʔi ʔápi yam hót·a ʔánʔikʔ ošàka
(today Ivy her maternal-grandmother played-with)
Today Ivy played with her grandmother.

A shorter sentence or clause may simply begin on (2) and drop to (1) at the end (Newman 1965: 14-15):

2   1
ʔápi ʔíya
(Ivy is-coming)
Ivy is coming.

Sometimes the de-emphasis entailed in the combination of weak stress and low pitch on the final syllable is carried a step further: the vowel may lose its voicing and the final consonant (if any) may become inaudible.

Cutting across these patterns of stress and pitch are what I like to call "lines," after the lines in written poetry. Each line is an uninterrupted sequence of sounds, falling between two silences.[4] The line is not to be confused with the "breath group." Many silences in extended discourse, Zuni or otherwise, are not accompanied by the taking of breath; indeed, they may be accompanied by the closing of the glottis. Nor is the line to be confused with the "utterance," which linguists treat as if it necessarily meshed directly with syntactical units. The line I am speaking of is the line as actually delivered. In the case of Zuni *télapnà·we* (tales), lines often end in the middle of a clause, sometimes even on a modifier whose noun or verb is delayed until the next line. In the following example (from Tedlock 1972), the two lines are separated by a pause of a little less than a second:

2   1   3   1 2
hǎnat·e tomʔa·n ténaʔu ni·šapak hom
(quick you sing-it mourning-doves my)
Quick, sing it, mourning doves made me

1   3   1
ténan ʔòk·ʔanàpka
(song caused-to-forget)
forget my song.

Conversely, a new clause or sentence may begin in the middle of a line:

2 1   3 1 2   1 2   1 3   1
kôp toʔ léyeʔa léʔ ʔánikʷap mǎʔ ho kǎwašeʔa
(what you doing that he-said-to-her well I am-winnowing)
"What are you doing?" He said to her. "Well, I'm winnowing."

In either situation the regular patterns of stress and pitch are usually undisturbed, as in the examples given. The effect of such lines, when they occur frequently in extended discourse, is analogous to that of syncopation in music: there are silences where notes might have been expected, or notes where silences might have been expected. In tale-telling, as in music, syncopation builds a kind of tension. It also occurs, if less frequently, in Zuni conversation, as in our own.

"Raising up" prayers

Zuni *téwusu péna·we* (sacred words), usually prayers, sound very different from tales or conversation. When prayers are intended to be heard and understood not only by an audience of *k'ápin ʔá·hoʔ·i* "raw people" (nonhuman beings) but by one of *tékʔohan·an ʔa·hoʔ·i* "daylight people" (humans) as well, stress, pitch, and line all come into concert in the mode of delivery known as "raising it right up." Each line is treated as if it were a clause (whether it is one or not), except that the sag to (1) after the initial (2) is now carried all the way to the penult of the final word, and the (3), instead of occurring on the first syllable of the final word, now occurs on the last. That same last syllable, instead of taking a weak stress or even being unvoiced, now takes the heaviest stress of the entire line, with a consequent lengthening of the vowel. Stresses which normally would be strong elsewhere in the line are reduced to the level of secondary stresses, and those which normally would be secondary stresses are reduced to weak stresses. These changes constitute an inversion: what would have been lowest becomes highest; what would have been highest becomes lowest; and what might have been the weakest syllable in the entire line now becomes the strongest.[5] Lines may still end within clauses, but they no longer separate modifier from noun or verb, and there are no longer shifts from one clause to another within lines. The following prayer to the Sun Father (adapted from Bunzel 1932b: 635) illustrates this "raised up" delivery of "sacred words":

$$
\overset{2}{lŭk·a}\ \overset{1}{yàton·}\overset{3}{ê·}
$$
(this day)
This day!

$$
\overset{2}{hŏm}\ yàtok·a\ \overset{1}{tǎ}\overset{3}{č·ú·}
$$
(my sun father)
My Sun Father!

$$
\overset{2}{yǎm}\ tèłaš·inak^{w}\overset{1}{i·}\overset{3}{}
$$
(your terrestrial-old-one-at)
To your holy place!

$$
\overset{2}{tŏ}\ yè·lana\ k^{w}àyik'ap·\overset{1}{á·}\overset{3}{}
$$
(you standing come-out)
You come out standing!

$$
\overset{2}{yǎm}\ k'àk^{w}i\ yà·na\ tè'on\overset{1}{á·}\overset{3}{}
$$
(our/your water-at become-whole that-which-is)
The water by which we live!

$\overset{2}{h\mathring{a}}lawtinan\cdot\overset{1}{\acute{e}\,}\overset{3}{}$
(prayer-meal)
Prayer meal!

$\overset{2}{l\mathring{i}}\cdot la\ tom\ ho?\ \overset{1}{l\grave{e}ya}?up\cdot\overset{3}{\mathring{a}}\cdot$
(here to-you I hand)
Here I hand to you!

$\overset{2}{y\mathring{a}m}\ ?ona\ y\grave{a}\cdot\overset{1}{nak\mathring{a}}\cdot\overset{3}{}$
(your/our road become-whole-instrument)
Your full road!

$\overset{2}{y\mathring{a}m}\ \overset{1}{la\check{s}}\cdot iyak\mathring{a}\cdot\overset{3}{}$
(your become-old-instrument)
Your old age!

$\overset{2}{y\mathring{a}m}\ k\overset{1}{?a\check{s}}im\mathring{a}\cdot\overset{3}{}$
(your waters)
Your waters!

$\overset{2}{y\mathring{a}m}\ t\grave{o}\cdot\check{s}onan\cdot\overset{1}{\acute{e}}\cdot\overset{3}{}$
(your seed)
Your seed!

$\overset{2}{y\mathring{a}m}\ ?\grave{u}tenan\cdot\overset{1}{\acute{e}}\cdot\overset{3}{}$
(your wealth)
Your wealth!

$\overset{2}{y\mathring{a}m}\ s\grave{a}wanik\mathring{a}\cdot$
(your become-powerful-instrument)
Your courage!

$\overset{2}{y\mathring{a}m}\ c\grave{e}mak^{w}in\ cum\cdot\overset{1}{\acute{e}}\cdot\overset{3}{}$
(your thoughts-at strength)
Your strength of mind!

$\overset{2}{t\grave{e}mla}\ hom\ to?\ ?\grave{a}nik\check{c}iyan\cdot\overset{1}{\mathring{a}}\cdot\overset{3}{}$
(all me you will-bless-with)
With all these you will bless me!

A prayer delivered before an audience may be answered with periodic affirmations, as when a man praying before the altar of a medicine society is answered by another man who sits behind the altar. Like the prayer itself, the response may be "raised right up": $?\grave{e}le\cdot t\acute{e}\cdot$ (instead of $?\acute{e}le\cdot te$) "Just so!" or, alternatively, $ha\check{c}\cdot\acute{i}\cdot$ (instead of $h\acute{a}\check{c}\cdot i$) "Indeed!"

There are times when a person delivering a prayer does not "raise it right up." This is especially likely to happen when there are people present other than the intended audience. A prayer is valuable and potent in inverse proportion to the number of people who know it (Bunzel 1932a: 493-94), and there is always a chance than an eavesdropper might steal it from its owner. This is the problem of a man who wishes a kachina dance to continue for another day, for example; he must go to the dance leader, right out in the plaza, and must preface his request with a prayer, but his prayer is intended for the dance leader, not for the general public. In addition to lowering his voice, he may return his stress pattern to something like that of tale-telling or conversation. In that case his pitch contour will also return to normal; in fact, it may even be flattened beyond the normal since long prayer clauses may be treated like the short clauses of conversation, that is, given an overall (2 . . . 1), without any (3). The fourth line of the above prayer, if it occurred in conversation, might be delivered as follows:

$$\overset{2}{to}{}^{\text{?}} \ \overset{1}{y\acute{e}\text{·}lana} \ k^w\overset{3}{\acute{a}}yik\overset{1}{{}^{\text{?}}ap}$$

But in lowered prayer delivery, the (3) might be flattened all the way down to (1). Moreover, this line might be run together with two or three others, with only the contrast between its final (1) and the initial (2) of the following clause to mark the spot where there might otherwise have been a pause.[6] The elimination of many pauses, together with the flattening of pitch, gives such a delivery the effect of a rapid paternoster.

As a rule, a person who prays in solitude, as a man does when he goes to his cornfield at sunrise, will use the flat and rapid delivery just described. But if, despite all this man's previous prayers and sacrifices, the "raw people" have failed to bring the expected summer rains to his field, he may use the "raised up" delivery, and even give the strong stresses a little more punch than usual. As one Zuni put it, "Sometimes you have to really tell them. The old man says, 'If they don't bring rain you might as well scold them'." Bunzel's statement that Zuni prayer "is never the spontaneous outpouring of the overburdened soul," but "more nearly a repetition of magical formulae" (1932b: 615) holds true only for the *wording*, not for the *delivery*.

Some prayers are so valuable to their owners that they are "said with the heart," without sound or even movement of the lips. This is the case, for example, with the prayers of dance leaders during the winter night performances of the Kachina (masked dance) Society. A prayer of this kind would be spoken aloud on only two occasions during the lifetime of a religious officeholder, the first when he learned it and the second when he trained his successor. Even a person praying in solitude will not risk the oral delivery of such a prayer, for, as one man put it, "You'll never know who might come around within a minute or two." In "saying it with the heart" we have a "speech event," if that is the word, which cannot be collected.

There are a few prayers which, even though valuable and potent, are intended to be heard by the public. These prayers are protected from being too widely known by their great length and by the fact that they are delivered only once a year (and in some cases only once in four years). Such is the case with the *péna tášana* (long talk) performed by the impersonator of the Long Horn kachina at the *šáʔlako* ceremony in December (Bunzel 1932b: 710-56), a prayer intended to benefit the entire community for the entire coming year. The delivery is an extreme form of "raising it right up." The line-initial (2) is maintained evenly, without any drop to (1), all the way up to the last syllable of the line, which is then delivered with a (3-1) glide lasting two seconds or so. During the pause before the next line, the performer shakes his rattle (a bunch of deer shoulder blades held in the hand) and simultaneously stomps his right foot. This combination of features brings us to the borderland between speech and song: the pitch control approaches that of the singing voice, though the "melody" is simple; the rattle provides a beat, if an unevenly spaced one; and the stomp of the foot suggests kachina dancing.[7]

"Sacred words" in a "secular" setting

Some *téwusu péna·we* (sacred words) are not prayers, that is, their audience is solely human except in the sense that "raw people" might be listening in. Again the pattern of delivery depends on the audience. When the impersonator of the *káklo* kachina gives a six-hour narration of the *čímikʔanàʔkowa* (origin story) before Kachina Society members, or when the Bow Priest announces a communal rabbit hunt to the whole village, they "raise it right up." But when the head of a household has a formal exchange with the medicine man whose services he is contracting, and when their words are not intended for others who may be in the room, the delivery is the flat and rapid one described earlier.

Although series of lines with stress and pitch inversion are usually found in settings which are clearly *téwusu* (sacred), such passages do occur in speech events which are only peripherally sacred. Episodes of the *čímikʔanàʔkowa* (origin story), for example, may be told in a hearthside setting, with some passages retaining a "raised up" delivery despite the secular occasion. Moreover, *télapnà·we* tales, which are not in and of themselves sacred at all, may contain "raised up" quotations of sacred words. In either kind of narrative, the lines in question usually involve formal exchanges (including greetings) between two parties, at least one of whom is either a "raw person" or a priest. In the following example a priest, after an exchange of greetings, asks a roomful of people why they called him to their house:

2   1   3
piʔła šiwani ʔi·tek·unak·a si·
(bow priest questioned-them now)
    The Bow Priest questioned them: "Now!

2   1   3
hom ʔà·tac̆·ú·
(my fathers)
    My fathers!

$\overset{2}{hom}\ \overset{\lor 1}{\check{c}aw}\overset{3}{\check{e}\cdot}$

(my children)

My children!

$k^{w}\overset{2}{\acute{a}}\text{?}\check{c}i\ k\acute{o}\text{?}\ \overset{1}{le}\ \overset{3}{\text{?}on}\ \overset{1}{\text{?}\acute{a}k\cdot a}$

(what thing which because-of)

For what reason

$\overset{2}{hom}\ to\text{?}\ \text{?}\overset{\lor}{a}nte\check{s}ema\cdot\overset{1}{w}\overset{3}{\acute{e}\cdot}$

(me you summon)

do you summon me?!"

At this point, or after another line or two, the quoted priest will pass to a less formal mode of delivery. (Note that he already did abandon "raised up" speech in the next-to-last line above, but then resumed it.) Then one of his hosts will reply with ?e· ?i·namiɬté· (Yes, in truth!) and perhaps a few more lines with stress and pitch inversion, again passing to a less formal mode before he finishes.

On rare occasions the hearthside narrator may "raise it right up" elsewhere than in quotations, as in this passage from the čímik?anà?kowa in which the twin war gods first learn that evil has come into the world:

$\overset{2}{\text{?}\acute{a}\cdot}\check{c}i\ lak^{w}\ \text{?}\acute{u}k^{w}\cdot ayika\ t\acute{e}k^{w}\cdot in\ t\overset{3}{\acute{e}\check{c}}\cdot\overset{1}{ip}$

(two there coming-out-instrument place come-to)

When the two come to the Place of Emergence

$\overset{2}{p\grave{o}}wayala\overset{1}{y}\overset{3}{\acute{e}\cdot}$

(is-sitting-on-the-ground)

there he sits!

$\overset{2}{\text{?}\grave{a}}mpe\text{?}\overset{1}{s}\overset{3}{\acute{a}y}$

(sorcerer)

A sorcerer!

$\overset{2}{ho}\text{?}\ \text{?}\grave{a}n\check{c}i\text{?}m\overset{1}{ow}\overset{3}{\acute{a}y}$

(person unclean)

Someone unclean!

$\overset{2}{ho}\text{?}\ \text{?}\grave{a}t\cdot an\cdot\overset{1}{i}\overset{3}{\cdot}$

(person dangerous)

Someone dangerous!

$\overset{2}{h}\overset{1}{\grave{a}}ɬik^{w}\overset{3}{i}\cdot$

(witch)

A witch!

The use of whole series of "raised up" lines formerly was limited to the kinds of religious and quasi-religious contexts just described. Public announcements always have been "raised up," but formerly they were delivered by the Bow Priest, who was unlikely to have any messages of a wholly secular nature. Today, however, public announcements are made by a civil official who brings news of an election or a fair, "raising it right up" in the old style but speaking into the microphone of a sound truck.

Exclamations and insistent speech

In secular speech events other than announcements, lines with stress and pitch inversion occur only singly, never in a series. In the nonreligious passages of tales and in the less formal narratives of conversations, such lines usually consist of a single onomatopoeic word or an interjection. In the case of onomatopoeia, the sound imitated in the "raised up" style is sudden, brief, and unrepeated: *hašán* is the sound of a large object, such as a rabbit, being swallowed at one gulp; *kolón* is the sound of a large gulp of liquid; *kolán* is the sound of a person entering a house precipitously; *tenén* is the sound of a body dropping to the ground in death or a faint. These words are never pronounced in any other way, even when they occur at the beginning of a long line instead of occupying a line of their own. A word imitating a continuous or repeated sound, on the other hand, never takes stress inversion: a hard rain, for example, is *ʔíš·akᵂakᵂa.*

The most frequent interjection in tales is *tíš·omah·á,* which expresses horror combined with a pleading attitude; a man might say it when he learns that his son is planning to exchange bodies with a man who died of an axe wound to the head, for example. Other interjections, almost always delivered as a single line with stress inversion, are frequently heard in everyday life. A woman may express sudden pain or anger with *ʔatú·* ; a man may express exasperation with *yaʔ·a·ná·* . Neither these nor any other Zuni interjections have any denotative meaning, unless it be said that they denote the emotions they express; they lack the religious reference carried by so many English interjections. Whereas English swearing opens up the boundary between the sacred and the secular, the Zuni interjection stands at the exact opposite pole from the most sacred Zuni prayer. Where the prayer "said with the heart" combines maximum content with lack of sound, the interjection combines lack of content with maximum sound.

Beyond these interjections, the uses of stress and pitch inversion in secular contexts include greetings, interrogations, descriptive exclamations of amazement, imperative statements, and sudden announcements of news. The most common greeting, *keš·é·* (Hello!) is nearly always delivered with final stress. Interrogatives, which normally carry first-syllable stress, may be given a sense of urgency and importance with stress inversion: *kᵂaʔpí·* (What?!), *hop·í·* (Where?!), *čúwapí·* (Who?!). A woman, trying to get her diversely occupied family to come to the dinner table, always says *ʔítona·wé·* (Eat!–plural subject); and if she has to repeat herself, she increases the final stress and widens her pitch intervals. A girl who sees a carful of visitors coming may run into the house and address everyone there with *čòlin ?a·wiyá·* (Jo Ann [and others] are coming!).

Exclamations of amazement commonly consist of *hiš* or *siš* (very) followed by a word which describes the thing or event remarked upon. Learning that a woman had paid sixty cents apiece for some cabbage seedlings, I said to her:

$\overset{2}{hi}\overset{3}{\check{s}}\ \overset{3}{t\acute{e}}hya\overset{1}{}$

How expensive.

She replied, as if correcting me or perhaps going me one better:

$\overset{2}{hi}\overset{}{\check{s}}\ \overset{1}{teh}y\overset{3}{\grave{a}}\cdot$

How expensive!

The "raised up" delivery in everyday life most frequently appears in the remarks which adults address to children. The commonest single item is *lesmá·* (Don't!). During a recorded interview, an older man was told by a child that someone had been throwing rocks at the screen door; he dealt with the matter as follows:

$\overset{2}{\check{c}}\overset{1}{u}wap\overset{3}{i}\cdot$

Who?!

(answer) $\overset{2}{?}\overset{1}{a}pi$

Ivy.

$\overset{2}{?}\overset{1}{a}pi\ lesm\overset{3}{\acute{a}}\cdot$

Ivy, don't!

Here are other lines which this same man addressed to Ivy (age three) when she interrupted interviews:

$\overset{2}{l}\grave{e}sma\ \overset{1}{pan}iy\overset{3}{\acute{u}}\cdot$
   (this-no get-down)
   Don't, get down!

$\overset{2}{l}\grave{e}sma\ l\grave{e}sma\ l\grave{e}sma\ l\grave{e}sma\ \overset{1}{les}m\overset{3}{\acute{a}}\cdot$
   (this-no this-no this-no this-no this-no)
   Don't, don't, don't, don't, DON'T!

$\overset{2}{h}\grave{o}p\cdot i\ \overset{1}{tam}\cdot\overset{3}{\acute{e}}\cdot$
   (where father-diminutive)
   Where's daddy?! (i.e., go away and find him)

$\overset{2}{hot}$·a les $\overset{1}{?an}\overset{\vee 3}{?ik?o\check{s}e}$·

(maternal-grandmother this-one play-with-hortatory)
Go on and play with grandmother!

$\overset{2}{si\check{s}}$ to$\overset{1}{?}$ pèye$\overset{}{?}a$ tèlok·$\overset{3}{?an\mathring{a}}$·
(very you talk be-quiet)
You talk too much, be quiet!

In most such scolding, the meaning is carried not only by the words and the "raised up" delivery, but by a tight and sharp voice quality as well.

The meaning of "raising it right up"

It remains to abstract the common features of all these examples of lines with stress and pitch inversion, ranging from prayer to reprimand. A Zuni man, asked to explain a narrative passage in which a quoted priest uses such lines, told me, "He's saying it in a way that is not ordinary. He's trying to stress, to bring out an important idea. It shows authority, and to have a complete thought at the same time, not just trailing off." In one way or another, these remarks can be applied to all the examples.

First of all, stress and pitch inversion attracts more attention than ordinary delivery and implies that what is being said is "important"; the speech event in question "is not ordinary," and it will take precedence over any other speech event that may already be in progress. Even a little girl can get the attention of an entire household, cutting right through the preoccupations of its members with her reversed delivery. In the case of ritual exchanges with a priest, inversion marks the beginning of a speech, but once the attention and importance have been established it is possible for the speaker to relax his delivery. In the case of the public prayer of Long Horn, on the other hand, every single line demands the same kind of attention that a little girl demands for only one line. The affirmations with which a "raised up" prayer may be answered are a subtler case: the affirming person is not trying to get attention or to be important, but to carry his assent beyond the lexical (Just so! or Indeed!) by *echoing* the stress and pitch inversion of the prayer, thus making a *phonological* assent. The use of onomatopoeic words by a narrator is also an echoing: it is not so much that he is trying to get attention (he already has it), but that he is imitating the attention-getting quality of sudden (and important) noises.

Second, stress and pitch inversion "shows authority." This is clear enough in the case of sacred words; in fact, sacred words carry authority in and of themselves, even when they are uttered by a person without priestly office. It is also clear in the case of orders and reprimands. In other cases, "authority" is present only in the sense that the speaker has a *temporary* right to demand attention in such a powerful fashion. In all contexts which are not even peripherally sacred, even including those which call for orders and reprimands, this right is limited to the delivery of a single line, after which ordinary speech is used. The sole exception to this is the public announcement delivered by a civil official.

Third, lines with stress and pitch inversion are clear and complete. They do not "trail off" into a low pitch, a weak stress, and even a loss of voicing, but rather stand in direct opposition to the most obvious weakness of everyday speech. This befits their importance and authority.

In the case of "saying it with the heart," importance and authority ride entirely on the lexical potency (as opposed to phonological potency) of the prayer and on the legitimacy of sacred office. These properties are sufficient to attract the attention of the "raw people," who are able to "listen" to thoughts.

It should be mentioned, before closing, that phenomena similar to Zuni stress and pitch inversion probably occur in all the other languages of the Pueblo Indians, though with some variation as to their exact use. I have heard heavy line-final stress, accompanied by high pitch and sometimes by a downward glide, in announcements made to spectators at Hopi and Jemez dances. It is also said that Tewa announcements are delivered in this manner, though prayers are not (Alfonso Ortiz, personal communication).

The place which the inversion of stress and pitch occupies in the total picture of Zuni speech points to the importance of a sociolinguistic approach, not only to "speech" but to "language" itself. If one were to include inversion in a description of Zuni phonology, it would be "low" (or late) in the list of rules. In fact, it is altogether absent from Zuni speech when there is no question of getting attention or expressing authority, and thus it is unlikely to appear under the circumstances of a formal linguistic interview (except as an interruption). The common greeting *keš·é·* (Hello!), when given out of context as a vocabulary item, is delivered as *kéš·e* or *kéš·i* (the latter is the form entered in Newman's dictionary, 1958). Newman catches "abnormal" stress only once in his dictionary (the entry for *ʔatú·*), and he does not discuss it at all in his grammar (1965).[8] Bunzel, for her part, treats line-final stress as a matter of literary style (1932b: 620). If we were to decide, however, that this device (if we noticed it at all) belonged somehow to the realm of style and "speech" rather than to that of grammar and "language," our grammar would fail to account not only for prayer, but for some of the most obvious features of speech in Zuni daily life, even including the way people said "Hello!"

NOTES

1. The orthography used here is that of Newman (1965: 13), except that I have followed Walker (1972: 259) in treating both the lengthening of vowels and the doubling of consonants as a single phoneme (·). The field work involved in this paper was supported, on separate occasions, by grants from the National Institute of Mental Health, the City University of New York, and the American Philosophical Society.

2. These two special modes of delivery are applicable not only to *péna·we* (words) but also to *téna·we* (songs). Of the five parts of a kachina song, AABBA, the first two A sections and the

first B section all have the same tonic, but the second B may be "raised up" higher and the final A still higher. It is never the case that an entire song is "raised up"; rather, *?ána k?éyato?u* describes the relationship between two adjoining sections of the same song. When a person *yam ?ík?e·nan·àk·a tén?a* (sings with his heart), on the other hand, the song is silent in its entirety, however many parts it may have.

3. It might be argued that there is really only one stress phoneme and that "weak stress" is its absence (Walker 1972: 247); the middle of the three pitches might similarly be treated as a sort of absence.

4. For a more extensive discussion of lines, see Tedlock 1971: 127-129.

5. This strengthening of the final vowel led Bunzel to suppose that there were special word endings for prayers: "Words ending with consonants—for example, the participles in *-nan* and *-ap*—take special forms . . . *-nana* and *-apa* when occurring finally" (1932b: 620n.). But these are not special forms: it is just that their final vowels, which are commonly unvoiced in everyday speech, came to her attention only in "raised up" delivery.

6. On the other hand, such pauses as there were would not be in positions other than those of a "raised up" delivery.

7. Long Horn's talk roughly fits List's description of "chant"; in the latter's map of the field of pitch variables connecting speech and song, chant lies closer to song than to speech (1963: 9, 11).

8. Newman does discuss one unusual type of Zuni intonation (1965: 15), involving the ideophonic lengthening of the final vowel of a verb, but this device, though it does involve a final (3), is not to be confused with the combination of stress and pitch inversion discussed here. The reason Newman caught the final stress of *?atú·* is that in the case of this and some other interjections, and in the case of the onomatopoeic words discussed earlier, final stress has become a feature of the word itself and no longer depends upon line delivery. These few words are, as it were, "raised up" every time they are delivered, even in an interview.

REFERENCES

Bunzel, Ruth L., 1932a, "Introduction to Zuni ceremonialism." *Annual Report of the Bureau of American Ethnology* 47: 467-544.

———, 1932b, "Zuni ritual poetry." *Annual Report of the Bureau of American Ethnology* 47: 611-835.

List, George, 1963, "The boundaries of speech and song." *Ethnomusicology* 7: 1-16.

Newman, Stanley, 1958, *Zuni Dictionary*. (Research Center in Anthropology, Folklore, and Linguistics, Pub. 6.) Bloomington: Indiana University.

———, 1965, *Zuni Grammar*. Albuquerque: University of New Mexico Publications in Anthropology, No. 14.

Tedlock, Dennis, 1971, "On the translation of style in oral narrative." *Journal of American Folklore* 84: 114-133.

———, 1972, *Finding the Center: Narrative Poetry of the Zuni Indians*. New York: Dial.

Walker, Willard, 1972, "Toward the sound pattern of Zuni." *International Journal of American Linguistics* 38: 240-259.

7 Divination as Model for Literary Form

Burke O. Long

Form criticism as a way of studying literary genres seeks to describe relationships between religious practice and literature. The results of this particular mode of inquiry have proved startling and exceedingly fruitful. Since the work of Gunkel (1933) and Mowinckel (1951), for example, the Biblical Psalms are no longer understood as literary pieces in the modern sense; they are for the most part seen as folk-creations originating in and preserved in ancient worship practices. Similarly, von Rad (1938) argued a thesis, which is still largely accepted, that the first six books of the Old Testament emerged in oral tradition, and were decisively shaped by a short, formulaic *credo* which had its life in the worship of the very earliest Israelites. Form critics have also detected a deep relationship between profane legal praxis and the literary forms utilized in worship and preaching (von Waldow 1963; Boecker 1970).

Examples of such studies could be multiplied. They all illustrate the perspectives which are available when this little sociological window is opened and one gazes at the culture lying behind the Biblical documents.

In this framework, I wish to raise another question of praxis and literature: the influence which divination had upon literary genres in Israel. I do not refer merely to the fact that narrators and speakers occasionally refer to mantic activity. Obviously there are texts which simply report language events relating to divination. And there are brief allusions to persons engaging a diviner. I am more interested, however, in those cases where narratives and poetry are defined, formally speaking, by practices which are at home in the mantic arts. In such cases, one will have evidence that divination has had direct influence in shaping, even creating, specific genres of literature. One might say that divinatory ritual and customary language have provided a model for constructing a literary genre, or if not genre, certainly conventional literary patterns. All this has happened despite the fact that the Bible as a whole is hostile toward mantic practices. A brief look, moreover, at the Mesopotamian evidence will illuminate further these aspects of the Israelite situation.

Practice of divination

Several studies (e.g., de Vaux 1961: 349-353; Eissfeldt 1966; Caquot 1968; and Lauer 1970) provide an up-to-date summary of what is generally known of ancient Israelite divination. The best attested form is the sacred lot, a priestly procedure (Robertson 1964; Lindblom 1962). The *locus classicus* for the institution is Num. 27: 21, where Joshua is invested with some of Moses' authority, and given the right to stand before the priest Eleazar, who shall in turn "inquire (*šā'al*) for him by the practice (*mišpāṭ*) of *Urim* before Yahweh." The text goes on to say, "At his word they shall go forth, and at his word they shall come in, both he and all the people of Israel with him" (verse 22). In other narrative contexts, this practice of oracular inquiry is frequently mentioned, always with "inquire of Yahweh" or "inquire of God" (*šā'al baYHWH* or *šā'al bē'lōhîm*).[1] There is remarkable consistency at this point, even when the reference is to a Babylonian king consulting omens, as in Ezek. 21: 26 (RSV 21: 21): "for the king of Babylon stands at the parting of the way, at the beginning point of the two ways, to observe the omens; he shakes the arrows, he inquires (*šā'al*) of the teraphim, he looks at the liver" (cf. Hosea 4: 12). The exact relationships with other forms of divination known to Israel, however, are not very clear.

Priestly consultation often took place at a sanctuary. Micah built a shrine for his personal priest: "and the man Micah had a house of god, and he made an ephod and teraphim and installed one of his sons as his own priest" (Judg. 17: 5). It is this priest who can be called upon for oracular guidance: "Inquire of God (*šĕ'al-nā'bē'lōhîm*) so that we will know whether the journey on which we are setting out will succeed" (Judg. 18: 5). If a priest could operate out of a local shrine, he apparently might divine elsewhere, too. David summons the priest out in the battlefield (I Sam. 23: 9-11; 30: 7-8) as did apparently Saul before him (I Sam. 14: 36-37). The occasion might be a military crisis (I Sam. 23: 2-12) or a question of assigning guilt (I Sam. 14: 40-42; cf. II Sam. 21: 1; Josh. 7: 13-18). One might even "inquire of God" in order to select a king, as Lods (1934: 91-100) has shown. This is most likely the meaning of I Sam. 10: 20-21:

Then Samuel brought all the tribes of Israel near, and the tribe of Benjamin was taken by lot. He brought the tribe of Benjamin near by its clans, and the clan of the Matrites was taken by lot; and Saul, son of Kish, was taken by lot.

Only a sketchy picture of the techniques can be drawn. Obviously the sacred lot (*'ûrîm w^{e}tummîm*) was a popular method, as already I Sam. 10: 20-21 and Num. 27: 21 show. But Micah's priest, after all, made for himself a graven image (*pesel*), molten image (*massēkāh*), ephod, and small idols (*t^{e}rāphîm*) (Judg. 18: 14). We know from I Sam. 30: 7-8 that the ephod, either a priestly garment or an object carried by a priest, was used in the inquiry or divinatory ceremony. And further, Zech. 10: 2 brings those small idols and divination together: "for the idols (*t^{e}rāphîm*) speak deception, the diviners see falsehood" (cf. also Ezek. 21: 26 = RSV 21: 21). Thus, at least this much can be said: ephod, sacred lot, and small idols were all used for divinatory ends. Precisely what these objects were, and how they would have been used, and whether or not other means might have been available to the priests, remain obscure (de Vaux 1961: 349-353; Friedrich 1968).

Evidence of ritual has practically vanished, too. There must have been such in use, however. Joshua commands the people to "sanctify" themselves in preparation for casting the lots (Josh. 7: 13). Something of what was involved is indicated by Judg. 20: 26. The battle has gone poorly and all the Israelites

> went up, and they came to Bethel, and they wept; and they sat there before Yahweh, and they fasted that day until evening. And they offered up burnt offerings and peace offerings. Then they inquired (*šā'al*) of Yahweh.

Moreover, in these military situations, stylized questions and oracular answers are frequently quoted, as for example, II Sam. 2:1:

> After this, David inquired (*šā'al*) of Yahweh, saying, "Shall I go up against one of the cities of Judah? " And Yahweh said to him, "Go up." And David said, "To which one shall I go up? " And he said, "To Hebron."

Almost identical questions and answers are reported in II Sam. 5: 19, Judg. 20: 18, 23. A variation is put into the mouth of David:

> Then David said, "Oh Yahweh, God of Israel! Your servant has surely heard that Saul seeks to come to Keilah, to destroy the city because of me. Will the men of Keilah surrender me into his hand? Will Saul come down as your servant has heard? Yahweh, God of Israel! Tell your servant" (I Sam. 23: 10-11).

These questions possibly represent no more than what various authors conceived of as having been spoken on such occasions. Even if that were so, the witness of the several, widely scattered texts nevertheless attests that some sort of direct question was put to the deity, a question which could in effect be answered by a "yes" or a "no." Of course, such questions would have been shaped by concrete circumstances while maintaining much of their stylized character as well.

There was another type of inquiry of Yahweh, apparently restricted to prophetism, and evidently employing different techniques (Johnson 1962; Guillaume 1938; Döller 1923; Jirku 1913; Hölscher 1914). The usual expression is: "so and so went to a prophet and sought Yahweh" (*dāraš 'et YHWH* or *'elōhîm*). Sometimes the text reads "sought an oracle of Yahweh" (*dāraš 'et d^{e}bar*

YHWH).[2] The precise relationships to other, less frequently mentioned forms of prophetic divination, or to those shamanistic actions recorded about Elijah and Elisha, are not clear. However, a similar expression is used for seeking an oracle from a deity other than Yahweh (II Kings 1: 2, 3, 6, 16; Isa. 19: 3), and also for seeking divinatory help from a necromancer (I Sam. 28: 7). Reference to Egyptian diviners in Isa. 19: 3 corresponds perfectly (Schmidtke 1967; Hoffner 1970).

I Kings 14 provides a fairly typical situation. The son of king Jeroboam has fallen sick, and the king sends his wife with gifts to the "man of God" (*'iš* *ᵉlōhîm*). She is to ask him for a divine oracle, whether or not the prince will recover (cf. II Kings 1; 8: 7-15). One might also seek out, or inquire of the deity about a military crisis (I Kings 22; II Kings 3), or a lost animal (I Sam. 9), or distress of a more religious kind (II Kings 22). In all these cases, the intent was for the prophet to reveal the future or to deliver a decision of the deity in a specified situation.

One might search out the seer (II Kings 1), or he might be sent for (I Kings 22). Men might gather in his house (II Kings 6: 32; cf. Ezek. 20: 1; 14: 1). The inquirer would ordinarily bring payment (I Kings 14: 3; II Kings 8: 8; I Sam. 9: 7). Although there is some evidence to suggest that these early 9th-Century prophetic figures were connected with the cult, there are no examples of inquiry taking place at a sanctuary. There is reason, however, to link oracular inquiry to holy spots of one kind or another (Gen. 12: 6-7; II Kings 4: 18-37).

The only hint as to the procedure followed to obtain an oracle comes in II Kings 3: 15 where music and an unspecified ecstatic experience play a role. Visions apparently were involved, too. Elisha says in response to the king seeking an oracle, " . . . Yahweh has made me see (*hir'anî*) that he [the king] will surely die" (II Kings 8: 10). In a similar inquiry situation, Michaiah ben Imla responds with an actual report of vision (I Kings 22: 17-23):

> I saw all Israel scattered upon the hillside, like sheep without a shepherd. And Yahweh said, "These have no master; let each return to his home in peace." . . . And Michaiah said, "Therefore hear the word of Yahweh: I saw Yahweh sitting on his throne, and all the host of heaven standing beside him on his right hand and on his left. . . ."

This shamanistic form of prophetic divination flourished in the 9th Century, and its popularity coincided with a waning of the priestly oracular functions (Cody 1969: 13-14, 44-48). But by the time of Jeremiah and Ezekiel, that is, the 6th Century, the meaning of the procedure is nuanced. Men apparently still went to the prophets for a word from Yahweh (Jer. 37: 17; 38: 14-23), but the procedure was now most akin to seeking political advice and religious comfort. The expression inquire of, or seek out, Yahweh in Jer. 21: 2, for example, already has in mind an intercessory prayer:

> Inquire (*dāraš*) of Yahweh on our behalf, for Nebuchadrezzar king of Babylon is making war against us. Perhaps Yahweh will deal with us according to all his marvelous deeds, and will make him withdraw from us.

Precisely the same picture emerges from Jer. 37: 3, 6:

> King Zedekiah sent Jehucal ... and Zephaniah the priest ... to Jeremiah the prophet, saying, "Pray on our behalf to Yahweh our God." ... Then the word of Yahweh came to Jeremiah the prophet: Thus says Yahweh, God of Israel: "Thus you shall say to the king of Judah who sent you to me to inquire of me ($l^e d\bar{a}r\check{s}\bar{e}n\hat{\imath}$, from $d\bar{a}ra\check{s}$): 'Behold, Pharaoh's army which came to help you will return to its own country, to Egypt.'"

Cf. further Ezek. 36: 37: "This also I will be prevailed upon ('$idd\bar{a}re\check{s}$ from $d\bar{a}ra\check{s}$) by the house of Israel to do for them." Actually II Kings 22: 13-20, a text worked over thoroughly by a late editor, fits in this context, too. In the 6th Century, therefore, prophetic divination was still practiced, as Micah 3: 5-7 and Isa. 8: 19 show. But for some of the classical prophets, the meaning of the procedure whereby one "inquires" of Yahweh embraces something akin to "call upon," "implore," "intercede before." This nuance likely emphasized a very old and long-standing tradition of intercessory prayer (cf. Gen. 20: 17; II Kings 4: 33, Jer. 15: 1).

We are much better informed, in general, about Mesopotamian divinatory practices, even though a great deal remains obscure. Complex historical developments, regional preferences, and diversity of method based on social status all add to our difficulties. The range of techniques apparently was much broader than in Israel, and the art much more developed and specialized. One hears of divining by oil on water (lecanomancy), by observing smoke (libanomancy), and by casting lots. The best attested techniques, however, involve observations of natural phenomena: astronomical features, birds, dreams, birth malformations, and inspection of animal entrails, including its specialization in liver omens (hepatoscopy). It is not necessary for my purposes to repeat the available summaries (Oppenheim 1964: 206-227; Nougayrol 1968). Suffice it to make two observations. First, the casting of lots, apparently so important in early Israel, never achieved firm cultic status in Mesopotamia, and may not even have been indigenous to the region. Secondly, inquiry of the gods was accomplished mainly through the $b\bar{a}r\hat{u}$ diviner, the specialist in hepatoscopy. In this function, he apparently was sharply distinguished from the shamanistic "seer" figure in the west and the northern fringes of Mesopotamia. The distinction should not be pressed too far, however. The few liver models found in Syro-Palestine from the 14th Century B.C. onwards, make it impossible to rule out other, more widespread cultural contacts (Tadmor and Landsberger 1964; Dietrich and Loretz 1968).

As in Israel, only the barest hints of divinatory ritual have been preserved. For the $b\bar{a}r\hat{u}$ diviner, apparently there was an animal sacrifice accompanied by prayers asking the gods of the omens to "write" their oracles in the bodies of the sacrificial body (Goetze 1968). There then followed the examination of the entrails, in a traditional sequence. This was followed by some declaration on the matter (Oppenheim 1964: 212), and perhaps even incantations to neutralize any evil omens observed (Saggs 1962: 325). We do not know precisely how the diviner determined his verdict. Judging from the sheer magnitude of the omen collections preserved, it must have involved a lengthy search for appropriate matching of phenomena and traditional interpretation. The later literary references have simplified the procedure drastically when they, for example, simply report that a king inquired of the gods through divination and received an answer (Borger 1956: 40, line 12-14):

> Thus did he inquire of Šamaš and Adad by divination, "Is this the heir to my throne?" And they answered him with a strong affirmative, "He is your replacement."

Literary reflex in Mesopotamia

What were the chief literary reflexes of this mantic activity? Aside from providing frequent allusions to kings consulting the omens (Gurney 1955; Böhl 1939; Pritchard 1969: 394-396; Schwally 1901), the Babylonians created special genres of texts expressly for use in the divinatory ritual. Well known are the collections of omens. Indeed, this is the best attested type of document for all of Mesopotamia. An omen collection typically consisted of a series of statements cast in protasis/apodosis form. One such compilation, *šumma ālu,* named for the incipit of the first tablet, "If a city is set on a hill," contains the following:

> If a city is set on a hill,
>   it will not be good for a dweller
>   in that town.
> If a city is set in a depression,
>   it will be good for a dweller
>   within that town.
> If there is seen in a house the dead
>   owner of the house,
>   his son will die.
> If there is seen in a house the dead
>   lady of the house,
>   the owner of the house will die
>   (Nötscher 1929; Saggs 1962: 321).

Dream omens were collected, too, although only fragments remain from Mesopotamian culture (Oppenheim 1956; 1969). Presumably, these texts formed the compendia from which the diviner would draw interpretations in various situations.

From a later period, we have detailed reports of extispicy, apparently designed to record the oracular guidance given the Assyrian kings. These reports have been published by Klauber (1913: 97-156). Some of them were treated earlier by Knudtzon (1893). Typically, this genre contained (1) an enumeration of omens observed upon examination of the exta, (2) a declaration, pronouncing the signs favorable or unfavorable, (3) a statement of the subject of inquiry, sometimes in the form of a question put by the king through the diviner, and (4) date and names of the diviners. (*Exta,* a Latin word, designates the "noble" internal organs, such as heart, lungs, and liver; *extispicy* is the inspection of the exta, as with tea leaves and the like, for divination or prophesying.) Here are examples from Klauber (1913: 103-105):

(1)   Given: a liver part, a twofold path, the left path lying upon the right path;
       The enemy will furiously vent his weapons over the weapons of the princes.
       Given: the KAL does not exist, [. . . .]
       Given: on the right side of the liver part a finger lies; ruin of the master
(5)   Or of the temple.
       Given: the left part of the gall bladder grows hard; your foot will trample (?) the
       enemy.

* * * * * * * *

(18) Five unfavorable (signs) here.
       Favorable (do) not appear.
       It is unfavorable.

Reverse

(1)   Nabû-bēl-šimâte from the land of the Sea
       Which does not pay attention to the largesse of Ashurbanipal
       King of Assyria . . .

* * * * * * * *

(5)   Now has Ashurbanipal, king of Assyria
       Your worshipper learned
       The following: the archers he has assembled in Elam.
       Will he go, will he
       With warriors, troops of Ashurbanipal,

* * * * * * * *

(13) Wage armed conflict, struggle
       And battle, fight with them?
       Not good.
       Disregard the fact that he goes and stops in the region of Elam
       Or in the environs of its land.
       Whether it be to stir up fear, or to help.
       For in that region he should not go.
(20) Fourth Nisan, Eponym of Sagab
       Ašur-dan-in-šarru Danai, reporter.
       The incantation took place in the new palace.

A similar genre was used in the Hittite culture as well (Pritchard 1969: 497-498):

We asked the temple officials and they said: "The house [. . . and] it is shaky." Is the god angry for that reason? Let the omina be favorable. . . . Unfavorable.

We asked the temple officials again and they said: "The [. . .] festival has been omitted; the cult stand is not adorned with discs." Is the god angry for that reason? Unfavorable. If it is only this, let the omina be favorable. Unfavorable.

A somewhat simpler text type, attested for the 7th-Century Assyrian kings, is the "query of the gods." The tablets are poorly preserved, but enough can be made out to describe their main characteristics (Klauber 1913: 1-96). They begin typically with an introductory plea: "Shamash, great Lord! What I ask of you, answer me with reliable consent." A question follows, stating the subject of the inquiry. This is followed by disclaimer—largely traditional—designed to insure that the divinatory ceremonies will be ritually correct: "disregard the fact that . . . so and so." Finally, the question is repeated, and a concluding formula added, which in prayer-like language asks Šamaš to communicate a favorable reply. The following example is typical (Klauber 1913: 29-31):

(1)   Šamaš, great Lord! What I ask of you, answer me with reliable consent.
Bartatua, King of Iškuza, who has [just] given his lands
To Asarhaddon, King of Assyria, for a princess
Even as Asarhaddon king of A[ssyria] has given him a princess
(5)   For a wife;
Will Bartatua, King of [I]škuza, speak truly
Efficacious words of friendship in trust,
Affirm the treaty of [As]ar[ha]ddon, King of Assyria
And do everything that is good for Asarhaddon, King of Assyria?
(10) Is it a [command in the mouth of your great divinity] Šamaš, great Lord—spoken,
affirmed?
Will it be [seen, will it be] heard?
* * * * * * * *
(15) Disregard the fact that the lamb of your great divinity which is viewed for omens,
is blemished, defective.

Reverse

(1)   Disregard the fact that it has eaten, drunk something unclean. . . .
* * * * * * * *
. . . . [I ask you Šamaš, grea]t [Lord]
(5)   Even as Asarhaddon [King of Assyria] has given
[A princess for a wi]fe to Bartatua, King of Iškuza
Whether Bartatua will affirm the treaty of Asarha[ddon, King of Assyria]
In trustworthiness speak efficacious words [of friendship]
With Asarhaddon, King of Assyria and do everything
That is good for [Asa]rhaddon, King of Assyria.

Apparently, this genre of text was customarily written prior to the actual divinatory ritual. Then, after omens had been obtained by examining the exta, they sometimes would be added to a given tablet, before or after the concluding formula. But when the actual omens are enumerated, which is by no means always the case, a declaration, favorable or unfavorable, is only very rarely recorded. The very absence of such declarations probably indicates that the "query tablet" typically functioned as a ritualistic complement to the divinatory ceremony, rather than as a record of the proceedings or their results.

The older Babylonian *tamītu* tablets also belong in this context (Lambert 1966). They are records of questions put to Shamash and Adad, questions about military campaigns, agriculture, even personal matters—such as a chariot driver who could not control his steeds, or a wife who had not yet borne a male heir, or etiquette surrounding a proposed marriage. Ordinarily the text begins with the rubric, "Shamash, lord of the decision, Adad, lord of the omens." There then follows a rather detailed listing of possible misfortunes, or a specific set of circumstances in the near future. These are really proposals put into the form of questions. Normally, they are followed by the oracular answer or verdict: "Šamaš and Adad (say, 'let him do') so." The entire text closes then with a tag line: *ta-mit* so and so ("a *tamītu* concerning so and so"). Very few of these texts have been published, so documentation is not very full.

A Mesopotamian genre which parallels the Israelite situation somewhat more closely is the so-called "Akkadian prophecy" (Grayson and Lambert 1964). On the surface, this type of text is reminiscent of the book of Daniel; it contains summaries of events, vaguely described, but cast in a predictive style. A small portion runs as follows (Pritchard 1969: 606):

(1)   [That ruler's days will be sh] ort. That land [will have another ruler.]

[A ruler will arise], he will rule for eighteen years.
The country will live safely, the interior of the country will be happy, the people will [have abun] dance.

* * * * * * * *

(8)   A ruler will arise, he will rule for thirteen years.
There will be an attack of Elam against Akkad, and
The booty of Akkad will be carried off.

Unfortunately, the end is broken. But Biggs (1967) noticed that the prologue to this text resembled the protasis in omen collections, and suggested that the so-called prophecies ought better to be called simply omen apodoses, that is, the interpretative readings of various omens. It is too early to settle the question, since so few of these texts have been recovered. Clearly the "prophecies" are not, formally speaking, exactly like the omen compendia. However, the latter may very well have served as literary model. In that case, the Akkadian prophecies would be related indirectly to the divinatory sequences reflected in omen compendia.

Israelite divination and literary form

In Israel, of course, no directly comparable genres of literature have survived. Nevertheless, one can detect, I believe, the literary influence of divinatory practices in various places. The institution of priestly inquiry of Yahweh, for example, helped shape several narratives of pre- and early monarchial times. Here one finds a schematic reporting of priestly inquiry as a structural motif in a larger narrative context. I Sam. 23: 1-5 is typical:

Now they told David, "Behold the Philistines are fighting against Keilah, and are robbing the threshing floors."

1. Report of inquiry (Divination)
2. Oracle

Therefore David inquired (šā'al) of Yahweh, "Shall I go and attack these Philistines?" And Yahweh said to David, "Go and attack the Philistines and save Keilah." But David's men said to him, "Behold we are afraid here in Judah; how much more, then, if we go to Keilah against the armies of the Philistines?"

1. Report of inquiry (Divination)
2. Oracle

Then David inquired (šā'al) of Yahweh again. And Yahweh answered him, "Arise, go down to Keilah; for I will give the Philistines into your hand." And David and his men went to Keilah, and fought with the Philistines, and

> brought away their cattle, and made a great
> slaughter among them. So David delivered the
> inhabitants of Keilah.

This passage is unusually full. In most cases, this schema never becomes more than a minor narrative element, reflecting in a schematic way the priestly institution lying behind it. (Cf. I Sam. 14: 36-37; II Sam. 2:1; 5:19, 22.) The closest Mesopotamian parallels, therefore, are those narrative texts in which brief allusions are made to divination.

On the other hand, the institution of prophetic inquiry appears to have left substantially more impress on the literature. This divinatory activity was also reflected in parts of narratives. More importantly, it left whole narratives and reports with a recognizable structure which may be called the "prophetic inquiry schema."

The clearest example comes in II Kings 8: 7-15, where the schema fully shaped the tradition. The constitutive elements are as follows:

A. Setting (situation) and preparation for inquiry (verses 7-9a)

Now Elisha came to Damascus. Ben-hadad the king of Syria was sick. And when it was told him, "The man of God has come here," the king said to Hazael: "Take a gift with you and go to meet the man of God, and inquire (*dāraš*) of Yahweh through him, saying, 'Shall I recover from this sickness?' " So Hazael went to meet him, and took a present with him, all kinds of goods from Damascus, forty camel loads.

B. Audience with prophet (verses 9b-13)
1. Request for oracle

When he came and stood before him, he said, "Your son Ben-hadad, king of Syria, has sent me to you, saying, *"Shall I recover from this sickness?"*

2. Delivery of oracle(s)

And Elisha said to him, *"Go, say to him, 'you shall certainly recover,' but Yahweh has shown me that he will surely die."* And he fixed his gaze and stared at him, until he was ashamed. And the man of God wept. Then Hazael said, "Why does my lord weep?" He answered, "Because I know the evil that you will do to the people of Israel; you will set on fire their fortresses and you will slay their young men with the sword, and dash in pieces their little ones, and rip up their women with child." And Hazael said, "What is your servant, who is but a dog, that he should do this great thing?"

Elisha answered, *"Yahweh has shown me that you are to be king over Syria."*

C.   Fulfillment of oracle
     (verses 14-15)

Then he departed from Elisha, and came to his master, who said to him, "What did Elisha say to you?" And he answered "He told me you would certainly recover." But on the morrow, he took the coverlet and dipped it in water and spread it over his face till he died. *And Hazael became king in his stead.*

Certain features of this schema are noteworthy. First, there is the verb *dāraš* "inquire" in the setting. A question is then put to the man of God by the messenger sent to inquire, and the answer comes in the form of oracle, reflecting here most probably visionary experience (*hir'anî YHWH kî* "Yahweh has made me see that . . ." verses 10, 13). The passage is fairly complex and contains further dialogue and pronouncements. The most important one, " . . . you are to be king over Syria," is fulfilled at the close in verse 15: "And Hazael became king in his stead."

It is important to observe that no narrative material falls outside the inquiry schema. The move from an initial narrative tension (Ben-hadad's illness) to its surprising outcome (Ben-hadad's murder) is fully structured by narrative elements modeled on sequences at home in prophetic divinatory activity.

I Kings 14: 1-18 shows this schema a bit less clearly. Yet in the earliest visible layer of tradition, verses 1-7 (7a), 12, 17 (Noth 1968: 310-311), the inquiry schema was very important in defining the structure of the material.

A.   Setting and preparation
     for inquiry (verses 1-5)

At that time Abijah the son of Jeroboam fell sick. And Jeroboam said to his wife, "Arise and disguise yourself, that it not be known that you are the wife of Jeroboam, and go to Shiloh. Behold, Ahijah the prophet is there, who said of me that I should be king over this people. Take with you ten loaves, some cakes, and a jar of honey, and go to him. He will reveal to you what will happen to the child."

Jeroboam's wife did so. She got up, and went to Shiloh, and came to the house of Ahijah. Now Ahijah could not see, for his eyes were dim because of his age. And Yahweh said to Ahijah, "Look, the wife of Jeroboam is coming to inquire of you concerning her son, for he is sick. Thus and thus shall you say to her."

When she came, she pretended to be another woman. But when Ahijah heard the sound of

B.	Audience with the prophet (verse 6)	her feet as she came in at the door, he said, "Come in, wife of Jeroboam. Why do you pretend to be another? I am charged with
	Delivery of oracle (verses 7a, 12)	heavy news for you. Go, tell Jeroboam, 'Thus says Yahweh . . . Arise, therefore, go to your house. When your feet enter the city, your child shall die. . . .' "
C.	Fulfillment of the oracle (verse 17)	Then Jeroboam's wife arose, and departed, and came to Tirzah. And as she came to the threshold of the house, the child died.

Of course variations are present, and the older tradition has been vastly expanded by a later editorial insertion (verses 8-11, 13-16). But the typical verb *dāraš* (inquire) occurs in verse 5, only this time in a dramatic revelatory scene in which the deity prescribes what Ahijah is to say to the wife of Jeroboam.

The prophetic inquiry schema also played an important role in I Kings 22: 4-23. The text is certainly composite as it now stands, and has undergone complex development (Würthwein 1967). The first two elements of the schema, however, the setting and the audience with prophet, appear in verses 4-6:

A.	Setting and preparation for inquiry (verses 4-5)	And he said to Jehoshaphat, "Will you go with me to battle at Ramoth Gilead?" And Jehoshaphat said to the king of Israel, "I am as you are, my people as your people, my horses as your horses." And Jehoshaphat said to the king of Israel, "Inquire first for the word of Yahweh."
B.	Audience with prophet(s) (verse 6)	Then the king of Israel gathered the prophets together, about 400 men, and said to them,
	1. Request for oracle	"Shall I go to battle against Ramoth Gilead, or shall I not?"
	2. Oracle	And they said, "Go up, for Yahweh will give it into the hand of the king."

The pattern seen here in verses 4-6, is repeated essentially in verses 7-9 and 15-18 as part of a three-fold dramatic dialogue. The surprising twist given by the last prophetic oracle (verses 15-18), namely that the battle will be lost, is fulfilled in verses 29-36. Thus despite the complexity, and the complicated growth of the passage, the inquiry schema stands out. It really provides the essential elements of structure for the narrative as a whole. Again, ritualistic sequences at home in prophetic divination have supplied a model for a literary text.

The prophetic inquiry schema was less important in shaping the narratives of II Kings 1: 2-18 and 22: 11-20. Compare also Isa. 37, although *dāraš* (inquire) is absent. It is worth noting that Gen. 25: 21-23, 24-26a, 27-28, 29-34 follows tolerably well the inquiry pattern. Here the setting involves Rebekah's pregnancy; she goes to inquire of Yahweh (*lidrōš 'et YHWH,* verse 22b), and receives an oracle (verse 23):

> Two nations are in your womb and two peoples, born of you shall be divided.
> The one shall be stronger than the other,
> The elder shall serve the younger.

The anecdotes reported in verses 24-34, describe the rivalry between Esau and Jacob and the dominance of the crafty Jacob over his brother. This surely pictures the fulfillment of the oracle given in verse 23. Of course, these series of anecdotes were likely independent of each other at one time and are very old. They now have been brought together by a redactor working in the 10th-9th Centuries B. C., a time when prophets, especially of the shamanistic type, were well attested and remembered. Thus it is understandable that the overall pattern of the editorial collection should suggest very strongly a comparable structure in stories about prophets.

Finally, the prophetic inquiry schema in II Kings 3 deserves special comment. Faced with revolt, King Jehoram amasses an army and goes to battle, only to run short of water and face impending defeat. He then seeks an oracle from Elisha. The inquiry schema comes in verses 11-25; there is the setting and preparation (verses 11-12), and the audience with the prophet (verses 13-19). Elisha predicts victory in an oracle. The fulfillment of the oracle resolves the crisis and Jehoram wins the battle. Note, too, the use of *dāraš 'et YHWH* (inquire of Yahweh) in verse 11.

I have argued elsewhere (Long 1973) that in the history of this tradition, the inquiry schema became a primary literary means of shaping the entire narrative. I believe that an earlier stage, somewhat reflected in verses 4-9a, (16), 20-24, 26-27, told simply of a battle in which the Israelites were denied complete victory. Later, new material that carried on the skeleton of the prophetic inquiry schema (verses 9b, 10-15, 17-19, 25) was fused with the old. The result was a composite tradition which resembled another group of stories which I have called oracle-actualization narrative. This is a type of narrative that portrays a crisis situation typically leading toward an oracle and miracle from the prophet. This in turn is followed by a confirmation, and acknowledgment of the correspondence between divine word and its actualization. Examples of this type of narrative would be I Kings 17: 8-16; II Kings 1: 1-17a, 2: 19-22, 4: 42-44. These stories differ from those in which the man of God performs wondrous acts (e.g., II Kings 2: 23-25; 4: 1-7, 38-41; 6: 1-7). The interest is not in venerating a holy man, but in demonstrating, fundamentally, a divine miracle: the quasi-magical power of Yahweh's spoken word, which once spoken must find its actualization.

If all this is correct, then one can justifiably say that the prophetic divinatory sequence, as reflected in the inquiry schema, provided a literary model for an important step in the growth of II Kings 3.

Apart from the influence of an inquiry schema upon narratives, prophetic divinatory practices seem also to be related to a pattern of preaching in Jeremiah and Ezekiel. There is a rhetorical question and answer in Jer. 23: 33; Yahweh speaks to the prophet:

> Setting: When one of this people asks you,
> Question: What is the oracle (*maśśā'*) of Yahweh?
> Answer: You shall say to them, "You are the burden (*maśśā'*), and I will cast you off," says Yahweh.

Allowing for minor variations, this basic pattern appears in Jer. 5: 19; 13: 12-14; 15: 1-4; 16: 10-13; 23: 33; Ezek. 21: 12; 37: 19.

Elsewhere I have dealt with these matters in some detail (Long 1971b). I need only comment here that the situation in which persons seek a word from the deity seems to have provided the raw material for this style of prophetic speech. Already the polysemy with *maśśā'* (burden and/or oracle) sets the question and answer in this context. Jer. 13: 12-14 offers a similar picture:

> And you shall say to them this word: "Thus says Yahweh, the God of Israel. 'Every jar shall be filled with wine.' " And they will question you, "Do we not indeed know that every jar will be filled with wine?" And you shall say to them: "Thus says Yahweh: 'See, I am filling all the inhabitants of this land . . . with drunkenness. And I am dashing them one against another . . . oracle of Yahweh.' "

In this passage, the deity commands an oracle, envisions the people asking for its significance, and prescribes the proper response.

In these two examples, as well as in the other passages cited, one can still detect the vestiges of the prophetic divinatory activity so widely attested in Israel. Furthermore, the tradition in I Kings 14, as we have seen, views the circumstances of prophetic inquiry as fully prescribed by Yahweh. Of course, the question-and-answer pattern in Jeremiah and Ezekiel is no longer directly related to that earlier setting. It is now quite free of genuine narrative, and divinatory contexts for that matter. It simply is a pattern of prophetic pronouncement. Only indirectly, therefore, did the divinatory actions suggest a model.

Possibly a parallel development took place in priestly circles, if one links early divination by sacred lot with later instructional activity. The link, however, is uncertain, and depends essentially upon the unsure derivation of *tôrāh* (instruction) from the verb *yrh* "to cast (lots)" (Cody 1969: 116-117). The question is not yet settled. However, it seems at least possible that priestly instruction was related to, and perhaps even evolved from, conventional ways of speaking in earlier inquiry situations (cf. Josh. 9:14). If so, then this early priestly divinatory practice has left its imprint in those few well known places where the priestly *tôrāh* has been preserved intact, as for example Hag. 2: 11-14:

> Thus says Yahweh of Hosts: "Ask the priests to decide this question: If one carries holy flesh in the skirt of his garment, and touches with his skirt bread, or pottage, or wine, or oil, or any kind of food, does it become holy? "

The priests answered, "No."

Then Haggai said, "If one who is unclean by contact with a dead body touches any of these, does it become unclean? "

The priests answered, "It does become unclean."

To summarize: It has become clear that divinatory ritual in ancient Israel, particularly in its early prophetic mode, had a striking influence upon Israelite literature. No text directly related to divination has survived in Israel. This contrasts sharply with Mesopotamia where omen collections, *tamītu* texts, reports of extispicy, and queries put to the gods were all preserved in the royal archives. But in Israel, prophetic divination apparently produced the next best thing: a narrative inquiry schema, modeled on divinatory ritual, which gave a structure to whole reports as well as decisively shaping the literary form of larger narratives. Furthermore, a later question-and-answer pattern of prophetic preaching found in Jeremiah and Ezekiel still shows its distant roots in those divinatory situations where persons would come to a man of God seeking an oracle. This inner Israelite literary process is at least as important to the phenomenologist of religion as hints of the ritual itself.

NOTES

1. Judg. 1:1; 18: 5; 20: 18, 23, 27; I Sam. 10: 22; 14: 37; 22: 10, 13, 15; 23: 2, 4, (6-12); 30: 8; II Sam. 2: 1; 5: 19, 23. cf. Josh. 9: 14; 19: 50; I Sam. 28: 6, 16; II Sam. 16: 23. Still useful is the study by Jastrow 1900.

2. Gen. 25: 22; Ex. 18: 15, I Sam. 9: 9; I Kings 14: 5; 22: 5, 8; II Kings 3: 11; 8: 8; 22: 13, 18; II Chron. 34: 21, 26; Jer. 21: 2; 37: 7; Ezek. 14: 3, 7.

REFERENCES

Begrich, J., 1936, "Die priesterliche Tora." Reprinted in *Gesammelte Studien zum Alten Testament,* ed. by Walter Zimmerli. Munich: Kaiser.

Biggs, R., 1967, "More Babylonian prophecies." *Iraq* 29: 117-132.

Boecker, Hans, 1964 [2nd edition, 1970], *Redeformen des Rechtslebens im Alten Testament.* Neukirchen-Vluyn: Neukirchener.

Böhl, F. M. Th., 1939, "Die Tochter des Königs Nabonid." In *Symbolae ad iura Orientis antiqui pertinentes Paulo Koschaker,* ed. by J. Friedrich. Leiden: E. J. Brill, 151-178.

Borger, R., 1956, *Die Inschriften Asarhaddons (Archiv für Orientforschung Beiheft, 9).*

Bouzon, E., 1968, *Die Prophtenkorporationen in Israel und im Orient.* Rome: Pontifical Biblical Institute.

Caquot, A., 1968, "La divination dans l'ancien Israël." In *La Divination,* ed. by A. Caquot and M. Leibovici. Paris: Presses Universitaires de France, 83-113.

Cody, A., 1969, *A History of the Old Testament Priesthood.* Rome: Pontifical Biblical Institute.

Craig, J., 1895, *Assyrian and Babylonian Religious Texts,* Vol. 1. Leipzig.

Dietrich, M. and O. Loretz, 1968, "Beschriftete Lungen- und Lebermodell aus Ugarit." *Ugaritica* 6: 165-179.

Döller, J., 1923, *Die Wahrsagerei im Alten Testament.* Münster: Aschendorff.

Eissfeldt, Otto, 1966, "Wahrsagung im Alten Testament." In *La Divination en Mésopotamie Ancienne et dans Les Régions Voisines* (Rencontre Assyriologique Internationale, 14). Paris: Presses Universitaires de France, 141-145.

Friedrich, I., 1968, *Ephod und Choschen im Lichte des Alten Orients*. Wien: Herder.

Goetze, A., 1968, "An old Babylonian prayer of the divination priest." *Journal of Cuneiform Studies* 22: 25-29.

Grayson, A., and W. G. Lambert, 1964, "Akkadian prophecies." *Journal of Cuneiform Studies* 18: 7-30.

Guillaume, A., 1938, *Prophecy and Divination Among the Hebrews and Other Semites.* London: Hodder and Stoughton.

Gunkel, Hermann, 1925, *Die Israelitische Literatur.* Leipzig.

———, 1933, *Einleitung in die Psalmen: Die Gattungen der Religiösen Lyrik Israels.* Göttingen: Vandenhoeck and Ruprecht.

Gurney, O., 1955, "The Cuthean legend of Naram-Sin." *Anatolian Studies* 5: 93-113.

Hallo, W., 1966, "Akkadian apocalypses." *Israel Exploration Journal* 16: 321-342.

Hoffner, H., 1970, " '*ôb.*" *Theologische Wörterbuch zum Alten Testament.* Stuttgart: Kohlhammer, 141-145.

Hölscher, G., 1914, *Die Propheten.* Leipzig.

Jastrow, M., 1900, "The name of Samuel and the stem *S'L.*" *Journal of Biblical Literature* 19: 82-105.

———, 1912, *Die Religion Babyloniens und Assyriens,* 2/1. Giessen: Töpelman.

Jirku, A., 1913, *Mantik im Alt-Israel.* Rostock.

Johnson, Aubrey, 1962, *The Cultic Prophet in Ancient Israel.* Cardiff: University of Wales.

Klauber, E. G., 1913, *Politisch-Religiöse Texte aus der Sargonidenzeit.* Leipzig: Pfeiffer.

Knudtzon, J., 1893, *Assyrische Gebete an den Sonnengott für Staat und Königliches Haus.* Leipzig.

Lambert, W. G., 1966, "The Tamitu texts." In *La Divination en Mésopotamie Ancienne et Dans Les Régions Voisines* (Rencontre Assyriologique Internationale, 14). Paris: Presses Universitaires de France, 119-123.

Lauer, W. Z., 1970, *La Divinazione nel VT.* (Dissertation No. 204 written at the Franciscan Institute of the Bible, Jerusalem.) Rome: Antonianum.

Lindblom, Johannes, 1962, "Lotcasting in the Old Testament." *Vetus Testamentum* 12: 164-178.

Lods, A., 1934, "Le rôle des oracles dans la nomination des rois, des prêtres et des magistrats chez les Israélites, les Egyptiens et les Grecs." In *Mélanges Maspero I* (Mémoires de l'Institut Français d'Archéologie Orientale du Caire). Paris, 91-100.

Long, Burke, 1971, "Two question-and-answer schemata in the Prophets." *Journal of Biblical Literature* 90: 129-139.

———, 1973, "2 Kings iii and genres of prophetic narrative." *Vetus Testamentum* 23: 337-348.

———, 1975. "The social setting for prophetic miracle stories." *Semeia* 3: 46-63.

Luck, U., 1959, *Hand und Hand Gottes.* Münster: Habilitationsschrift.

Mowinckel, Sigmund, 1962, *The Psalms in Israel's Worship.* Nashville: Abingdon.

Noth, Martin, 1968, *Könige I.* Neukirchen: Neukirchener Verlag.

Nötscher, F., 1929, "Die Omen-serie šumma ālu." *Orientalia* 31: 39-42; 32: 51-54.

Nougayrol, J., 1968, "La divination babylonienne." In Caquot 1968: 25-81.

Oppenheim, A. Leo, 1956, *The Interpretation of Dreams in the Ancient Near East* (Transactions of the American Philosophical Society, 46/2). Philadelphia.

———, 1964, *Ancient Mesopotamia.* Chicago: University of Chicago Press.

———, 1969, "New fragments of the Assyrian Dream Book." *Iraq* 31: 153-165.

Pritchard, James, 1969, *Ancient Near Eastern Texts Relating to the Old Testament.* Princeton: Princeton University Press.

von Rad, Gerhard, 1938, *Das formgeschichtliche Problem des Hexateuch.* Stuttgart: Kohlhammer. (Now available in the author's *The Problem of the Hexateuch and Other Essays.* New York: McGraw-Hill, 1966, 1-78.)

Richter, W., 1966, *Traditionsgeschichtliche Untersuchungen zum Richterbuch.* Bonn: Hanstein.

Robertson, E., 1964, "The urim and tummim." *Vetus Testamentum* 14: 67-74.

Saggs, H. W. F., 1962, *The Greatness That Was Babylon.* London: Sidgwick and Jackson.

Schmidtke, F., 1967, "Träume, Orakel, und Totengeister als Künder der Zukunft in Israel und Babylonien." *Biblische Zeitschrift* 11: 240-246.

Schüpphaus, J., 1967, *Richter- und Prophetengeschichten als Glieder der Geschichtsdarstellung der Richter- und Königszeit.* Bonn: Unpublished doctoral dissertation at the University of Bonn.

Schwally, F., 1901, *Semitische Kriegsaltertümer.* Leipzig.

Tadmor, H. and B. Landsberger, 1964, "Fragments of clay liver models at Hazor." *Israel Exploration Journal* 14: 201-217.

de Vaux, Roland, 1961, *Ancient Israel: Its Life and Institutions.* New York: McGraw-Hill.

von Waldow, Eberhard, 1963, *Der Traditionsgeschichtliche Hintergrund der Prophetischen Gerichtsreden.* Berlin: Töpelman.

Würthwein, Ernst, 1967, "Zur Komposition von I Reg. 22: 1-38." In *Festschrift für Leonard Rost* (Beihefte zur Zeitschrift für Alttestamentliche Wissenschaft, 105). Berlin: W. de Gruyter, 245-254.

8 The Collect as a Form of Discourse

Charles A. Ferguson

The points made in this paper emerged from work done on the Subcommittee on Prayers of the Liturgical Texts Committee of the Inter-Lutheran Commission on Worship during 1970-1971, and I would like to express my appreciation of the opportunity to work with the members of these bodies as they create and adapt liturgical texts. This paper will be published in substantially the same form in the Festschrift in Honor of A. A. Hill, *ed. by Edgar Polomé, W. Winter, and M. Jazeyery.*

Linguists and grammarians through the centuries have generally regarded a grammar as a characterization of the possible (i.e., grammatical, pronounceable, writable) utterances of a particular language. Sometimes this aim has been reduced, as when a linguist has tried to characterize only a limited corpus; sometimes it has been expanded, as when a linguist has tried to characterize a set of dialects or languages by the same grammar. Recently the notion of grammar has been consciously extended, in a direction sometimes implicitly suggested in the past, to a characterization of the utterances appropriate or acceptable under various sociolinguistic, psychological, or communicative conditions. No matter which of these views is taken, the linguist faces the same crucial question. What is the locus of the grammar; exactly what is this "language" which he is characterizing? The problem of how to define a language as opposed to a dialect or a family of languages is an old one which remains inadequately resolved (see, for example, Ferguson and Gumperz, 1960, or many other treatments), but it will not be examined here.

An even more troublesome problem is the existence of systematic conditions on grammaticality or acceptability which cut across what every linguist would regard as separate languages or seem to have a quite nonlinguistic locus. We will examine this question by making some observations about a particular form of discourse, a very slight example, but one which may nevertheless be instructive: the collect.

Contemporary attempts at discourse analysis have generally been intended to show features of a particular language which should be incorporated in a total grammar of the language, although some also have been intended to suggest universal features of grammar. Only rarely have linguists been interested in characterizing the changes in a particular form of discourse as it continues through time, or tracing the features of a form of discourse as it passes from one language to another. These latter interests have been more evident in the work of folklorists and students of comparative literature. The present paper is intended as a very small exercise in showing continuity of a form of discourse across a language boundary and through the history of a language.

The form of discourse to be discussed is the traditional brief prayer, uttered by the minister on behalf of the congregation near the beginning of the mass, which generally sets the theme for the day or season being observed. This prayer, which is a characteristic of the Western Church, apparently first emerged in Latin sometime in the 3rd to 5th Centuries of the Christian era, the earliest known collection being the Leonine Sacramentary (named after Pope Leo the Great, 440-461 A. D.). From the earliest examples to the present day, this prayer, called simply "the prayer" (*oratio*) or "the collect" (*collecta, collectio,* origin disputed), has exhibited a very clear structure of form and content. A full collect has five parts:

(1) an invocation, i.e., an address to God;

(2) a "basis" for petition, i.e., some quality of God or some action attributed to him;

(3) the petition or desire itself;

(4) the purpose or reason for making the request, i.e., the good result which would follow the granting of the petition; and

(5) a formulaic ending.

Of these five parts, the second or the fourth is sometimes absent, and occasionally both are missing. This structure is represented by Formula One.

(1) Collect → Invocation (+ Basis) + Petition (+ Purpose) + Ending

Details about the range of variation possible within each part and correlations among the form or content of the parts will be discussed only to the extent necessary for our purpose here. There is a sizeable literature on these matters and they are evidently amenable to rigorous formal analysis.[1]

The collects have had a long and complex history in the Roman Church, in some places or at some times being greatly expanded, but always the basic structure outlined above has been present, and in fact many collects have been retained without change since the Leonine Sacramentary.

At the time of the Reformation those Churches which kept the main features of the mass, such as the Church of England and the Lutheran Churches of the continent, translated and adapted the historic collects for use in vernacular services of worship. The first collection of these prayers to appear in English was in the Prayer Book of 1549, and many of them appear in the same form—apart from modernization of spelling and punctuation—in Anglican, Lutheran, and other English-language service books in use at the present time. Translations and adaptations of Reformation collects are also to be found in dozens of other languages, sometimes dating back to the 16th Century, often prepared in the 19th Century in connection with Protestant missionary efforts.

In recent decades, movements of liturgical renewal have given rise to new collects and new variations of old collects in many different modern languages, for use by Christians of many denominational affiliations. In this chapter we will pay some attention to all three major layers of collects: Latin, Reformation, and contemporary.

Discourse grammar

Formula One above could be regarded as a kind of phrase-structure rule specifying the base form of a collect. If we assume that the constituents are ordered as listed, we could then identify possible expansions and appropriate lexical categories, and we could devise transformational rules which would characterize the full range of acceptable orders and constructions which appear in collects.[2]

For example, in Latin collects the Invocation may consist of a single word, e.g., *Deus* (God) as in the collects for Christmas (midnight), Ash Wednesday, Epiphany, 1st, 2nd and 4th Sundays in Lent, etc., or it may be expanded in typical noun-phrase fashion, e.g., *Omnipotens sempiterne Deus* (Almighty everlasting God) as in the collects for Christmas (early), 2nd and 3rd Sundays after Epiphany, or Palm Sunday.

The Invocation may be preceded by certain other elements outside the noun phrase, most commonly an imperative (sometimes followed by a pronominal object), less commonly a direct object with its modifiers (very rarely a direct object alone). Another preposeable element *quaesumus* (we beg, please!) is quite rare as the first word, but frequently appears in second position between the preposed imperative or direct object and the Invocation.

As a kind of surface constraint, we may note that the maximum amount of material that may precede the noun of the Invocation seems to be direct object (or imperative) + *quaesumus* + Adjective, and, in this case, apparently only a single adjective occurs, not two or more:

Excita, Domine . . . (Stir-up, O-Lord) 2nd Sunday in Advent
Converte nos, Deus salutaris noster . . . (Change us, God salvation our) 1st Sunday in Lent
Ecclesiam tuem, Domine . . . (Church your, O-Lord) St. John
Concede, quaesumus, omnipotens Deus . . . (Grant, we-beg, Almighty God) Christmas
Preces nostras, quaesumus, Domine . . . (Prayers our, we-beg, O-Lord) Quinquagesima

In spite of the fact that indefinitely many different collects may be composed, it is abundantly clear that there are severe, systematic constraints on order and construction, and the form of the collect could probably be captured by some kind of sentence grammar.

It is not immediately apparent, however, where this particular sentence grammar belongs in a full grammar of Latin sentences, since some of its rules would be closely related to, or even subsumed under, rules of very general applicability, while others would be limited to related forms of discourse (e.g., prayers in general) or only valid for the collect itself. The collect poses one of the dilemmas of the sentence-vs.-discourse issue in a very clear way. Theoreticians have tended to see the function of grammar writing as the characterization or generation of sentences, and discourse analysis as concerned with utterances larger than sentences. Elsewhere (Ferguson 1967) I have given a clear example of grammaticality of the typical sentence-syntax sort which goes beyond a single sentence. Here I draw attention to the piece of discourse analysis which is limited to single sentences. Sentencehood is not the crucial differentiator between grammar in the usual sense and discourse "grammar," or else the differentiation itself is questionable.[3]

Transfer grammar

When Archbishop Cranmer and his associates undertook to render the Latin collects into English equivalents for use in public worship, they faced all the usual problems of the translator. The two languages—like any pair of languages—differed in phonology, syntax, and lexicon; and in the relations between semantic value and the respective linguistic systems. The whole question of the commensurateness of linguistic systems has been discussed from many points of view (contrastive analysis, machine translation, language universals), and it will not be treated here. Also, of course, the existence of doctrinal differences interfered with direct translation. But in this section let us examine differences which are neither narrowly linguistic nor theological.[4]

One important difference between the Latin collects and Reformation English collects is the question of style, or perhaps better, register. What special features of the respective languages are appropriate for use in public prayers as opposed to other uses of language? Some stylistic features are common to both, such as the use of paranomasia or word play in which, for example, the stem or root appears in several places with different endings or an affix is echoed with different stems. This will of course differ in detail: for example, the Early-Modern English (EME) prayer register had more alliterative repetition while Latin had more complex interlocking patterns of word order. Also, a word play in one language often cannot be reproduced in the other simply because of the lexical and phonological differences.

The feature which we will examine here is the EME practice of word pairing, in which two synonymous words or phrases are used in direct coordination or in a parallel or chiastic position apparently to express a single notion. This is part of a more general registral difference of conciseness vs. elaboration in the Latin and

EME prayer languages. The Roman collect, like some other parts of the liturgy, tended to be very terse: a minimum of words tightly arranged with clause-final cadences (*cursus*); the Reformation English collect, like the vernacular devotional literature on which it was based, was free and expansive, somewhat wordy with a rhythmic flow involving sequences of short and long words. Latin collect style also had characteristic word pairs, but they were fewer in number and more often antitheses rather than synonyms. The word pairing which characterizes Reformation-English collects and prayer-book style in general may have originated in the pairing of Romance loanwords with the Anglo-Saxon glosses attested for Middle English, but in any case it was a striking feature of elaboration compared to the Latin originals. An example cited by Brook (1965: 129-130) illustrates these registral differences (traditional collect for 1st Sunday after Epiphany, now replaced in Roman usage):

> ... *ut et quae agenda sunt videant et ad implenda quae viderint convalescant* ...
> ... that they may both perceive and know what things they ought to do and have grace and power faithfully to fulfil the same ...

For word play: *videant, viderint; faithfully, fulfil.* For pairs of words: *perceive and know; grace and power.*

It is of some interest to note that this English pairing, whatever its origin, is very similar to the word pairing found in the poetic portions of the Old Testament, particularly the Psalms,[5] and in all likelihood the two kinds of pairing were mutually reinforcing in the development of "liturgical English."

What is of particular interest in this chapter, however, is where the description of registral features belongs in a grammar. Registral and stylistic features may cut across the various components of a grammar (phonology, syntax, lexicon) in complex ways, but clearly the identification of registers begins very early in child language development (cf. Weeks 1970) and some of the fundamental registral differences may be universally present in the linguistic competence of the members of a speech community. In any case, we need to try experimental versions of registral "grammars" either in the form of tagging appropriate elements and rules of a conventional grammar or in the direct formulation of registral constraints and regularities.

Diachronic grammar

Collects have been translated into English or composed directly in English since medieval times, and English collects are still being produced at the present time. As mentioned above, the two great periods of English collect composition are the 16th Century and the 20th. During the course of the four centuries between these periods, the English language changed in many respects, not only in linguistically well-recognized ways such as phonology or syntax but also in the characteristics and distribution of registers and styles. As an example of more narrowly linguistic change, we may note that second-person relative clauses, which were perfectly acceptable in the 16th-Century English, now are marginal or nonexistent for most speakers of English. As an example of registral stylistic change, we may note that the current preference in prayers is for greater simplicity, in the sense of fewer words and fewer subordinate clauses.

The commonest way of expressing the Basis component of the collect in Latin is a relative clause dependent on the noun of the Invocation. For example, the collect for Epiphany begins:

> *Deus qui hodierna die unigenitum tuum gentibus stella duce revelasti . . .*

which was translated into EME:

> O God, who on this day by the leading of a star didst reveal thine only-begotten Son to the Gentiles, . . .

In modern English this kind of clause is at the very margins of acceptability. When second-person relative clauses appear in contemporary liturgical texts they often have third-person agreement (Almighty God, who knows us to be . . .); usually they are avoided altogether. A contemporary Roman Catholic version of the Epiphany collect reads: "O God, on this day you revealed your Son to the peoples of the earth through the guidance of a star . . ." The syntactic change eliminating such second-person clauses is relatively unimportant in the total historical syntax of English, but it has great effect on the collect as a form of discourse.[6] In the first place, it often results in breaking the collect into something more than one sentence, and, in some cases, it is probably the direct cause of the elimination or revision of the Basis in a collect.

Some contemporary versions of collects have removed the Basis from the collect and set it separately as a kind of introductory statement or "bid" to prayer preceding the collect itself. This change is chiefly due to the unacceptability of second-person relative clauses. Thus, two Experimental versions of a new collect for the Thursday after Ash Wednesday begin:

(1)   Lord, our God,
you walk before us and give us guidance in everything we do.
Stay with us, and be our . . .

(2)   Let us pray to the Lord, our God, who walks before us
and gives us guidance in everything we do.
Stay with us, and be our . . .

Once a new format with preceding bid is attempted, it then becomes possible to set the Purpose in that position rather than the Basis, as is done in some contemporary versions, and this move toward a major alteration in the basic structure of the collect was apparently triggered by the syntactic change.

The general preference for simplicity, interestingly enough, tends to take contemporary English collects nearer to the original Latin forms in wordiness and total length although the grammatical structure of English is still a bar to the kind of tight arrangement typical of the Latin style. The use of word pairing, however, has become so much a part of liturgical English that it frequently persists in contemporary collects, and the simplification comes more from omission of adjectives and adverbs and the dropping of other elements such as the resumptive "the same" (through the same thy Son, Jesus Christ our Lord, . . .) in the ending formula for collects in which Christ has been mentioned.[7]

The writing of diachronic grammar is often viewed as the specifying of successive stages, and this may be done by providing relatively static grammars and statements of relationship between them or by giving a baseline grammar and succession of changes. In writing a diachronic "grammar" of the English collect, both these procedures would be possible and instructive, but at least one other kind of grammar would be of obvious value: a characterization of the structure common to all periods. Such a grammar would serve to place the English collect within the universe of all collects and at the same time specify its differences from non-English collects.

Perhaps the fundamental problem here, as in all treatments of variation, is how to recognize and present the significant equivalences. At one level, the second-person relative clause of EME is equivalent to the contemporary independent declarative sentence, but at another level it is different and the EME structure is closer to the Latin. The attempt to write a diachronic grammar of a small form of discourse such as the collect might be revealing and instructive for the writing of larger-scale diachronic grammar, whether of the sentence type, discourse type, or more pronounced sociolinguistic focus.

Locus of the grammar

In each of the preceding sections we have commented on structural regularities which could be presented in the form of a grammar, but in each case the locus of the grammar has not been a homogeneous, full, natural language. It has been a form of discourse in a particular language, a form of discourse in two languages, or a form of discourse at different stages of the same language. Indeed, a very natural object-language for a grammar would be the class of all possible collects in any language of Christian worship at any time from the 3rd to 20th Centuries. The definition of this "language" is hardly more problematic than the definition of a homogeneous, full, natural language, and the latter as well requires a sociological component.

Among the many variables of interest are code (i.e., which language or language variety is used), time period (e.g., century), doctrine, day or occasion, liturgical setting. We have already seen how different languages and different historical periods would correlate with differences in collect grammars. Differences in doctrine explain, for example, the radical shift in collects for saints' days between Latin collects and Reformation collects in any language, all reference to intercession of saints being removed from the latter. Differences in day or season account for such general textual differences as the alleluia qualities of collects in the Easter season, and are, of course, a crucial factor in determining the wording of particular collects. Differences in liturgical setting refer to the relation of the collect to other variable parts of the liturgy, to the formulaic expressions which precede and follow collects, to whether the collect is intoned or spoken by the minister or read aloud in unison by the congregation, and many other similar phenomena. Differences in this realm are also related to variation in the actual texts of collects.

In the point of view adopted here, much of the basic grammar of the collect is independent of the variables given above, but the range of variation to be covered by the total grammar must be in terms of variables such as these. Perhaps the most novel point for the linguist is the notion that most of the basic grammar and even some fairly superficial details of this form of discourse are essentially language independent. For the collect as a form of discourse we might start with a definition of the sociolinguistic setting (assembly of Christians, leader, theme-prayer of day or season, etc.) and then construct a grammar and a set of conditions under which specified variation takes place.

In her important early paper on sociolinguistic variables, Ervin-Tripp noted: "One of the major problems for sociolinguists will be the discovery of independent and reliable methods for defining settings" (Ervin-Tripp 1964). This problem is just as difficult as ever, but it still holds as much promise now as it did then. The present study has merely suggested it, giving a simple example, and has suggested that sociolinguists might regard the setting as the locus for a kind of grammar. A sociolinguistically located grammar, although at present far beyond our techniques of analysis and presentation, must be an ultimate goal for linguists who see themselves as students of language in society.

NOTES

1. Cf. Suter 1940; Reed 1947: 227-287, 567-622; Kulp 1955; and the references they cite.

2. For a sample generative grammar of Early-Modern English based on the text of the Lord's Prayer, see Bloomfield and Newmark 1963: 237-285. The presentation there alludes to forms of discourse, but its aims are different from those of the present study and it does not make explicitly the four points offered here. For a basic analysis somewhat different from Formula One see Kulp 1955: 388ff. and references.

3. See Traugott (forthcoming), for a stimulating discussion of discourse analysis in relation to current sentence-based grammatical models. Although her discussion is focused on literary texts and the stylistics of particular works or authors, her approach has many points of contact with the approach suggested here.

4. For a recent discussion of the problems involved in translating Latin collects into the English of the Prayer Book, see Brook 1965: 126-136.

5. This word pairing is a striking feature of early Canaanite poetry, well attested in Ugaritic and Hebrew poetic texts. Cf. Dahood 1966-1970, I: xxxiii-xxxv; III: 445-456; and references.

6. The status of first- and second-person relative clauses may well be an important typological question, of value in cross-language analysis following the research strategy of "language universals," as in Schwartz 1971. For example how widespread is the repetition (or nonsuppression) of the second person pronoun in the relative clause, which is obligatory in German and hence a feature of German collects?

7. The formulaic ending of the collect has generally been the most rigidly constrained part. In one tradition of Reformation English collects, for example, the basic form is " . . . through Jesus Christ thy Son our Lord, who liveth and reigneth with thee and the Holy Ghost, one God, world without end, . . ." and this has prescribed variants if the Son or the Spirit is addressed or mentioned in the prayer, and a shortened form for when the collect is used as a secondary prayer or "commemoration." Luther, in his own numerous translations and adaptations of collects, used a great variety of endings, but Lutheran usage soon stabilized again. It is interesting to note greater variety again in some contemporary collects. Cf. *Prayers of the Day and Season* 1971.

REFERENCES

Bloomfield, Morton W. and Leonard Newmark, 1963, *A Linguistic Introduction to the History of English.* New York: Knopf.

Brook, Stella, 1965, *The Language of the Book of Common Prayer.* New York: Oxford University Press.

Dahood, Mitchell, S. J. (trans. and ed.), 1966/1968/1970, *Anchor Bible: Psalms* (three volumes). New York: Doubleday.

Ervin-Tripp, Susan M., 1964, "An analysis of the interaction of language, topic, and listener." *American Anthropologist* 66: 86-102.

Feltoe, Charles L. (ed.), 1896, *Sacramentarium Leonianum.* Cambridge: Cambridge University Press.

Ferguson, Charles A., 1967, "Root-echo responses in Syrian Arabic politeness formulas." In *Linguistic Studies in Memory of Richard Slade Harrell,* ed. by Don G. Stuart. Washington, D. C.: Georgetown University Press, 35-45.

Ferguson, Charles A. and John J. Gumperz, 1960, "Introduction." In *Linguistic Diversity in South Asia,* ed. by Ferguson and Gumperz. Bloomington: Indiana University Research Center in Anthropology, Folklore, and Linguistics. (*International Journal of American Linguistics,* Vol. 26, No. 3, Pub. 13), 1-18.

Inter-Lutheran Commission on Worship, 1971, *Prayers of the Day and Season.* New York: Multilithed.

Kulp, Hans-Ludwig, 1955. "Das Gemeindegebet in christlichen Gottesdienst." In *Leiturgia: Handbuch des evangelischen Gottesdienstes. Vol. 2: Gestalt und Formen des evangelischen Gottesdienstes 1. Der Haupt-gottesdienst,* ed. by Karl F. Muller and Walter Blankenburg. Kassel: Johannes Standor-Verlag, 355-419.

Reed, Luther D., 1947. *The Lutheran Liturgy.* Philadelphia: Muhlenberg Press.

Schwartz, Arthur, 1971, "General aspects of relative clause formation." *Working Papers on Language Universals* (Stanford University) 6: 139-171.

Suter, John Wallace, Jr., 1940, *The Book of English Collects.* New York: Harper.

Traugott, Elizabeth Closs, forthcoming, " 'Style' as chameleon: remarks on the implications of transformational grammar and the generative semantics for the concept of style." In *Festschrift in Honor of A. A. Hill,* ed. by Edgar Polomé, et al.

Weeks, Thelma, 1970, "Speech registers in young children." *Papers and Reports on Child Language Development* (Stanford University) 1: 22-42.

PART III

Tradition

Religion very often is associated with strong language attitudes. This is not necessarily true only of religions of "higher" civilizations or of literate societies. Gossen's account in the first part of this book, for example, describes how the Chamula see their language as being the best of all possible languages, and the best with which to commune with the gods in a world where–unlike the explanation in Genesis–linguistic diversity was created by the gods so that people could learn to live in harmony with each other. But the language-religion link leads to a privileged position where the tradition is a long one, as with Arabic, Latin, Hebrew, and Sanskrit. Normativeness is not the only consequence of the superiority of the religious standard. Where it is accompanied by plurilingualism (including varieties of the same language as well as different languages), there are possibilities for gross as well as finely nuanced functional variation. There are competition and accommodation between varieties of speech forms with relation to many of the social variables recognized in sociolinguistics. The effects of this plurilingualism are seen not only in religious behavior (as with the problem of the vernacularization of the Roman Catholic mass), but in profane as well; not only in interpersonal relations but also at the level of political states. In this section we have passed from looking primarily at speech acts and discourse genres to looking also at the macrosociolinguistic implications of religiously tinted plurilingualism.

India is an extremely complex area, and to characterize its principal religion as "Hinduism" is one instance of gross oversimplification, as Christian (Patterns of Telugu religious language) points out. Even when she selects one language area, there is bound to be a wide range of speech patterns. Sanskrit is a dominant language not only because of its religious ancestry, but also because of linguistic (or folklinguistic) and metaphysical notions like Sanskrit's ostensible priority over all Indian languages in a geneological sense and its power in sacred verses. There *are, therefore, highly Sanskritized forms of Telugu, which is a Dravidian language, but there also are forms of Telugu, even in religious usage, that are relatively free of Sanskritization. Using amount of Sanskritization as one of the features, as well as phonology, prosody, and kinesics, Christian identifies several different religious styles of Telugu. Observations are also made on the social dynamics of language acquisition and use—such as education, literacy, and the cinema—at the interface of the sacred and the profane.*

It would be more than an oversimplification—it would be erroneous—to say that the sacred language of Judaism is Hebrew. Rabin (Liturgy and language in Judaism) *demonstrates the importance of Aramaic in the study of religious texts, in prayers, and even in the use of Modern Israeli Hebrew. Moreover, Hebrew came in forms that differed according to the distribution of the Jewish communities. The social values of these variants were brought into focus during the Jewish "Enlightenment" and the establishment of the state of Israel. Rabin discusses the consequences of this plurilingual legacy with respect to the emergence of a standard Modern Israeli and for public religious practice. Not excluded in the discussion is the acquired language of modern Judaism, Yiddish.*

Although the question of a national language in Israel is settled, and the politics of language seeks now for the standardization of language usage, the language question for the Christian minority is, according to Lapide (The use of Hebrew by Christians in Israel), *far from settled. Although Hebrew, as language of the "Old Testament," is also sacred for Christians, the State language has not yet been wholeheartedly adopted by all Christian residents of Israel. Lapide shows how such factors as ethnicity (the sense of social oneness) and translatability (a problem in linguistic acculturation) contribute to this ambivalent attitude.* Editor

9 Patterns of Telugu Religious Language

Jane M. Christian

Analysis of the social uses of speech progresses in an irregular fashion from consideration and synthesis of data from known languages and social contexts, to efforts to create some sort of comprehensive etic grid serving these, to projection of a tentative etic grid or at least a notes-and-queries framework into new field study or re-analysis of old data. Recently the projection of such dimensions and paradigmatic contrasts, and indeed componential analysis, have been called into question. This is because of the (necessarily) subjective nature of the components or dimensions chosen to form a grid, and difficulty of finding proof positive in, for example, psychological reality for one's choices. Another problem found in many specific componential analyses is that of incomparability of dimensions: along even one axis they may be on different levels or may differ in complexity. A further difficulty in some analyses is an artificial and misleading dichotomization of contrasts which simply may not fit a plus-minus model, but constitute a multidimensional set, points on a continuum, etc. In any case, greater awareness of the complexity and subtlety of social verbal rules and interaction (see Ervin-Tripp 1964; Hymes 1964, and Gumperz and Hymes 1972), and of our own inescapable subjectivity as measuring instruments, can lead to further refinement of models and more sensitive fieldwork.

At least two major facts emerge from recent work in this area. First, however variables of sociolinguistic analysis may be defined, it is increasingly apparent that their interaction is rule-governed just as are grammar and phonology, and that these rules are at least in many cases ordered and hierarchical. This applies also to semantics, a central sociolinguistic concern (Steinberg and Jakobovits 1971). Secondly, it is becoming clear that no description, let alone theory, of language can stand in ignorance of the rules of sociolinguistics.

A third appraisal will be defended here: that a competence model incising grammar from its matrix of cultural meaning and activity can only be distorted, as would be a grammar based solely on the sentence element, or one arbitrarily assigning primacy to syntax over semantics. It will be my thesis, in the context of religious patterns of language use in South India

(1) That any competence model must be firmly based in the factors encountered and defined in the field and found necessary for construction of a performance model;

(2) That competence and performance are too much involved in dynamic mutual feedback connections to be well served by a separate or a state model in either case;

(3) That a combined process model, however distant just now, must be the aim for theory.

Religious value of Sanskrit

India is an ideal laboratory in which to study a wide variety of phenomena associated with language and with religion, and especially with the multitudes of patterns resulting from these in combination. It is also most unusual in the sophistication, conscious elaboration, and analysis of some of its own religious linguistic codes.

India's languages number in the hundreds, her official state languages at fourteen. Throughout the north and much of central India Indo-Aryan family languages and dialects are spoken. The Dravidian family takes in the entire south plus some of the central Deccan Plateau. Formerly Dravidian languages were much more widespread, slowly receding before the Indo-Aryan impact over at least the last 3,500 years. Traditionally most of their mutual influences are supposed to have informed Dravidian changes according to Indo-Aryan's sacred Sanskritic norms. Undoubtedly much such influence has taken place and continues to do so along well worn pathways of religious and social aspiration. However, influences in the other direction are also very evident to the linguist. The sociolinguistic importance of Sanskrit is clearly marked by the forceful insistence not only of present Indo-Aryan speakers but of Dravidian speakers that Sanskrit is the basis for all modern Indian languages. Virtually all functionally literate people point out Sanskrit-based lexemes, and most others are aware of the Sanskritic phonological influences. Even illiterate villagers insist holy Sanskrit must be the base of all educated speech and deprecate their own deviance from Sanskritic norms.

Though numerous types of Hindu belief account for well over eighty percent of the population, Shia and Sunni Muslims comprise nearly ten percent. Jains, Sikhs, Parsis, Christians, Mahāyāna and Theravada Buddhists, Jews, and followers of several tribal religions actively contribute to the heterogeneity and complexity of religion in India. Hindus themselves are in many respects so diverse as to beggar the simple foreign rubric Hinduism. Besides variance by region, caste,[1] and class, Hindus comprise many diverse yet overlapping sects such as *śaiva, vaiṣṇava,* and *śakta,* encompassing everything from animism to highly abstract monism, and six major philosophical systems. Religion guides one in India through the stages of life from before birth to after death by means of *karma, dharma,*[2] and the evolutionary *saṃskara* concept of transmigration of souls toward the goal of *mokṣa* or liberation in union with the absolute.

In this extraordinarily religious land language itself is essentially sacred, being inherently possessed of divine nature and power. This is *mantrikāśakti,* one of seven basic powers or *śakti,* and is manifested in syllables, speech, and music as a sort of kinetic energy; in verbal thought and writing as potential energy. Here too, in the beginning was the Word or *vāk* often symbolized as the goddess Sarasvati, consort or *śakti* of Brahma as creator. The potently sacred syllable *aum* or *ōm* itself calls forth all creation from the void, and is used daily to bring forth the godhead in ritual and prayer. There is immanent power in literally thousands of sacred verses or *mantralu* in the Sanskrit *śloka*-s or sixteen-syllable poetic doublets, and in many other ritually sanctified verbal forms. Syllables themselves have basic powers of different sorts and perforce create their meanings. For the purposes of religion-philosophy the essential duality of patterning of human languages is partially denied for Sanskrit: each sound is identified with power and basic transcendent meaning. A syllable becomes for this purpose what could equally well be called a morpheme and a sememe; its character indeed is a necessary combination of these.

Larger utterances often are built up by means of a word-play technique creating layers of double or triple meanings. Each syllable imposes its meaning modified by each of the others. Superimposed on this is the more conventional meaning of the words and syntactic forms those sounds normally constitute. Use of this Sanskrit form is extensively borrowed into Telugu. The whole is meant to be taken as exemplification of the unity of all that is perceived, through and by means of its very diversity. This sort of case serves to underline the idea of direct divinity of religious language, an immanence of divine nature in all things.

Spoken and written Telugu

Sanskrit has been used as a vehicle of religion, learning, and communication, and has been a main medium for religious and philosophical works by Dravidians for at least some two thousand years, and even before Sanskritized Dravidian languages and scripts gained currency for these purposes. The Dravidian languages, some twenty-five in number, are today found mainly in South India. Here by far the greatest number of speakers and the whole Dravidian literary tradition are carried by the three main Southern Dravidian languages—Tamiḷ, Kannaḍa, and Malayālam—and by Telugu, a Central Dravidian language of Andhra Pradesh with more than forty million mother-tongue speakers. The Kannaḍa-Telugu division is traced back to the 9th Century B. C., that between Tamiḷ and Telugu to the 10th Century B. C. (Kameswari 1969). Though contacts have always been strong among some speakers[3] of all these languages and between these languages and Sanskrit, Pāli, and Prakrits speech infiltrating from further north and west (Katre 1964), nevertheless regional adherence to a local dialect and multilingualism rather than convergence have been the rules.

Most people have traveled rarely; when they do it is very often for religious reasons. Most people have been and many remain ill able to participate directly in the Telugu written heritage; to the extent they do, it has most often been for religious reasons. Their main access to the literary tradition is still through well-established local channels which filter through some aspects of this heritage. Local specialists and itinerant religious players and story tellers, a lively folksong tradition incorporating much material from literary sources, and active participation in numerous religious events all foster a selective spread and mutation of ideas and their linguistic forms.

Telugu has a distinctive script and a mainly religious written literature dating back to the 9th Century A. D. when epic translations were made from Sanskrit and much Telugu poetry was written. Presumably the Sanskritic influence on spoken Telugu is many centuries older: phonology and lexicon of the first written Telugu are already heavily Sanskritized, and there are some influences on grammar as well as style. One wonders under these circumstances at just what date, and in just what manners the ordinary vernacular dialects of Telugu began to be Sanskritized, as they rarely appear in written form even now. Certainly in current standard Telugu, especially that of the eastern coastal districts, a sizeable proportion of lexemes derives from Sanskrit.

In all of Andhra Pradesh, some four hundred miles both north-south and east-west, Telugu dialects and influences vary from the coastal Godāvari to the Urdū-influenced Telangana of Hyderabad, to southeastern Tamiḷ-influenced Chittoor, to southwestern Kannaḍa-influenced and somewhat archaic Rayala-seema, to mention only the most important varieties. Godāvari, influenced by Oriya in its far north, is generally considered to be the most elite. Its greater evidence of Sanskrit influence and wealth of literature underlie this attitude. The Rayalaseema variety of spoken Telugu contains fewer Sanskrit borrowings, virtually no influences from Sanskrit phonology, and very little from its grammar. It is considered the farthest from an elite pattern.

All Telugu children beginning school (and often before) learn to recite the Telugu syllabary, which is based explicitly and consciously upon the Sanskrit model. Sanskrit phonemes in the standard Telugu syllabary, however, generally belie actual usage except in very formal public or religious speech settings, and some formal school recitation.[4] In other words, Sanskrit intonation patterns, canonical forms, and phonology in general, plus a large number of lexemes for which functional equivalents exist in ordinary Telugu—all are considered both prestigious and somewhat holy. At the same time they generally are limited to a minority of the population and to usage primarily in situations of religious connotation.

Literary Telugu is then almost to be identified with religious Sanskritic Telugu. Nearly all writing in Telugu until well into this century was religious in form and content. Furthermore, the remainder—government documents, etc.—had little currency, while the religious literary forms have been reaching a larger audience and are increasingly known and valued, even by people who have a very limited or nonexistent power to reproduce them.

The enormous epic *Mahābhārata*, dear to South Indians, was the first Sanskrit translated into Telugu prose and poetry. Nannayya is said to have rendered the first part of it in the early 11th Century, Tikkana to have nearly completed it in the 13th Century, and Errapragada to have finished the remainder nearly a hundred years later. This *kavitrayam* or trinity of poets, as could have been expected from the values of the time, set the precedent for writing in a highly Sanskritized Telugu. Meanwhile, several others wrote *śaiva*, and *vaiṣnava* religious and philosophical treatises, poetry, and translations of *Ramāyaṇa, Bhāgavata Purāṇa*, and other popular works. Some uniquely Telugu literary forms appeared in the next three centuries: the mystic yet incisive *śakata* style of Vemana and others—still most popular even in remote villages and among older children; *yakṣagana* folklore, *desi* songs, and others. After a decline in productivity during Muslim and European invasions and rule, Telugu literature revived during the late 19th Century.

Recent trends include numerous nonreligious items as well as many traditionally oriented religious works, *avadhanam* verse and *asukavita* or extempore religious verse—both of the latter uniquely Telugu and very popular. A few modern writers have experimented with spoken Telugu in novels, but no religious literature has been written in this manner. The government-sponsored Telugu Bhasha Samiti has nearly completed *Andhra Vijñāna Sarvasvamu,* a highly Sanskritized seventeen-volume encyclopedia of Telugu culture and history, a considerable portion devoted to language and religion. Similarly sponsored Telugu Akademi prepares Telugu textbooks in very Sanskritized style, though some current effort is being devoted to making it for the early grades more similar in style to standard spoken Telugu.[5] For government radio broadcasts a very Sanskritized standard Telugu is clearly preferred.

Modern Telugu movies are either "social" or derived from myths and religious events. Even "social" films generally contain some religious settings and episodes complete with religious styles of language (some of which can even be burlesqued in comedies by characters portraying false piety, etc.). Both varieties of film are very popular indeed, and attendance at religious movies sometimes adds to or substitutes for temple visits. At such occasions as the *śivarātri* festival hundreds of coconuts may be broken by devotees before the screening of a religious film.

Religious movies are composed in standard, slightly Sanskritized Telugu, with Sanskrit or highly Sanskritized Telugu used for religious discourse and by religious specialists. Film songs, somewhat—to considerably—Sanskritized, are extremely

popular and are heard everywhere from cities to remote villages, sung by virtually
all young people and older children besides a surprising number of older people.
By my count a large majority of the themes are religious. The words are published
in cheap pamphlets and sold widely from small stalls in all towns or fair-sized
villages. These are purchased especially by boys and young men, seconded by
women and girls, and are passed around by friends and families until threadbare.
They can be sung on almost any friendly or holy occasion and are in some cases
pre-empting the place of older religious folksongs. I would hazard the guess that
these exceedingly popular religious movies and film songs may well affect ongoing
changes in the local varieties of spoken religious Telugu, and may tend toward
their convergence.

In all India Sanskrit knowledge and use, with the philosophies, beliefs, laws,
ritual, and procedures enshrined in it, is still not only highly prestigious but also a
prime unifying force for this very heterogeneous country. The brahmans'
prerogatives for knowledge and performance of this elite style nearly everywhere
are acknowledged though both competence and, to a lesser extent, performance
actually extend broadly beyond their sphere of control. It seems evident that this
competence also is expanding rapidly with the influence of movies attended by all
castes, radio broadcasts listened to by all, and the insistence of the government
(not heeded strictly in all cases) that all temples be freely open to all castes. Most
people, assuming the basic importance of Sanskrit and its related ritual in religion,
try to incorporate them, to the best of their knowledge, in their own religious
observances in certain but not all ways. Sanskritized speech and ritual have
filtered quite pervasively through most types of religious performances in Telugu
country, while they are highly valued even by the large number of people who feel
themselves incompetent to produce them. Extensive pure Sanskrit is understood
by only a few—generally those who can also produce it; but most levels of
Sanskritized Telugu, incorporating a few *mantra*-s or Sanskrit *śloka*-s, are widely
understood and increasingly widely used in the restricted contexts described
above.

A strong popular trend, evidently very old and stemming from the other,
strictly Telugu direction, indicates the use not only of non- or minimally-
Sanskritized Telugu in individual prayer and other personal observances, but of
the intimate form of ordinary spoken Telugu, and of intimate or casual references
to deities and their milieu. Both direct address and reference to close personal
deities by individuals alone and in casually gathered groups tend to be phrased in
intimate, nonrespect style, Sanskritized only or mainly where no functional
equivalent for the Sanskrit exists in Telugu. The lack of Sanskritic education has
never hampered the religious expression of millions of Telugu speakers; indeed the
intimacy and immediacy of supplication and song in the familiar form of Telugu
provide an expression of direct contact between man and god, or between the
seen and unseen. Telugu film songs, lexically Sanskritized, combine standard
Telugu grammar in largely intimate forms of supplication and description. Perhaps
the immense popularity of these songs derives directly from their very

combination of organizationally sanctioned and prestigious Sanskritization with its implication of direct identity with the divine and the opposite closeness of familiar and intimate forms. This ambiguity is perhaps not ambiguous at all, but a statement again that unity subsumes diversity as in so much of Hindu religion. Perhaps here again is the unity implied by the serpent with its tail in its mouth.

At a lower level of abstraction there is also a significant popular attitude of ridicule or deprecation for Sanskrit-quoting false piety, or any brahmanic suggestion of superiority in dealing with the supernatural which is felt to be unwarranted.

Vernacular religious forms vary widely throughout India and even within Telugu country, along the dimensions outlined above, just as do Sanskritized forms. Language forms are particularized among folk religious specialists such as some curers, diviners, mendicants, folk musicians, and practitioners of magic, some of whom are associated with local forms of major Hindu deities. Many remain in fixed locations, often holy spots, while others are itinerant—following fixed circular itineraries from market to market or religious fair to fair or in some cases making long irregular journeys. These people vary considerably in the prestige or disrepute in which they are generally held; and vary in their professional use of Telugu both because of their needs to communicate, sometimes over a considerable region, and in association with their particular callings. Some follow rigid and distinctive forms very different indeed from Sanskrit.

Religious styles

There are definite phonological-level differences among the religious styles considered here as among their nonreligious counterparts. Deep-level choice of intonational patterning and of features such as canonical forms, aspiration of consonants, consonant clusters, etc., imply a definite mixture of levels. All phonological choice is not late or surface but intimately combined with basic meaning and intent. Basic phonological patterns shape whole utterances and discourse forms. A clear and direct tie here between meaning and sound in some cases can secondarily shape grammar.

In phonological terms we may tentatively specify four major religious styles used by speakers of Telugu, with the reservation that different minor forms do exist, and that variations and approximations do occur between styles. Three of these are named in Telugu; the other is not lexically designated but is recognized and described by Telugu speakers. Still another, *japamu,* participated in by literally everyone from two-year-old children up, represents at least the muttering of *mantramulu* or *mantra*-s, repeated names of deities and prayers, and may include recitation of passages from the *veda*-s; there is no hearer or audience except possibly a deity.

Within *japamu* are further modifications relative to at least the four main styles. Of these major styles first is *sanskrutamu* or pure Sanskrit as it is recited all over India. It may be inserted in or interspersed with discourse segments of the second, *panditudu bhāṣṇamu* or highly Sanskritized Telugu, the elevated speech of pandits. The third style is unnamed but very common. It consists essentially in Dravidian-based Telugu plus selected approximations of Sanskritized Telugu at all levels, and has an interesting combination of these with folk religion intonation patterns, paralinguistic features, and kinesics. The fourth style is referred to as *tsaduvani māṭalu* or *vidyaleni māṭalu,* and is not at all Sanskritized. The first indicates speech of one who has not studied formally; the second implies lack of religious wisdom conferred by Sanskritic study. Sanskrit and Sanskritized Telugu are noted for precise and full analysis of verbal forms and uses. It seems clear that all these names, or the lack of them, derive from a view placing a high value on Sanskrit and Sanskritization. *Bhāṣṇamu,* derived from Sanskrit, implies an elevated religious use of language and further Sanskritization. *Māṭalu* is purely Dravidian, has no necessary connection with religion, and in the case of its use with *vidyaleni* implies lack of Sanskritization. It is interesting that this last is not used by the people to whom it is applied.

Relevant aspects of Sanskrit phonology, including intonation patterns and paralinguistic features, contain at least the following:

(1) high concentration of $C_1 C_2 (C_3)$ clusters such as *tr, dr, tv, dv, ty, dy, jñ, jv, dhr, dhy, dhv, ny, pr, br, ry, bhr, ml, mṛ, kṣ, kṛṣṇ, śy, sv, sy, śn, sn, śv, śr, sph, smr, sth,* etc., used initially and medially. (In these formulas C stands for consonant and V for vowel.)

(2) such canonical forms incorporating these as $C_1 C_2 (C_3) V C_4 C_5$.

(3) a plus-minus aspiration distinction for all stops and most fricatives, with considerable frequency of the aspirated consonants; and aspiration occurring alone as the consonant *h* initially and medially but considered separately as *ahā* finally.

(4) a three-way distinction among spirants *s, ṣ,* and *ś.*

(5) *sunna* or environmentally conditioned preconsonantal nasalization.

(6) assumption of a primary unmarked syllable Ca (or cluster) which can be marked by vowel substitutions treated as additions.

(7) *sandhi* or syncopation and assimilation in connected speech, as opposed to citation forms.

(8) *svaramu* or intonation patterns of rigid type as, for example, the pitch, length, stress, and juncture requirements carrying through each half of a *śloka.*

I have heard extended recitation of Sanskrit incorporating most of these features, whole or somewhat attenuated, even from an eleven-year-old boy, son of a *śudra* silk dyer in a remote small town in the Rayalaseema area of Andhra. He was learning from his father, whose Sanskrit fulfilled these requirements and, of course, more, though his Telugu was only very slightly Sanskritized. The child hesitated and made false starts occasionally, and lacked some details of pitch and rhythm in generally correct intonation patterns. He substituted his unaspirated

Telugu consonants for the Sanskrit aspirated set and coalesced the spirant set to s but was able to produce most consonant clusters. Usually he produced a typical Telugu -V where the Sanskrit requires -$\bar{V}$ (long vowel).

At the opposite extreme of Sanskrit usage by Telugu speakers we may take as example a brahman of the coastal Godāvari area who learned Sanskrit as a child from his grandfather and father, a well known Telugu poet. He has published his own volume of Sanskrit poetry and for years has served as a very popular commentator on Sanskrit and Telugu scriptures and other works in a temple of his city. He is considered to be a very competent *vyākhyānakarta* or commentator, and *kavi*, poet. With an extensive repertoire of memorized Sanskrit he can easily hold forth for hours of narration and explanation in Telugu liberally interspersed with Sanskrit quotations, delivered with technical perfection and even dramatic finesse.

This same individual may serve as example of *panḍituḍu bhāṣṇamu* used in his temple expositions and other formal renditions of religious discourse. In both Sanskrit and Telugu he has what Basil Bernstein would call an elaborated code. In his extensive use of Sanskrit-derived lexemes (including very many with Dravidian Telugu functional equivalents) he uses precisely all the elements enumerated above. However, these lexemes incorporated into this code of Telugu have lost their long final vowels, so that sometimes the same item in a Sanskrit context, e.g., Sītā wife of Rām, will become Sīta a minute later in the Telugu rendition. Telugu morphemes are regularly added to Sanskrit formants with almost unlimited freedom, as below. Regular contrasts in this style of Telugu also are ts with c and dz with j; s, $ṣ$, and $ś$; and m with $ṃ$. Aspiration, alone and following consonants in Dravidian Telugu, seems quite clearly to indicate emphasis or forcefulness and thus to be semantically based.[6] This applies both to religious speech and secular.

The third religious style differs from the above in several ways. Telugu patterns of single or geminated consonants predominate, often in the place of Sanskrit C_1C_2 clusters or aspirated consonants. Where such clusters remain they may be modified, as with $kṣ$ becoming ts. The consonant v-, which rarely is used otherwise in Telugu, automatically precedes any initial back vowel; similarly y- automatically precedes any front or central initial vowel except in rare cases of Sanskrit borrowings. Sankaranarayana (1964: 1033) lists $yādi$ but as a "wrong" form of $ādi$ (cause).

Nearly all aspiration is an indicator of emphasis: with most speakers it is altogether omitted from Sanskrit borrowings except for explicitly religious items. It seems in fact to be a sort of marker for religious words: thus *Brahmuḍu* or Brahma, *bhakta* or devotee, *bhārati* or eloquence (also a name of the goddess Sarasvati). The same informant who produced these words in religious context responded elsewhere with *bārata* to a question using the Sanskritized *bhārata,* India. He aspirated *bhōjanam,* a ceremonial meal, in this case a meal partaken by the gods, but in the next sentence produced *bōn'cēsindi,* a frequent Telugu syncopation of *bhōjanam* in the context of an ordinary or special meal being prepared. Initial aspiration is retained more frequently even in these items, e.g., *ātmabōdhamu* or spiritual knowledge is rendered *ātmabōdamu*. It is interesting in this connection that the aspirated consonants used for emphasis in Telugu are nearly all initially placed. It is also interesting that the above speaker used aspiration much more when deliberately and slowly starting a religious discourse, and almost altogether abandoned it in Sanskrit-derived terms when he became excited about the narrative, talking louder, faster and with much more variation in intonation patterns, paralinguistic features and gestures. (These latter however, were most characteristic of this religious style in Telugu.) Within the same discourse he quoted several short Telugu poems modeled after and delivered in Sanskrit *śloka* style. Though this informant, a building contractor from Chittoor District, had no formal training in Sanskrit, he had four years of government schooling in his village. He was the first in his family to receive education and to become functionally literate, but far from the first to be exposed to Sanskritized Telugu and Sanskrit produced by others.

With regard to writing and aspiration, a surprising phenomenon occurs in this religious style. Unaspirated Sanskrit-derived words generally (not always) are written in Telugu script as unaspirated; but when they are transliterated into English script, they regularly turn up with misplaced aspiration. Some examples of *t* becoming *th* are: Sitha, Ganapathi, Parvathi (all deities), thillana, shanthi, ashtapathi, sathyam, moorthi, bharatha, jothi (< jyoti), manthramu, etc. City and town names, especially pilgrimage centers, are also thus written: Thanjavur, Tirupathi, Pennathur, etc. Rarely is any consonant except *th* thus employed, for reasons I have not yet been able to determine.[7] In any case it appears as if aspiration in and of itself is taken as connoting religious meaning in discourse and writing in this style of Telugu.

Other phonological characteristics of this style include the coalescence of sibilants to *s* and *ś* in religious speech and their further coalescence to *s* in ordinary speech. This is paralleled by *m* and *ṃ* collapsing to *m*, *ts* and *c* to *c*, and *dz* and *j* to *j*.

The fourth style and last to be considered here depends entirely upon Dravidian Telugu phonology for its religious discourse. Sanskrit-derived lexemes are thoroughly incorporated into Telugu, though they still are much more frequent in speech associated with religion. A distinctively Dravidian system of intonation as well as paralinguistic and kinesic features marks this as religious style. It is louder overall and of a more staccato rhythm. Utterances and whole discourses tend to be markedly shorter, though the range of pitch, length, and stress features is greater than in ordinary speech. Without recourse to the intermediate priestly class of Sanskritic formulae it seems to represent a direct contact and supplication from man to god. Much of this occurs also in the third style, but it is more characteristic of this fourth. Complete Dravidianization of some Sanskrit names and terms is exemplified by the transformation of the deity Nṛsiṃha's name in Telugu. In Andhra, where Nṛsiṃha is extremely popular, his name is followed by Sanskrit svāmī, but both these words undergo several modifications besides being fused. Consonant clusters are reduced to single and geminated consonants, aspiration is lost, r is incorporated in r, the final vowel is shortened, and the central vowel a is introduced between the consonants of erstwhile $C_1 C_2$ clusters—producing Narasimmāsmi.

Little of Sanskrit grammar immediately influences modern Telugu, but with the adoption of so much of the Sanskritic religious lexicon there is morphological adaptation to Telugu in each of the above styles. Overall, a strong tendency adds Telugu -*u* or -*mu* to nouns in direct form. Thus *darśan* or vision granted by a deity becomes *darśanamu*, and *śrāddha* or a rite for the souls of ancestors becomes *śrāddhamu* or *sraddamu*. Also the -*ru* plural-and/or-respect marker for verbs and pronouns is never used for single deities or saints, etc., but the plural marker for nouns may be so used. Thus the sage Saṇkarācarya is often called Śrī Sankarulu, here incorporating the honorific *śrī*. Another honorific often used alone or with *śrī* in religious reference and address is the Indo-Aryan particle -*jī*, often realized as -*ji*. More common is the addition of -*du*, the neutral or even intimate status masculine marker, to names of deities or saints. This produces Sankaruḍu, Viṣnuḍu, Īśvaruḍu Brahmuḍu, and even Aśōkuḍu and Buddhuḍu. Similarly -*amma*, separately meaning "mother," marks *devi*-s (goddesses). Nearly all persons are named thus for deities, except for those given names with other religious connotations, to which -*du* and -*amma* are not always added. Other highly respectful titles of address and reference given for religious reasons occasionally are Sanskrit-derived: *mahātma* (exalted soul) and *mahākavi* (great poet).

The postfixes -*garu* for respectful reference and -*andi* for respectful address, though the latter is added more to verbs than to nouns, are extensively used in polite secular Telugu, but are rarely used for specifically religious reasons. From a different point of view, all foreign words adapted to Telugu are positively eschewed in religious discourse, though they are frequent indeed in ordinary speech at virtually all levels. A few examples are *bukku*, *kāru*, *pennu*, *pensilu*, *sinema*, *ṭīcaru*, *eskūlu*, *fōṭo*, *ṭaymu*, and *rēḍiyo*, none of which could be semantically excluded from religious contexts except for their foreign origins. (It should not be difficult to recognize these as "book," "car," "pen," etc.)

Nonlinguistic features

Common to all religious discourse in terms of paralinguistic and kinesic features is the speaker's extensive and complex use of the "clean" right arm and hand in both large and small gestures. The left can be secondarily used, can echo, or can draw in that part of the audience to the left of the speaker. To do otherwise would be highly inappropriate and insulting. Similarly the hand or arm is not stiffened much as is seen often in secular gesturing. Common to all is a frequent side-to-side motion of the head indicating affirmation or assent generally, and here apparently showing affirmation of the religious context and events. To sit crosslegged and very erect, slightly forward, with one's hands palm-up on the thighs when not being used for gestures, closing the eyes for emphasis, pausing for dramatic effect, smiling or chuckling where appropriate in a narrative; to combine and synchronize gestures, facial expressions, posture variations, and verbal stress, length and pitch patterns for both syntactic and semantic uses—bringing all patterns together to small and large series of climaxes, and reverting to quietude in all—is to perform appropriately and well in all forms of religious discourse discussed here. For Sanskrit recitation a formal, sober demeanor is maintained, and the speaker's gesture, paralanguage, and intonation are rather rigidly restricted to a few patterns considered appropriate for Sanskrit all over India. The sitting posture is as described above.

The second, or pandits' style in Telugu, differs from Sanskrit in allowing far more latitude in all these dimensions and much speaker-hearer-audience contact and mutual reinforcement. It differs from those styles which follow it in a lesser overall voice volume and speed, and a greater range of pitch variations. It consists in series of complex, concatenated sentences whose syntax is matched and varied to indicate maintenance and shift of subject or emphasis.

The third style varies more with individual speakers and the amount and kind of their experience in religious discourse. Settings also can vary more for this style and modify its characteristics. Sanskrit is not used except for very short utterances, but paralinguistic and kinesic behavior is somewhat similarly modified for the quoting of Telugu poetry. Posture conforms fairly closely to that of the second style, but facial expression is less similar to the controlled *bhāvalu* or precisely defined expressions of classic dance-drama and tends more towards patterns used for supplication and for less intricately rule-governed narrative. The same is true of gestures which lack some of the fine detail of the second style and conform more to secular gesturing. Discourses often are longer in this style, though they may not include more semantic content. They are generally less abstract and less tightly systematized. Sentence structures and their uses are similar to those of the second style, but their delivery is perhaps more forceful, sometimes causing the speaker to gasp on his breath intake. This style may be modified either for a speaker and audience or a one-to-one speaker-listener relationship, and in the case, for example, of the professional religious storyteller, the main speaker may have a second as spokesman and professional listener-reactor who leads the audience and weaves the whole group and speaker-response patterning together. In the case of one speaker to one listener, there is a necessary and quite rigid periodic pause by the speaker after each major sentence or small group of them, which the listener fills necessarily by murmuring the Telugu informal *āā* affirmative with falling pitch while slightly tilting his head from side to side and briefly closing both eyes. Without this response the discourse cannot continue.

Only speaker-audience relationships obtain for the first two styles. In the second a very close speaker-audience tie is the ideal, but the pauses are less frequent and less marked and the response depends more on slight gestures of assent, their intensity and combination with verbal signals depending upon cues from the speaker. Wherever a speaker-audience relationship obtains in the first three styles the speaker is separated from the rest by sitting on a raised platform facing them. The audience is massed closely, sitting similarly on the floor or ground below, men and women clearly divided.

Wherever a performer-audience relationship is found in the fourth style it is likely to result from an impromptu crowd gathering on the call of the religious specialist. The crowd is more likely to surround the performer than to sit at his feet, to engage in informal and sometimes extraneous conversation, and not to wait for dismissal if they wish to leave. The audience is often called on to respond not verbally but by donations; the one-to-one speech-response relationship, if it exists, consists of the major performer and his helper. Verbal behavior and style of delivery are generally governed by quite rigid and narrow rules, and often involve singing, chanting, and similar responses. Very often drum, rattle, string or even flute music calls the audience and forms an important part of the performance. The repertoire in this style is generally much more restricted than in the other three styles. The same may be said when it is used between two individuals, or by one individual worshiping alone. Of the latter it may be said that he expects to be more a listener in public than a speaker, though religious explanation and narration he gives in a home setting may be extensive. These sentences are likely to be shorter and less bound in long or complex sequences; they are likely to lack some diversity of structure found in other styles, and in general to conform fairly closely to Bernstein's idea of a restricted code.

Settings and performers

Settings for religious discourse in terms of place and time are clearly important but perhaps not primary. Just being in or near a holy place does not trigger a shift to religious style of speech; nor does, say, a market place preclude it. The crucial point seems to be the topic; whatever the time or place, religious speech must accompany the expression of material semantically connected with religion. However, some settings are considered more appropriate than others for certain types of religious speech or discourse. And the many religious festivals call forth some unique types.

Every home (and virtually every shop, public conveyance, etc.) has a place set aside for daily worship, always in the early morning and sometimes in the evening. This may be simply a special corner of the main or only room with a shelf holding *dēvudi bommalu*—picture, plaster, wooden, or brass icons—oil lamp, incense, and other paraphernalia of worship or *pūja*. Generally the eldest active woman of the home cares for the shrine and conducts her worship there; the eldest man equally well may do so; and the whole family shares more passively in worship especially of the *intidēvudu* or family tutelary deity. Middle-class homes usually have a whole room set aside for worship, and wealthier homes may have fairly elaborate shrines. The extent of home worship depends partly on *varna* and family position, but more on individual piety. It consists most typically of prayer and recitation.

Small neighborhood and village shrines are everywhere, and are open daily for worship at morning and evening hours; many have non-brahman caretakers or priests, but worship is mainly conducted individually, similarly to that of the home. Somewhat larger temples with brahman priests are likely to have more elaborate worship with recitation of Sanskrit; acceptance, blessing, and return of offerings; and often organized *arithi* or *bhajan* performances of music and prayer-songs by interested devotees. These can be on certain days of the week, or on selected festivals. Usually they are in the evening, but may sometimes continue day and night for a festival. Any man, woman or child of a wide variety of castes can and do come to worship individually and in small groups of relatives or friends at small shrines and large temples. They come at their leisure whenever the temple is open. Pilgrims come from far away and sometimes in multitudes to particularly holy spots, most especially the hill temple of Śrī Venkateśvara at Tirupati in southeastern Andhra. (This is a main center of pilgrimage for all of South India, and has been the focus for more than one study of organization and practices. It is enormous and complex, with an army of priests and other religious specialists to conduct regular and special sorts of worship.) At such pilgrimage centers most devotees remain several days, often conducting rites of passage in these holy surroundings; usually they purchase paper or other books of religious poetry or scriptures.

Religious performers may be considered along a sort of rough continuum as can the styles of religious speech from the most Sanskritized to completely lacking in Sanskritization; or, from the other direction, the most local small group styles in all their plenitude to the much more unified Sanskritic tradition whose members function in a much broader religious world spatially and temporally. In a very rough way we also can say that the population increases in the first direction.

Group (1). Style one coalesces with its performers, all of whom are also competent in style two in Telugu country. These include Sanskrit scholars, religious literary figures, philosophers, teachers, commentators, etc.

(2). Next are main priests of large temples whose command of Sanskrit and Telugu is extensive but rarely creative.

(3). Brahman *pūjāri*-s of smaller temples or minor officials in the larger ones generally possess a very limited code in Sanskrit, and their Telugu varies between styles two and three. This group also includes very many professional or semi-professional pandits, the main religious instructors of youth outside of the family, and professional guides and instructors of pilgrims in holy places.

(4). Group three partly overlaps with group four which includes various professional holy men such as *sādhu*-s who wander or attach themselves to temples and lead a group or solitary life of meditation. Some few of these take a vow of silence and utter no word for many years, an interesting alternative to the great amount and variety of religious speech produced by others. From this point few people use more Sanskrit than a small number of *mantramalu* at the most, and all use styles three or four of religious speech.

(5). We may tentatively group together as five, pious laymen, who spend much time in the study of scriptures in Telugu and sometimes effectively organize the building of shrines, and non-brahman priests of minor temples and shrines. This fifth group varies from use of style three to four, and is quite heterogeneous in several respects. There are very many here whose only religious book consists of an inexpensive breviary committed to memory and recited daily.

(6). In group six are the religious mendicants and practitioners of minor cults, magic, etc., who use style four in all its variety and heterogeneity. Most often nonliterate, their verbal repertoire is often quite restricted, as is the code in which it is couched.

(7). Group seven, the last for our purposes, includes an enormous number of pious lay users of style four. Nonliterate for the most part, they participate in family and community ceremonies and festivals, go on sometimes extensive pilgrimages, and always conduct family and personal worship at home and in local shrines. Many can expound for hours at a time on stories of the deities and their meanings.

This account perforce omits some aspects and types of Telugu religious language and its uses and some groups of its practitioners such as women, individuals in the various stages of life, etc. Language use in household rites, rites of passage, and calendrical festivals constitutes another important area for study, as does the use by various groups which congregate at centers of pilgrimage. Far more elaborate comparative and in-depth studies of these styles and their groups of performers could well start where these general and preliminary remarks end. Some points briefly mentioned here might with care be developed in further study to shed light upon the question of interdependencies of the various aspects of language and its use.

NOTES

1. Regarding caste in its religious context, the following over-simplifications may help a bit to clarify the situation. It consists of thousands of *jātī*-s (Telugu *kulamulu*), occupationally based but varying also by several measures of a pollution-purity hierarchy. These are contained, for the most part, within the four-level *varna (varnamu)* system. Of these *varna* the first three classes are *dviya* (Telugu *dvijudu*) or twiceborn, ritually instructed and initiated into sacred knowledge and practice, and sanctioned to wear the sacred thread which proclaims their high status. Highest are ritually pure brahmans—traditionally priests, teachers, and keepers of the vast sacred knowledge and law, including the venerated Sanskrit language in which they are couched. Brahmans also participate in other ritually clean occupations. Second, the *ksatriya* (Telugu *ksatramu*) or administrator-warrior-ruler *varna* participate in somewhat less sacred knowledge and ritual, and on a nonprofessional basis. They often study Sanskrit. The vaisya include predominantly castes with commercial interests; their ritual participation is in some cases more attenuated. Fourthly, the *ādviya* śudra comprise a very large bulk of artisan castes who do not traditionally learn Sanskrit or conduct Sanskrit-based worship. Some śudra now raise their status by acquisition of Sanskrit, though this learning is probably more often related to the piety of individual śudra. The harijan ex-untouchables comprise the remaining *kulamulu*. Traditionally they were debarred from the study or use of Sanskrit or major sacred texts. Like many within the *varnamu* some harijan groups seek to augment their ritual, economic and political status by Sanskritizing their behavior, conforming to the sacred Hindu law with regard to dietary, family, occupational, and ritual restrictions. Some *kulamulu* thus manage to successfully assert membership in higher *varnamu,* especially when they can acquire traditional and modern education.

Individuals and groups can define and raise their social status by making stylistic changes in their communicative behavior, specifically by making it more consonant with the esteemed ritual language and related forms. This total effort to increase prestige by traditionalization of behavior is so closely identified with the language that it has been effectively labeled "Sanskritization" by Mysore N. Srinivas, well-known South Indian anthropologist.

2. *Karma* may be very briefly defined as that individual fate attaching to man as a result of all past lives, deeds, and thoughts; and as that experience which comes because of need to understand poorly grasped aspects or principles of life. *Dharma* is partially dependent upon one's *karma*, and is that social responsibility within the framework of each life to which one is born. One must therefore fulfil his *dharma* in order to progress in *karma* towards the goal of *mokṣa* (liberation). As for other terms used here: *śaiva* are devotees of *śiva*, *vaisnava* devotees of Viṣṇu in various of his incarnations or *avatar*-s such as Kṛṣṇa and Rām, and *śakta* devotees of power as devi (goddess) in such forms as Durgā, Kālī, Pārvatī, etc. Devotees are not mutually exclusive. They normally worship many other deities in their seasons.

3. These have been traders, merchants, government emissaries, immigrants, etc. as well as pilgrims, wandering religious mendicants, priests, saints, scholars, teachers, and artists.

4. Nearly all knowledge and traditional skills are imparted via intentional or unintentional demonstration by elders, with the child observing and, then or later, imitating. Traditional Sanskritized religious instruction differs markedly from this pattern, as it alone is precisely and deliberately taught by verbal means, in a pattern of its own which varies little over India. Traditionally young *dvijuḍu* boys are formally initiated into their first study of sacred language and scriptures via a special religious ceremony. Their exact language study even includes repetition backwards, syllable by syllable, of Sanskrit passages, in order to achieve the necessary perfection of enunciation and intonation. Of course, not all *dvijuḍu* boys were actually taught in this prescribed manner at any time, least of all perhaps at present. On the other hand, many non-*dvijuḍu* boys and even a few girls are given this instruction either by a qualified family elder or a *panḍituḍu* especially hired for this purpose. Interestingly, modern secular government schools continue many of the time- and religion-honored techniques for instruction, such as ceremonial beginnings and close repetition in a quasi-sacred atmosphere.

5. Few students in school learn Sanskrit; it is to be learned at home if at all, in the view of many people, and for religious reasons exclusively. However, it would be unthinkable to write most textbooks in ordinary spoken Telugu, as it would imply disrespect to those who read it and to the formal school situation. Textbooks include much religious content as well in terms of myth fragments, poems, and descriptions of festivals, etc., since education used to be almost exclusively religious. With emergence of a secular state at the time of Independence the implementation of a universal secular educational program posed unique problems and resulted in a sort of compromise. Though removed as the driving force behind education, religion has remained strong within it. An interesting adaptation to changing times is the incorporation of description of Muslim festivals or Buddhist figures and ideas to early readers in Telugu.

6. Strong aspiration accompanied by stress is typically added to the first consonant of a word to be emphasized. Many common interjections are characterized by their combination of aspiration, vowel length, and stress: *ohō* (Is that so!), *hā* (ah!, oh!), *hō* (hey! hello!), *hihī* (scorn, disgust). A dictionary inventory of aspirated consonant-initial Telugu words yields an overwhelming proportion semantically associated with emphasis, superlative quality or quantity, and onomatopoeia. A few examined at random indicate such things as murder, injury, riot, frustration, destruction, great strain, redoubling of sound or brilliance, frightful, diabolical, slander, ruin, gang robber, multitude, and such noises as clash of arms, thundering, roaring, shrieking, ringing, cascading, twanging, grunting, drumming, etc.

7. It is perhaps pertinent that *th* is quite rare in Dravidian Telugu, and, not having been pre-empted for the purpose of indicating emphasis, may have been the only aspirated consonant free for Sanskritization purposes.

REFERENCES

Annamalai, E., 1968, "Onomatopoetic resistance to sound change in Dravidian." In *Studies in Indian Linguistics* (Professor M. B. Emeneau ṣaṣṭipurti felicitation volume). Poona: Linguistic Society of India.

Bach, Emmon and Robert T. Harms (eds.), 1968, *Universals in Linguistic Theory*. New York: Holt, Rinehart and Winston.

Bernstein, Basil, 1972, "A sociolinguistic approach to socialization; with some reference to educability." In Gumperz and Hymes 1972: 465-497.

Bhattacharya, Bishnupada, 1962, *A Study in Language and Meaning: a Critical Examination of Some Aspects of Indian Semantics*. Calcutta: Progressive Publishers.

Birdwhistell, Ray L., 1970, *Kinesics and Context: Essays on Body Motion Communication*. Philadelphia: University of Pennsylvania Press.

Chafe, Wallace L., 1970, *Meaning and the Structure of Language*. Chicago: University of Chicago Press.

Christian, Jane M., "Learning the gods in Hindustan." Paper read at the annual meeting of the American Anthropological Association, 1970.

———, "Hanumān worship in India: popular vs. pandit views." Paper read at the annual meeting of the American Anthropological Association, 1971.

———, "Style and dialect selection by Hindi-Bhojpuri speaking children." In *Proceedings of the Conference on Child Language, 1971*, ed. by Theodore Anderson. Chicago: International Association of Applied Linguistics. (In press.)

———, "The end is the beginning: a chain of semantically connected calendrical festivals in southern Andhra Pradesh." In *Festivals of South India*, ed. by Guy R. Welbon.

Emeneau, Murray B. and T. Burrow, 1961, *A Dravidian Etymological Dictionary*. Oxford: The Clarendon Press.

———, 1962, *Dravidian Borrowings from Indo-Aryan* (University of California Publications in Linguistics, 26). Los Angeles and Berkeley: University of California Press.

Ervin-Tripp, Susan M., 1964, "An analysis of the interaction of language, topic, and listener." *American Anthropologist* 66 (Part 2): 86-102 (*The Ethnography of Communication*, Special Publication, ed. by John J. Gumperz and Dell Hymes).

Gumperz, John J. and Dell Hymes (eds.), 1972, *Directions in Sociolinguistics*. New York: Holt, Rinehart and Winston.

Hymes, Dell, 1964, "Introduction: Toward ethnographies of communication." *American Anthropologist* 66 (Part 2): 1-34.

Kameswari, T. M., 1969, "The chronology of Dravidian languages." In *Dravidian Linguistics*, ed. by S. Agesthialingom and N. Kumaraswami Raja. Annamalainagar: Annamalai University.

Katre, S. M., 1964, *Prakrit Languages and their Contribution to Indian Culture*. Poona: Deccan College Postgraduate and Research Institute.

Ramanujan, A. K., 1967, "The structure of variation: a study in caste dialects." In *Social Structure and Social Change in India*, ed. by Bernard Cohn and Milton Singer. Chicago: Aldine.

Reddy, G. N., 1966, *A Study of Telugu Semantics*. Tirupati, A. P.: Sri Venkateswara University.

Sankaranarayana, P. (2nd rev. ed.), 1964, *A Telugu-English Dictionary*. Madras: V. Ramaswamy Sastrulu and Sons.

Steinberg, Danny D. and Leon A. Jakobovits (eds.), 1971, *Semantics: an Interdisciplinary Reader in Philosophy, Linguistics and Psychology*. Cambridge: Cambridge University Press.

10 Liturgy and Language in Judaism

Chaim Rabin

I should like to thank Dr. Joseph Heinemann for reading through the manuscript of this paper and for his valuable suggestions.

This chapter deals with the broad type of Judaism usually called Traditional Judaism. It has many varieties, and one of the matters in which these varieties differ most from each other is the composition and content of the liturgy. On the other hand, there is little difference in the language aspect of liturgy. There are also within Traditional Judaism wide variations in the individual practice of the liturgy ("learning," for example, is far from universally practiced), but if any particular kind of liturgical activity is performed, this is done in the language described here. Our description does not apply in full to the types of Judaism on either end of the scale, namely, Reform Judaism, where the use of Hebrew is much restricted, and extreme orthodox and mystical (Hassidic) groups, though in the matter of liturgical language the latter resemble Traditional Judaism and their usage will be mentioned in various connections.

Traditional Judaism has been more affected than the extreme orthodox groups by the formation of a modern Jewish national entity in Palestine and the foundation of the state of Israel. This process has led to considerable differences in the forms of religious life between the Jewish community of Israel and the Jews living outside Israel, the *diaspora.* The two principal factors in this dichotomy are the use of Hebrew as an all-purpose language in Israel, while in the diaspora it still is to a large extent a language of liturgy; and the fact that in the diaspora the synagogue is the main institution through which the Jew can identify himself with his community. Such a person may be little interested in the liturgical aspects of the synagogue. In Israel, however, Jewish identity is expressed in secular patterns, and those who attend a synagogue do so because they wish to participate in its liturgical activities.

The dichotomy between Israel and the diaspora began to develop in the 1880s. Until then there was only the diaspora, ever since the destruction of Jerusalem in 70 A. D.; the small Jewish community in Palestine was sociologically the same as the communities in other lands. We shall refer to this period as the Exile.

Ritual activity in Judaism falls into four classes: prayer, required readings, free individual devotion, and "learning."

Ritual practices

Prayer.

This includes the statutory daily prayers (three on weekdays, four on Sabbaths and holidays, and five on the Day of Atonement), which normally should be said in a congregation of at least ten men (not necessarily in a synagogue building) but can be said in private. The Blessings are short formulas pronounced on a wide variety of occasions. Certain Blessings are longer texts and constitute a form of domestic service, such as the grace after a meal, the Sanctification (*Kiddush*) before the main Sabbath and festival meals, and the Distinction (*Havdalah*) marking the end of Sabbath or a festival. Special among these domestic ceremonies are the rite on Passover eve (*Haggadah*—in the diaspora repeated on the following night) and the wedding rite.[1]

The common feature of all prayers is the absolute fixity of text and sequence within a given community (see below). There is no room for individual choice: a man may say a prayer or neglect to say it, but he cannot say it unless the occasion for saying it is present. To say an uncalled-for prayer or blessing is a sin.

Required readings.

The Pentateuch is divided into an appropriate number of "portions." These are read out in sequence throughout the weeks of the year, in part on Monday and Thursday, and in full on Sabbath morning. Each weekly portion has its appropriate section from the Prophets, read out immediately after the Pentateuch portion. On certain days in the year, prescribed passages from the Pentateuch—as well as the books of Esther, Lamentations, and Jonah—are read aloud. All these readings can only be performed before a congregation of at least ten men. The Pentateuch and the book of Esther have to be read from parchment scrolls written in a prescribed way. The books of Canticles and Ruth are also read as part of certain festival services, but without the formality described.

Free individual devotion.

The recitation of Psalms is performed by many as an act of devotion, but such recitation is also in the more traditional circles believed to have effects such as averting danger or curing illness. (The non-stop recitation of Psalms is sometimes a feature of orthodox demonstrations against institutions in Israel.) During Sabbath meals it is customary to sing or recite one's individual selection of poems (*Zemiroth*).[2] There are forms of *Kiddush*, but without a Blessing, for those who wish to recite them before such Sabbath meals for which no *Kiddush* is prescribed. Among the Hassidim, there are numerous voluntary additions to prayers and blessings, meant to lend their performance more inwardness. For example, before saying a Blessing, one may recite the Biblical verse prescribing the action which occasions the Blessing. In the course of history quite a few such voluntary forms of devotion became incorporated into regular services, and thus obligatory. An outstanding example are the Psalms recited before the prayer on Sabbath eve, the "Reception of the Sabbath" (*Kabbalat shabbat*), originally performed by 16th-Century mystics at Safed by going out into the fields and "receiving the bride."[3]

"Learning."

The simplest example of "learning," the reading of certain texts individually or in company, is the custom of reading individually the weekly Pentateuch "portion" in Hebrew and in the Aramaic translation (*Targum*). Usually this is done with a traditional commentary of one's choice. "Learning" depends upon the individual's level of Jewish education, and within that level, upon his preferences. Those who can, "learn" the Talmud, a legal, ritual, and ethical compilation in Hebrew and Aramaic justly renowned for its difficulty. Out of its sixty "tractates" one has free individual choice; some hardy learners work through the whole Talmud once or several times in their lives.[4] Those who cannot follow the Talmud can learn *Eyn Yaakov*,[5] a selection containing only the ethical passages from the Talmud and the legends, or the *Mishnah*, the Hebrew legal compilation to which the Talmud is a commentary. (For an English translation of the *Mishnah* see Danby 1933.) Men of mystical bent can learn the *Zohar*, a vast medieval Aramaic work.

I deliberately do not use the verb "study" but "learn," the term used among English-speaking Jews, which is an English adaptation of the Yiddish *lernen*. "Learning" implies reciting the text audibly, in a traditional sing-song melody, with a rhythmic forward swaying of the upper part of the body, which is traditionally also performed during prayer. The learner is supposed to understand the text; there always is a commentary on the page to help him along. One who learns much will acquire greater facility and a stock of quotations. The professed purpose of "learning," however, is not to acquire knowledge for practical purposes. Quite the contrary, in many circles the person who studies Talmud in order to become a rabbi is looked upon as someone who "makes the Law a mattock to dig with";[6] and a learned orthodox man will not take money for teaching Mishnah or Talmud, but only accept payment as compensation for "waste of time" which would otherwise be spent on "learning."

The purpose of "learning" is to occupy oneself for a certain time with the sacred text, for the sole reason that God commanded "thou shalt ponder it day and night" (Joshua 1: 8). One should set aside for it fixed times, as for prayer. The ideal is to spend all one's waking hours in "learning," and those who do this, existing on charity or on the labor of their wives, enjoy a standing somewhat similar to that of monks.[7] Orthodox ideology stresses the character of "learning" as a form of worship and makes the claim that those who devote their lives to it—or, using a phrase from the Talmud, "kill themselves for it"—do so vicariously for the rest of the Jews who will not or cannot study continuously.

To illustrate the ritual character of "learning," I quote from *Tanya,* the basic work of the influential Habad (Lubavitch) movement, Book I, Chapter 34: (a man must say to himself) "Let me build for God a temple and a place for Him to dwell, that is by occupying myself with the study of the Law according to the free time available to me, fixing regular times by day and by night . . . and thus his heart will rejoice and he will give thanks for having been privileged to be host to the Divine Power twice each day . . . moreover, at the time when a man 'learns' and prays, he offers as a sacrifice to God all that he eats and drinks and enjoys for the health of his body after having given one fifth for charity." In the public debate about the practice of absolving from military service in Israel Talmud students who were attending a Yeshiva (higher institution for Talmud study), the argument was advanced that they were in fact participating in the war effort by ensuring God's favor through their continuous study.

During the mourning period and on anniversaries for the dead, it is customary to invite people for "learning," and some mourners pay another person to "learn" regularly in memory of the deceased. After "learning," a form of *Kaddish* (see below) is said, as after a statutory prayer. In many statutory prayers, passages or "learning" are incorporated. In Eastern Europe, the same room served both as a house of "learning" (*Bet Midrash*) and for community prayer, the Hebrew word doing service for both concepts.

I think the facts cited suffice to show that "learning" in Traditional Judaism is a ritual activity, not a pursuit of knowledge, though of course the intellectual pleasure it offers and the status it bestows are additional factors not to be neglected. The liturgic "learner" is behaving quite differently from the serious Talmud student, who will go over passages repeatedly, compare them with other Talmudic passages on the same subject, discuss what he has read and be examined on it, and aim to commit material to memory and to develop acumen in solving problems and in discovering unsuspected difficulties.

For the Talmud student there is, at least theoretically, the legitimate aspiration of obtaining "permission to decide cases," the rabbinical diploma, or of writing learned books. It was, and still is, quite common for men to hold a rabbinical diploma without intending to take up a position as a rabbi, but simply as proof of achievement. The holding of such a diploma entitles one to be addressed as "rabbi" and confers considerable social status. Traditionally, such a diploma can be conferred by anyone who already has one, but in many western countries, the conferral is institutionalized.

The rabbinical diploma implies ability to derive from a combined study of the Talmud and the medieval "decisors" what the law is in each case. (These latter are writers who discuss problems left open by the Talmud or which have arisen since the time when the Talmud was concluded.) The ordinary "learner" is not qualified to derive this, the only practical benefit, from his study of the text. If he needs to know a point of ritual or law, he will take recourse to a work of the class of "The Well-laid Table" (*Shulkan Arukh,* 1565 A. D.) or its 19th-Century condensation. The division between "learning" and studying is, of course, not absolute. In order to "learn" one has first to study, and the serious Talmud student often becomes ultimately a high-level "learner," but then, as we shall see, the Jewish child also has to study in order to pray, and the prayers may form a subject of study; for instance, before festivals, some people will peruse the difficult *Piyyut* prayers with a commentary. It is not claimed that the individual is always conscious of which of the two activities he is engaged in. We may add that the Hebrew language uses the same verb (*lamad*) for both studying and "learning," but then Hebrew also uses for the accomplished scholar the same basic word as for the beginning student (*talmid*), adding to it only the adjective "wise" (*talmid hakham*).

Prayer in a congregation is performed invariably with the assistance of an "emissary of the congregation" (cantor; in German Jewish usage *Vorbeter* "prayer leader") who recites aloud certain parts of the prayers which are said also by each member of the congregation. In addition the cantor has prayers which only he recites. In a similar way "learning" can be performed in a congregation with the assistance of a scholar who reads aloud the text everyone has before him, often providing explanations to it which may range from a Yiddish or other vernacular summary of the printed commentary to learned or moral disquisitions. This is called a lesson (*shi'ur*), and may with the less educated take the place of individual "learning." The traditional sermon is nothing but such a lesson on a single verse or Talmudic item with more elaborate discussion and somewhere a reference linking it to the "matter of the day," i.e., the festival, the wedding, the consecration, or the funeral which occasions the sermon.

The languages of liturgy

Jewish liturgy uses two distinct, though related, languages: Hebrew and Aramaic. This applies in the diaspora only to Orthodox and Traditional Judaism. Reform Judaism (and to a much more limited extent, Conservative Judaism) allows part of the public prayers to be performed in the language of the country.

Hebrew was from about 1200 B. C. to about 200 A. D. the spoken language of the Jews living in Palestine. It is the language of most of the Old Testament (henceforth referred to as the Bible) and of the Mishnah and related literature; Hebrew passages also appear, closely interwoven with Aramaic passages, in the Talmud. The Hebrew of Mishnah and Talmud is a distinct later development, called Mishnaic Hebrew. After Hebrew ceased to be spoken, it continued as a written language, used in various Jewish communities and at different periods either as sole vehicle of reading and writing, or side by side with another language, the uses of the two languages being regulated by custom. The uses of Hebrew were in part secular, such as private correspondence or poetry on nonreligious subjects. It produced a literature of about the same size as medieval Latin literature. In fact, the diglossia situation with regard to Hebrew among medieval Jews was analogous to the situation obtaining in western Christendom with Latin, in eastern European Christendom with Greek, and later with Church Slavonic; in Islamic countries with Classical Arabic, and in India with Sanskrit.[8] The difference was not structural, but quantitative, owing to the fact that post-Biblical Judaism does not have a priestly class and that prayer and "learning" are incumbent on every male.[9] Literacy and a modicum of command of Hebrew were well-nigh universal among Jews, at least where males were concerned (see below).

The diglossic situation lasted into the 19th Century, when it became more common among Jews to employ the literary languages of their countries of residence, using them also for written communication in religious matters. The liturgical use of Hebrew has not lapsed entirely, however. It continues in full in the more traditional forms of Judaism, and to some extent even in the most extreme Reform communities; and original writings on religious subjects appear currently outside Israel, even in groups unconnected with, or hostile to the Jewish national renaissance or the revival of the Hebrew language. For example, the Brooklyn-based extreme-orthodox leader, Rabbi Joel Teitelbaum (the Rebbe of Satmar) published a fifty-page dissertation directed against the belief that speaking Hebrew was a meritorious religious act (Teitelbaum 1961: 403-453). Like all his works, this is written in fluent and elegant traditional Hebrew.

From 1880 onwards, Hebrew began to be spoken again, both in Palestine and in the diaspora, at first by small groups. In Israel today it is the cultural, administrative, and public language of the Jewish population, the language of daily use of a large percentage of it, and the mother tongue—and often the sole language—of practically all younger Palestine-born Jews. For Israel, there is thus no diglossia (though there are language situations of immigrant groups), except within the extreme Orthodox groups who maintain a Yiddish-Hebrew diglossia of the traditional type and employ Israeli spoken Hebrew as a foreign language in their contacts with outsiders.

In the diaspora, the situation is complex. In some circles, spoken (and secular written) Hebrew still exists as a result of the diaspora branch of the revival. Members of these circles are often highly critical of Israeli spoken and written Hebrew and consider their own Hebrew purer. One reason for thinking so is that they use new diaspora-made Hebrew formations for a number of items for which international words are used in Israel. Other circles use Israeli spoken Hebrew as part of identification with Israel. In both these groups Hebrew is spoken only occasionally, but there are families where only Hebrew is spoken in the home. A third group is formed by Israeli emigrants and Israelis temporarily abroad, where Hebrew is an immigrant language. Interplay is involved, one aspect of which derives from the large number of Israeli emigrants and temporary residents employed in teaching religious and spoken Hebrew (see below) in local Jewish communities and working there in collaboration and competition with teachers belonging to the first group.

Aramaic originally was spoken in an area extending from the northern borders of Palestine into southeastern Turkey and into northern Iraq.[10] By 600 B. C. it had replaced Assyrian-Babylonian as spoken language in Mesopotamia. After the 8th Century it spread over additional areas, including Palestine, because of the Assyrian and Babylonian policy of transferring entire conquered populations. It was perhaps used at first as lingua franca between populations thus brought into contact, and penetrated into daily use.

After 539 B. C., Aramaic was adopted as administrative language for the western part of the Persian empire. In Palestine it inherited by 200 A. D., together with Greek, the place of Hebrew in speech and partly in writing. The Jews of "Babylonia" (the area of modern Iraq) used Aramaic in speaking and writing, with Hebrew restricted to liturgy. The Palestinian and Babylonian communities each produced a Talmud, but the Babylonian Talmud became ultimately the authoritative one. The Aramaic passages in each represent in all probability the actual spoken language, closely resembling that of the non-Jewish population of the respective country, except for the specific Jewish vocabulary. After the Arab conquest in the 7th Century A. D., Aramaic gradually receded and died out, except for the mountainous regions of Kurdistan, where it is spoken and written by Christians (under the name of "Assyrian") and Jews (under the name of "Kurdish" or "Targum"); and in some villages of southern Syria. The Aramaic-speaking Christians of northern Iraq fled in the 1930s, and are now mostly living in South and North America.

Within the Old Testament, six chapters of Daniel and less than three chapters of Ezra are in an Aramaic resembling (with orthographic differences) the Imperial Aramaic of the Persian Empire. During the period 539 B. C.-200 A. D., most of the Bible was translated into an Aramaic which is probably a compromise between Imperial Aramaic and the spoken language. These translations, the *Targum,* were recited in synagogues in connection with the liturgical reading of Pentateuch and Prophets and are still recited. (For a general survey of the Targum see Déaut 1966; and Rabin 1968: 17 for an attempt at sociolinguistic appreciation.) Also from the time when Aramaic was still a spoken language among the Jews, there date a small number of Aramaic prayers couched in the type of language used in the Targum. Thus, at the beginning of the domestic service for Passover eve, the participants recite with great solemnity in Aramaic: "This (the unleavened bread) is the bread of misery, which our forefathers ate," etc. After the reading of the Bible portions on Sabbath morning, two prayers in Aramaic are said for the well-being of the community. Before the beginning of the prayers on the eve of the Day of Atonement, an Aramaic declaration (*Kol Nidre*) is recited three times, absolving the congregants from rashly-made religious vows. This prayer—recited with the Ark open[11] and the two leading members of the congregation[12] holding Scrolls, flanking the cantor—is sung in an impressive and moving melody, and is probably for a majority of Jews the most important prayer of the year.

The most prominent one of the Aramaic prayers, however, is the Sanctification, *Kaddish,*[13] beginning with "Magnified and sanctified be His great, mighty name in the world which He created according to His will. May He establish His kingdom during your lifetime," etc. This short prayer is repeated by the cantor at important junctions in each service. Important enough in itself, its importance grew when in the Middle Ages it became usual for mourners to recite the *Kaddish* at the open grave, during the year of mourning daily, and each year on the anniversary of their relatives' death. *Kaddish* can only be said before a congregation of at least ten men. For many religiously indifferent Jews today, *Kaddish* (and perhaps the *Kol Nidre*) is the only prayer they know and perform.

Thus it will be seen that the Aramaic prayers, though few, hold a very important emotional position within the liturgy. For the large majority, whose religious studies do not extend as far as the Talmud, Aramaic is of course unintelligible, though on the other hand many of its words hauntingly evoke the sound of well-known Hebrew words, and thus provide an aura of mystical half-understanding. For example, at the beginning of the *Kaddish*: (1) *shmeh* (his name) = Hebrew *shmo*; (2) *rabba* (great) = Hebrew *rav* (much, great); (3) *alma* (world) = Hebrew *olam*. The Hebrew words mentioned are known to those who have learned little Hebrew.

Even after Aramaic ceased to be spoken, it continued as a kind of auxiliary holy language. Targums to some books, e.g., Psalms, were composed centuries later. About 1300 A.D. a north-Spanish mystic wrote the *Zohar* in an Aramaic similar to that of the Targums. (For the *Zohar* see Scholem 1946: 156-190. The language has been analyzed by Kaddari 1956.) The *Zohar* is a pseudepigraphal work consisting of utterances attributed to teachers of the 1st Century A.D., but the Aramaic is not part of the period trappings, as the teachers in question are all represented in the sources with sayings in Hebrew. Rather "the artificial patina of his Aramaic, with its strangeness and its solemnity" (Scholem 1946: 201) seems to be inspired by such ideas as that the angels do not understand Aramaic—which thus serves as a nonmonitorable vehicle of communication between God and man.[14] Indeed, according to a somewhat later source, Aramaic was the language in which God communicated with the Biblical prophets (Ginzberg 1938: 45, note 242). There can be no doubt, however, that the existence of the Aramaic *Zohar* did a great deal to reinforce the feeling that Aramaic was a language of divine mysteries. At a later date, passages from the *Zohar* were incorporated into the prayers. The liturgy also contains Aramaic poems in the Targum-Zohar dialect written in the Middle Ages.

The main active use of Aramaic in the Middle Ages and early modern times was in legal and ritual discussions where the implications of Talmud statements were argued in the language of the Talmud itself. From the 16th Century onwards, Talmud study was carried on through the method of *Pilpul*, lit. "peppering," in which the learner was encouraged to discover difficulties in the argument and to suggest daring solutions for them. These discussions were carried on in the spoken languages, but the Talmudic technical terms were not translated and were incorporated in their original form. In this way the Jewish languages, and with them Hebrew, absorbed hundreds of Aramaic terms.

Many hundreds more were absorbed by modern written Hebrew or deliberately incorporated by the men and institutions that charged themselves with expanding its vocabulary. Aramaic plays a role vis-à-vis Hebrew like that of Greek and Latin vis-à-vis European languages—as a reservoir for learned word formation. In present-day Israel an ability to handle Aramaic expressions and proverbs is a hallmark of those who "really know Hebrew." The role playing of Aramaic is not yet exhausted. In the 19th Century westernized Hebrew writers drew an analogy between Yiddish, the popular language of their day, and Aramaic, the popular language of ancient times, and in translating colloquialisms of Russian or Yiddish literature, drew freely upon Talmudic Aramaic. Thus Aramaic functions, albeit in different literary spheres, as a vehicle for mystery, for erudition, and for familiarity at one and the same time.

Language education

Diglossia necessitates an efficient system of language education for those who are expected to handle the superior language: in traditional Judaism, this means every male, in order that he may pray and "learn." In Eastern Europe, boys started school at the age of three, and the school day was thirteen hours. No secular subjects were studied. The boy learned the letters and vowel signs, practiced briefly on the prayer book without translation, and then began to read and translate word for word from the weekly portion of the Pentateuch, covering some part of it during the week, and jumping next week to the beginning of the succeeding portion. When he had made some progress in word-for-word translation, he would begin to read with each verse the 11th-Century commentary of Rashi which, like all books written for adults, appeared in his text without the vowel points.[15] It was read, but not translated word for word, though some translation could be demanded. Eventually, the boy would proceed to studying the Mishnah. If he was sufficiently gifted, or his parents insisted, he would be initiated to the Talmud, picking up the Aramaic much as he had picked up the Hebrew of the Bible, by translation, word for word or phrase by phrase.

Men who studied in the traditional way have informed me they were not even told that the Talmud was mainly written in a different language. As one put it: "Just as we knew that *bo* was translated 'come here,' we knew that *ta* (Aramaic) had to be translated 'come here.' " Thus the Aramaic words were just additional synonyms. Grammar was not used in teaching either Hebrew or Aramaic; learning Hebrew grammar was looked upon as a sign of having become antireligious. (It might be interesting to investigate at which stage traditional learners became aware of Aramaic as a different language.) The main method for learning the Talmud was by a kind of communal self study, all pupils sitting or standing in the same room and each reading the text and commentaries aloud to himself. This self study was controlled by examinations and deepened by lessons based on the prepared texts.

The translation was done, of course, into the spoken language of the pupil. The language of translation often gained an importance and holiness of its own. The vernacular equivalents of words and constructions were handed down orally from one generation of teachers to the next, and remained fairly constant, so that in course of time many of these renderings ceased to be used in common speech and became unintelligible. (For a complete presentation of such a tradition see Banitt 1972.) Some of the words and constructions, being slavish renderings of the Hebrew, were probably only half-intelligible from the outset. The recurrence in different languages of the same peculiar renderings of certain Hebrew words is an eloquent witness for the rigidity of tradition in the teaching of Hebrew.

A famous example of a "fossil" word is the Yiddish *pipernuter*. Originally the rendering of Hebrew *shefifon* (Genesis 49: 17), in the King James Version "adder" (*nuter* = German *Natter* "adder"), *pipernuter* became a word meaning anything bizarre, an "outsider," etc. Yet such words were not replaced. The same thing is found, of course, in the Christian religion where words such as *loving-kindness* are employed. Enquiries among children reveal that they have no idea what that word means and are not interested in knowing. I am not sure of any systematic research on the use of unintelligible words in sacred texts (the Koran is a well known instance). In making such an investigation, translations of such texts may well provide many interesting insights.

Since the language of translation is itself part of liturgical usage, a problem arises when a Jewish group changes its language. This problem can be observed nowadays in communities composed of former Yiddish speakers. Although their children can no longer speak Yiddish fluently or at all, such communities often feel that the Pentateuch and the Talmud must continue to be taught through the medium of Yiddish. Children thus are taught Yiddish before they embark on Hebrew, and the Pentateuch is translated with them into the accustomed archaic Yiddish. Some enlightened teachers first teach the Yiddish renderings and then make the children translate these into the local language.

Parents often insist that children recite at the Passover-eve ceremony the "four questions" both in Hebrew and Yiddish, as was done "at home." These four questions begin with "Why is this night different from all other nights? " and refer to striking customs of the celebration. They are asked by the youngest child, in order to enable the head of the family to fulfill the commandment—"When thy son asks thee" (Exodus 13: 14)—and to relate the story of the Exodus. This being the first liturgical performance in the life of a child, a great deal is made of it. In communities where there is a strong and influential former Yiddish-speaking component, this procedure has led to the practice of teaching the Yiddish translations even to children in whose homes no Yiddish is spoken. In India many families which came generations ago from Iraq read out the "four questions" in Hebrew, Arabic, and English.

No doubt this persistence of nonfunctional translation languages is in some measure due to the traditional children's teacher. Knowing the translation by heart is their chief professional asset. Since they possess no theoretical superstructure, such as formal grammar or the ability to consult a dictionary, it is difficult for them to adapt their technique to another language. The religious teachers also are often the least assimilated part of the immigrant community, hence least expert in the new language and at the same time most aware of the danger of linguistic inexactitude. The objective difficulties are at times sublimated into a theory that the new language is less suitable for translating from the Hebrew than the old one. This point of view was once succinctly summed up for me by a teacher recently arrived in Northern Ireland from Hungary: "How can the Belfast children learn the Pentateuch when they don't know Yiddish? " In another case, an English Yeshiva accepted boys from Morocco but taught them Yiddish before they were taught Talmud. In Israel many Yeshiva teachers felt that replacing Yiddish by Hebrew as language of translation in teaching Talmud took a lot out of the spirit of the subject. Among the glosses for Hebrew words given by French Jewish commentators (writing in Hebrew) in the 11th to 13th Centuries, are quite a few Provençal words. These must have been brought in by teachers from the south of France, where Hebrew learning had been established earlier and kept on for centuries, because these renderings were felt to be more appropriate than the corresponding French forms.

In the older traditional course, the prayers were part of the curriculum only as reading practice after learning the letters. They were not translated. In modern "Hebrew classes" and Jewish day schools a great deal of time is given over to translating prayers. The effect upon the efficiency of the acquisition of Hebrew is negative, as the language and thought of the prayers is too abstract for children at the age of six or eight, and the text does not, like the Pentateuch, divide naturally into small sections that can be discussed so as to impress the vocabulary upon the memory. Word-for-word translation is still used and somehow seems to be the only way in which such a text can be taught when there is not proper linguistic preparation. In many of the above institutions, modern methods of language teaching as well as teaching aids are employed, but the use of these is linked to modern Hebrew. They are thus more successful in turning out modern Hebrew speakers than in preparing their pupils for understanding the prayers, let alone for "learning" as defined above.

Few parents outside extreme Orthodox circles in the diaspora are nowadays willing to sacrifice general or technical education in order to give their children the number of hours needed to bring them up to the standard where they can "learn." Many stop the Hebrew education immediately after the boy has reached the age of thirteen, at which time he is initiated into full religious manhood. This is marked by calling the boy up on a Sabbath to read from the Pentateuch. In contrast to the usual practice—that a person called up only recites the Blessing, and the text is read by a skilled reader—most of these boys read the text themselves; and thus the preparation for the *Bar-Mitzvah* (lit. "obliged to perform the commandments") includes the study of the proper cantillation of the reading. From thirteen onwards the boy is bound to keep all commandments and is counted as one of the required minimum of ten for public prayer. (For girls, see below.)

A widely chosen way out of the dilemma imposed by religious diglossia is to replace the learning of religious Hebrew in fact (though rarely officially) by a course focused on the acquisition of Modern Hebrew. Modern Hebrew, if properly taught, is probably no more difficult to acquire than Russian or German. The assumption is that a child able to read Modern Hebrew fluently will find it easy also to learn to understand religious texts. The instruction often is given in Hebrew, and where there is a competent teacher, good standards are often achieved by this combination of spoken Hebrew as medium of instruction and discussion with the traditional religious texts. This applies especially to day schools, where many hours each week are given in this way. The condition is, of course, that the course is long enough and so designed as to lead to the ability to read Modern Hebrew and not just to carry on simple conversation in it.

We have mentioned repeatedly the statutory minimum of ten men over thirteen years old for performing public prayer. Women do not make up any part of that number. In Orthodox synagogues women sit in a separate part of the hall or on a balcony, screened off so that they cannot be seen by the men. In many oriental communities no accommodation at all is provided for women in synagogues. In religious law, women are required to say the Blessings as occasion arises, but they are not required to pray, though they are allowed to. In western communities it is common for women to share in the prayers from behind the screen (in Conservative congregations most sit with their men), but in Eastern Europe often only young girls and old women came to the synagogue, mainly on Sabbath and festivals, while younger married women stayed at home, except for the Day of Atonement.

As for "learning" on the part of women, opposition to it is widespread, and justified by quoting the statement of Rabbi Eliezar (ca. 100 A. D.): "If a man teaches his daughter to study the Law, it is as if he were teaching her to trifle."[16] It is true that this statement was never taken to mean outright prohibition and that we hear at different periods of women learned in Jewish lore and even in sacred Law. On the whole, however, it did mean that girls were simply not educated. They learned the alphabet, but used it mainly to write Yiddish or whatever language they spoke. A semi-cursive font used to be called in Eastern Europe *Weiber-teitsh,* i.e., "(script used for) translations for women." In oriental Jewish communities alphabetization was thought unnecessary. Statistics collected in Israel suggest that about fifty percent of the women in these communities were illiterate. In more enlightened times and circles, where education was provided for girls, it was usually not Hebrew education, but in the language they spoke. Thus a literature in Yiddish arose which was ostensibly only addressed to women, though we know that it was read also by less-educated men. One of the first products of the Hebrew printing press, the Yiddish epic on the lives of Samuel, David, and Saul, was said on the title page to be destined for "women and pious maidens." Parts of the Bible were printed in Yiddish as "women's translations." In 1616 there was printed in Poland a Yiddish book of devotion which offered an anthology from various works of "learning" and was printed more than one hundred times. This work is by Jacob Ashkenazy and is called *Tsena u-re'ena* "Go ye forth and look" (Song of Songs 3: 11). It has recently been translated into English.

While in the 2nd Century A. D. a rabbi advised anyone who wanted his son to learn Greek "to teach him at an hour which is neither day nor night," so as not to waste time that might be used for "learning," one of his contemporaries stated, "A man is permitted to have his daughter taught Greek, because it is an adornment for her."[17] Middle-class parents felt free in more modern times to give their daughters a general education and teach them music and art. In 19th-Century Russia girls of Orthodox wealthy families learned Russian and even had French governesses. In circles close to the Hebrew "Enlightenment" girls learned to write Hebrew letters, read Modern Hebrew literature, and even were taught Bible at a time when for a man reading any part of the Bible outside Pentateuch and Psalms was a sign of having broken with Orthodoxy. Thus there came into being numerous families in which the husband was ignorant of literature and manners outside Jewish tradition, while his wife might be well read and genteel in her manners. For anything concerned with Jewish religious life, such women were of course totally dependent on the guidance of their husbands.

In modern times, mainly under the influence of German Neo-Orthodoxy,[18] it has become customary to give girls a religious education. Care is taken, however, that the education of girls always remains one step behind the stage aimed at for boys from the same group: where boys learn no further than the Pentateuch, girls will only be taught prayers; where boys study the Mishnah, girls will study the Pentateuch with Rashi's commentary; where boys are initiated into the Talmud, girls will learn Mishnah. In Orthodox circles Talmud is considered entirely unsuitable for girls. Lately, however, some Religious State Schools in Israel, and an Orthodox Jewish School in Boston, have been teaching Talmud to their girl pupils. At modern Jewish institutions of college and university level the practice is not always the same, but on the whole women students are admitted to the study of Talmud.

Modern westernizing Orthodoxy permits parents to celebrate a girl's reaching the age of twelve, at which she is under Jewish Law bound to keep the commandments. These celebrations (called *Bat-Mitzva*), are modeled on the *Bar-Mitzva* celebrations of boys at thirteen, and the girls often will give a learned lecture. In Reform synagogues and in many Conservative synagogues she will be "called up" to have a part of the weekly portion of the Pentateuch read to her. The American Reform community consecrated in 1972 its first woman rabbi.

In Orthodox circles, it has become quite common in recent years to institute "lessons" for women. These are given either by men or by women, especially by rabbis' wives, who are thus enabled to utilize their often considerable religious learning in the same way as men do. This development, together with the increasing number of women teaching religious Hebrew at all types of institutions to children, is slowly changing the role women play in liturgy in the wider sense.

In Israel, there is no diglossia (except for the Aramaic of the Talmud). The Hebrew-speaking Israeli child can pray as soon as it can read. Unlike Classical and modern Dhimotiki Greek, Biblical and Modern Hebrew are "mutually intelligible." About ninety percent of the Biblical vocabulary is employed today, most of it with only minor changes of meaning. Out of the 1,000 most frequent words, 800 occur in the Bible. A check of average news items in the daily press shows that sixty to seventy percent of the words employed are Biblical, while Mishnaic Hebrew words make up about twenty percent. In the Ten Commandments (Exodus 20: 2-17) there occur only six words not current in present-day literary Hebrew; out of these, five are easily guessed morphological or semantic variants, and the only one which is not understood is *amah* "maidservant."

Small children are taught to say some Blessings; toddlers of five in kindergartens have Bible verses or Bible stories read aloud to them in the original and understand them in the same way as they make sense out of the elegant Modern Hebrew affected in the stories written for small children. From the beginning of its school career, the Israeli child reads the Bible.

There are three Hebrew school systems in Israel: State Schools, Religious State Schools, and the (state-supported) "Independent Education" of the Orthodox party *Agudat Israel*. The extreme Orthodox groups do not send their children to any of these, but maintain for their boys separate schools of a strictly traditional pattern (*cheder*), where Yiddish is the language of instruction and no "secular" subjects are taught. These private schools are subsidized by local authorities. In the first-mentioned three school systems there is a balance between secular and religious education. The State Schools devote much time to the Bible, but teach also some Mishnah and Midrash and a subject called "Jewish Consciousness," an important element of which is an introduction to the prayer book and to prayer customs. In the two religious networks, the Bible is studied extensively as well, with more attention to the traditional commentaries, and Mishnah and Talmud (for boys) are taught. At the high school level, there are so-called "Yeshiva High Schools," where half a day is given over to the normal curriculum and half a day to advanced Talmud study.

The frequent complaints about the ignorance in liturgical matters of State School-educated young people reflect partly the complexity of the content of Jewish learning and partly the results of the in-group attitudes of Israeli synagogue congregations, where a person not fluent in the sequence and manner of praying feels like an outsider. At any rate there is no linguistic barrier involved.

Language differences in liturgical varieties

Jewish liturgy varies a great deal according to regions or even towns. The localization of liturgic rites may be the actual habitat or a country from which a group emigrated recently, e.g., the Italian or Yemenite rites (with their local varieties). It may, however, be a country which the group left a long time ago. Thus the Spanish Jews (Sephardim) left Spain before 1942, but maintain a Sephardi rite in all countries where they have since settled. Most of the Jews of Eastern Europe descend from people who emigrated there from western and southern Germany before and about 1348, but have a basically common German

(Ashkenazi) rite. The Ashkenazi rite, however, is divided into the German, which was used in the areas corresponding to the early medieval Frankish kingdom, and the "Polish" rite east of it. The Hebrew names Sepharad for Spain (probably because of the similarity of the first two consonants) and Ashkenaz for the Frankish empire came to be used for Jews whose ancestors had once lived in those areas. The original meaning of Sepharad (Obadia 20) is almost certainly Sardis on Asia Minor; Ashkenaz (Jeremiah 51: 27) is possibly Scythia.

Besides the differences in wording, order, and identity of the prayers and readings, there are also considerable differences in the pronunciation of Hebrew.[19] Two isoglosses (dialect boundaries) run across Jewry and create the main divisions:

(1) the line between Western Jews (Ashkenazim and European Sephardim) who do not sound the two pharyngeals, ^{c} and h and the three emphatics, t, s, and q, and the Oriental Jews (in particular the Yemenites)[20] who sound some or all of these; and

(2) the line between Ashkenazim and Yemenites who pronounce historical lengthened $\bar{a}$ (Qamas) as [o] and historical long or lengthened $\bar{o}$ as a diphthong such as [ay, öi, oi], and all the rest who pronounce $\bar{a}$ as [a] and $\bar{o}$ as [o]. (The ancient Hebrew vowel system distinguished three degrees of length, and these are still written in the present system of vowel signs. No Hebrew pronunciation today distinguishes length, and probably none has done so since at least the 9th Century A. D.) It is usual to refer to the a/o pronunciation as "Sephardi" and to the o/au pronunciation as "Ashkenazi," while the sounding of pharyngeals and emphatics is referred to as the "oriental" or "Semitic" pronunciation.

European Renaissance Hebraists seem to have had scant regard for the Hebrew of the Ashkenazim amongst whom they lived and whom they knew as a ghetto-bound, zealously traditionalist group with no knowledge of formal grammar. They were more disposed to turn for guidance to Spanish refugees who, as a group, were more urbane and westernized and had access to the great grammatical tradition developed in Spain and southern France from Judah Ḥayyūj (10th Century) to David Kimḥi (1160-1235). Most important, their a/o pronunciation closely resembled the form in which the Hebrew names were transcribed in the Vulgate and the Septuagint. Thus the western Sephardi pronunciation (without pharyngeals and emphatics) became the "scientific" pronunciation of Hebrew taught at universities. From the second half of the 19th Century onwards, enlightened Jews in Central and Eastern Europe also acknowledged it as a pronunciation superior to their own Ashkenazi one.

In mid-19th Century, a somewhat rudimentary Hebrew came to be established as a lingua franca between different Jewish communities in Jerusalem and other "holy cities" of Palestine. The pronunciation used was Sephardi in type, probably owing to the fact that Sephardi and oriental Jews both predominated in the trading class and dominated the Jewish representative bodies under the Turkish administration. When Eliezar Ben-Yehuda (1857-1922), the theoretician and charismatic personality of the revival of spoken Hebrew, began to operate in

Palestine in 1881, he was all the more willing to adopt as his standard this actual and scientific variety because he had a great admiration for oriental Jews. Thus Israeli spoken Hebrew became established with a pronunciation which differed from every traditional prayer pronunciation in use at the time, for by then oriental Sephardim had accepted the oriental pharyngeals and emphatics, and the few western Sephardic communities had introduced features not found in the "scientific" variety. It has been said that the success of the Hebrew revival was to some extent due to the fact that it was not spoken by any part of Jewry, and thus no group had to give up its own language for that of another group (Poliak 1945: 27-34). It may well be that the success of the Israeli pronunciation was assured by its neutrality as to existing prayer pronunciations. In fact, as we shall see, the standard remained neutral with regard to the sounding versus substitution of pharyngeals and emphatics.

During the many population shifts typical of diaspora history, each community on the whole held tenaciously both to its prayer rites and prayer pronunciations. (There are, however, some striking exceptions. The o/au pronunciation was imported from Palestine into Northwest Europe only in the 12th Century A. D. In the 18th Century the Hassidim of Eastern Europe adopted a modified version of the Sephardi prayer rite, though retaining their Ashkenazi pronunciation.) In many countries, e.g., the United States and Canada, there still exist two major networks of synagogues differing in rite and pronunciation, as well as numerous small synagogues preserving the rite of some city in Europe. On the other hand, there has been taking place in the diaspora, and even more so in Israel, a process of polarization into a binary Ashkenazi-Sephardi opposition. This is largely due to the prestigious group of "pure Sephardim" becoming the spokesman and model of oriental and South-European Jewry as a whole. Among other factors, there also has been the easy availability of prayer books printed at Livorno according to the Spanish rite while it is difficult to maintain in print local prayer books.

In Israel today it is usual for a man from any oriental community to refer to himself as a Sephardi. After an initial tendency of oriental Jews to change over to the nonpharyngeal pronunciation of the speakers of Ashkenazi origin, the 1950s initiated not only a trend towards maintaining a distinct Sephardi speech, but also a trend for oriental communities that traditionally did not pronounce the pharyngeals to introduce them into their speech. This restitution did not, however, include the emphatics. Today Israeli Hebrew is spoken in two varieties, of approximately equal numerical strength: the oriental or Sephardi with pharyngeals, lingual trilled r, and a tendency to sound historical e in certain positions as [e] or [a], versus the Ashkenazi or European origin variety which sounds ^{c} as zero, h as [x], uvular r, and historical e as zero to a much wider extent than the oriental pronunciation. It will be seen that the names Sephardi and Ashkenazi have acquired several meanings each. The situation is further complicated by the widely held view, subscribed to also by the Hebrew Language Academy, that it is correct and desirable to sound the pharyngeals, since they exist in the spelling and have some influence on grammar.[21] As a consequence, the Israel radio demands that its announcers sound the pharyngeals.[22] The average Israel-born "Ashkenazi" is able to produce pharyngeals and will occasionally do so in order to make his meaning clear, but only a few enthusiasts adopt oriental speech in public and even fewer in private life. The majority is well aware of the social implications of the two varieties of pronunciation.

The Israeli pronunciation, in its two varieties, has almost completely replaced in liturgical use the traditional pronunciations of the various countries of origin. Only older people and the extreme Orthodox still use forms of Ashkenazi pronunciation in liturgy (prayer and "learning"). On the oriental side it is only the Yemenite community that makes some effort to teach its children the traditional Yemenite pronunciation for use in prayer and is said to insist upon its use at least in the public reading of the Pentateuch portion. The younger Israeli prays and "learns" according to the pronunciation in which he carries on his daily affairs.

Israel has two chief rabbis, one Sephardi and one Ashkenazi. In each large town there is both a Sephardi and an Ashkenazi main rabbi. Synagogues are for the most part either Sephardi or Ashkenazi. The Sephardi synagogues are usually attached to a community of common extra-Israeli origin, such as Syria, Aleppo, Iraq, northern Iraq, etc., but the rite in all of these is common Sephardi, except for a small minority of the Yemenite synagogues. Ashkenazi synagogues usually have given up the special rite of the country of origin and are also much more mixed in their attendance than the Sephardi ones, so that most of them are just generally Ashkenazi. There is, however, a difference in rite between Hassidic and non-Hassidic synagogues, and amongst the extreme Orthodox each Hassidic subgroup has its own synagogue(s) with differences of custom, though even in the small Hassidic *shtiblach* (little rooms) different types of Ashkenazi pronunciation will be heard. (In contrast to synagogues built for the purpose, which tend to be more formal, a *shtibel* is a room, often in a private home, with a plain Ark and a few tables, chairs, and benches, in which prayer proceeds informally, and the individual worshipper can "let himself go.")

There has, however, developed an "Israeli rite" on a predominantly Ashkenazi basis. Since the army chaplaincy uses this rite for all services as a means of unifying the men in the ranks, younger men often prefer it to traditional rites, and it is slowly penetrating into synagogues. In some villages the younger men hold Sabbath services apart from the older generation, and at such services use the Israeli rite and the Israeli spoken-style pronunciation. Also in the cities, some of the larger synagogues use the Israeli rite or some modification of it and have a mixed Ashkenazi-Sephardi attendance. In all such places each person who in turn acts as prayer leader or as reader from the Pentateuch will pronounce according to the Israeli oriental or the Israeli European-origin pronunciation, but these differences have no liturgical significance. Indeed, it may well happen that an older person will lead the prayers in traditional Ashkenazi pronunciation, while the responses of the congregation will be given in Israeli Hebrew.

The European-origin style of Israeli pronunciation is gradually penetrating also into the liturgy in the diaspora. The causes for this are complex. As we saw, the teaching of Modern Hebrew is, for purely pedagogical reasons, becoming widely accepted as part of the curriculum of religious schooling. There were, indeed, as late as the 1930s, some educators who taught their pupils to speak Modern Hebrew in the Ashkenazi pronunciation. However, the absurdity of teaching a modern language in a pronunciation that could not be employed in talking with its native speakers, soon led to the general acceptance of the Israeli pronunciation for the modern language texts. At the same time many schools insisted on continuing to teach the sacred texts in the Ashkenazi pronunciation as used in the local synagogue, in spite of the burden imposed upon pupil and teacher alike by the simultaneous use of two different ways of sounding the same letters.

The establishment of the state of Israel in 1948 was followed by a wave of enthusiasm for Hebrew in the diaspora. In many communities, the rabbis organized or themselves gave classes in spoken Hebrew. The Department for Education and Culture and the Department for Torah Education of the Jewish Agency sent Israeli teachers to diaspora communities in an effort to reconstruct Jewish religious education after the damages wrought in World War II. These teachers tended to use the Israeli pronunciation in the classroom as well as in the liturgy and in the reading of sacred texts. Within a short time praying in the Israeli pronunciation became not only a matter of habit with young people, but also a means of demonstrating identification with Israel. It was common to hear young people pronounce the blessings over readings from the weekly portion (which are said aloud) in Israeli pronunciation, or, as it was called, Sephardi. At times a Sephardi pronunciation would be used by the person reading the Pentateuchal portion or leading the prayers. A prayer for the well-being of the state of Israel was introduced in synagogues and was often said in the Israeli pronunciation within the framework of a service otherwise completely conducted in Ashkenazi.

In the 1950s one of the larger synagogues in London officially announced its decision to henceforth conduct its services in the Sephardi pronunciation. The Chief Rabbi reacted in his capacity of chief religious judge by declaring that pronunciation was an integral part of religious custom, and that Jewish law prohibited changing local custom. (A religious custom and a prayer rite are both denoted by the Hebrew word *minhag.*) The synagogue in question, and others which had made the change less publicly, had to revert to the Anglo-Ashkenazi pronunciation. To some extent this was also enforced in religious teaching.

When Hebrew was being revived in speech, the "direct method" of language teaching was in vogue. It was enthusiastically adopted by Hebrew teachers, both because it conformed with Ben-Yehuda's principle of Hebrew as language of instruction and because it was the opposite of the word-for-word translation current in the traditional schools. Under the name of "Hebrew through Hebrew" (*Ivrit be-Ivrit*) it has been connected in the popular mind ever since then with the acquisition of living Hebrew. Once the rudiments of Hebrew had been acquired through the direct method, with only Hebrew spoken in the classroom, it was natural that the religious texts would also be taught through the medium of Hebrew, without the translation into the pupil's mother tongue. Especially in

North America this is now the habit in a large number of Jewish part-time and full-time schools. In the latter general subjects are taught in English, Jewish subjects in Hebrew. Many teachers' colleges and adult continuation institutions (Jewish Colleges), as well as rabbinical seminaries apply this procedure which has practical advantages: it provides constant practice in Hebrew, makes it easier and more natural to employ Israeli teachers, and at the higher levels prepares the student for reading Hebrew research literature and eases the question of terminology. Sociolinguistically, it produces a close linkage in the pupil's mind between "learning" and spoken Hebrew in the Israeli pronunciation.

Liturgical literature

The Jewish prayer liturgy consists of a number of distinct items, usually printed in separate volumes:

(1) the daily and Sabbath prayers (*Siddur*);

(2) five distinct sets of festival prayers (*Maḥzor*)—this terminological distinction between Siddur and Maḥzor being purely Ashkenazi;

(3) the penitentiary prayers recited before the Day of Atonement (*Seliḥot*);

(4) the domestic service for Passover eve (*Haggadah*);

(5) the dirges for the anniversary of the destruction of Jerusalem (*Qinot*).

There are commentaries on all of these, over fifty on the Haggadah. It is a status symbol to use at least Maḥzor and Haggadah in editions provided with commentaries, thus linking prayer with "learning."

The material in these volumes was formed in many layers. Psalms, which form an important section of the morning prayers and part of many others, date partly from before 586 B. C., certainly wholly from before 100 B. C. The bulk of the basic prayers dates from about 200 B. C.-300 A. D. The Biblical Psalms are composed in the poetical variety of Biblical Hebrew. In part they contain a higher concentration of archaizing forms than other Biblical poetry, so that we have some justification in assuming that a special prayer register existed. With regard to the basic prayers, there can be no doubt about this. Their language constitutes a mixture between Mishnaic Hebrew (see below) spoken at the time of their composition and Biblical Hebrew. In particular, it uses many words that occur rarely in the Bible. It is clear that this language was never spoken, but was formed in order to serve in the prayers.

In the festival prayers of the Ashkenazi communities, a striking element is provided by the *Piyyuṭ* (from Greek *poiētēs*), hymns with an elaborate structure of rhythm, rhyme, and acrostic, many of them exhibiting deep messianic fervor. They were written in Palestine, Italy, and Germany, in that chronological order, from 300 or 500 A. D. until the 12th Century. The earlier beginning date is suggested by Schirmann (1953), the later by Fleischer (1970). Both agree that the Piyyut started in Palestine and spread from there to other countries. Zunz (1855) dated the beginning of this poetry about 770 A. D., and placed it in Italy.

The earlier Piyyut writers were cantors in synagogues. They not only used the existing Biblical and Mishnaic vocabulary to the full, but also created thousands of new words. The result is that they are often difficult to understand. Certain Piyyut hymns are sung aloud by cantor and congregation, with the Ark opened and the congregation standing. The words and the haunting melodies are likely to form the most memorable religious experience of the service, especially on the Day of Atonement when even the religiously indifferent attend services and there is an atmosphere of awe. To those who know some Hebrew, part of the *frisson* no doubt derives from the strange words and recondite allusions which mark these poems. Within the spectrum of registers used in Jewish prayer, this is the most numinal one. Since about 1950, the Piyyut language has exercised a deep influence on the language of some of the younger Israeli poets.

In the Sephardi prayer books, most of the Piyyut hymns were removed as a result of the criticism by 12th-Century Spanish Hebrew grammarians that their language was ungrammatical. Their place was taken by poems composed in Spain and southern Europe in meters derived from the Arabic and in pure Biblical language. Some of these also found their way into Ashkenazi liturgy where they hold an honored place and are recited at prominent places of services in an antiphony similar to that of the Piyyut, but without opening the Ark. Thus, the song "Go forth, my friend" is sung on Sabbath eve, while at the beginning of services and at the end of the Sabbath services there are sung either "Lord of the Universe" or "The Living God is great," the latter a rhymed version of the thirteen articles of faith according to the Sephardi philosopher Maimonides (1135-1205). As a poem, "Go forth, my friend" was composed by Solomon Alkabeṣ (1505-1584) from Salonica, while he was living at Safed in Palestine, probably under the influence of the mystic Isaac Luria who was active there 1570-1572. (For these poems see Singer 1890: 2-3.)

In the mystical ferment of the 16th-17th Centuries, many further additions were made to the prayer book. Linguistically, these are important in being closely modeled upon the language of the basic prayers. Thus, after the departures from that language in Piyyut and in Spanish religious poetry, it now came to be clearly established that the prayer idiom of Mishnaic times was the only suitable vehicle for liturgy.

In the diaspora, until the revival of spoken Hebrew, the language of prayer was indeed a register clearly set apart. Likewise, the various types of Hebrew in the works used for "learning" were connected with that activity only. Hebrew was written in a variety of forms for religious and secular purposes, but none of these was identical with any type of language used in prayer or learning. The only point of contact might be found in Hebrew poetry, which during the later Middle Ages and into modern times was written in an imitation of Biblical Hebrew. However, it seems that in fact the contact was not felt, because only Pentateuch and Psalms formed part of the liturgical corpus, while the poetry drew largely on Biblical books such as the Prophets, Job, or Proverbs. Only when the "Enlightenment" literature of the 18th-19th Centuries drew for its prose, too, on the Bible, a nonliturgical style was created which resembled Biblical—and especially Penta-teuchal—narrative. But then the Enlighteners treated the Bible as literature, and thus started a process towards effacing the clear demarcation between liturgy and nonliturgical language.

This process was completed as a result of the linguistic tendencies connected with the revival. Here we must distinguish two separate trends. One is represented by a purely literary development. While the Enlighteners used for their narrative prose pure Biblical Hebrew, Mendele Mokher Sefarim (S. J. Abramowitsch 1836-1917) introduced into the style of his satirical and picaresque novels words and phrases from Mishnaic Hebrew and Talmudic Aramaic.[23] This was intensified by his pupils and successors. C. N. Bialik introduced elements from "learning" literature into his poetry, part of which was devoted to the glorification of "learning" and the Bet ha-Midrash. J. D. Berkovitz (born 1884) translated the Yiddish story writer Sholem Aleikhem (1859-1916), using Talmudic Aramaic words and phrases as substitutes for juicy Yiddish idioms on the principle that Aramaic was the popular speech of its time, and therefore a suitable equivalent for the popular speech of our time. A similar procedure was adopted by translators of modern Russian novels in order to render the colloquial idioms of the dialogue. From these the "popular" Aramaisms spread into picaresque Israeli novels. Sholem Aleikhem is widely read in Israeli schools, so that nowadays the language of the most revered "learning" texts curiously resembles the language of modern classical works recommended for imitation. This is further reinforced by the Israeli practice of teaching idioms in schools. The various idiom dictionaries contain a high percentage of Talmudic Aramaic phrases.

The speakers of Hebrew and the school teachers in the villages of Palestine in the 1880s were neither learned in classical literature, nor did many of them seem to have belonged to the inner circle of Enlighteners with their mastery of writing Biblical Hebrew. In fact, the established writers of the period, including Mendele Mokher Sefarim, were almost to a man opposed to speaking Hebrew and to Ben Yehuda's "word factory." The early settlers from Eastern Europe came mainly from middle-class families on the periphery of the Enlightenment. They had enjoyed the standard Jewish education: they understood the more frequent prayers and probably knew them by heart, were familiar with the Pentateuch (with Rashi's commentary), and could "learn" Mishnah and perhaps the most popular one of two Talmudic tractates. It was this knowledge that they activated when they began to speak Hebrew. As a result, the syntax of Modern Hebrew resembles that of the basic prayers (with an overlay of European influence) rather than the syntax of either Biblical or Mishnaic Hebrew. The mixture of words, too, is not unlike that of the prayers, with a very high proportion of Biblical words among the more frequent items. Where there are Biblical and Mishnaic synonyms, in most cases the Mishnaic member of the pair functions in elevated style, the Biblical in everyday speech.

Thus the language structure of the daily and Sabbath prayers is not too different from standard written Hebrew. As we have seen, it is also pronounced the same way. Where it differs is in rhythm: short sentences, often in parallel sets of structure and meaning; few subordinate clauses; chains of synonyms or near synonyms. These, however, mark prayer language only by virtue of their concentration and can all be found in elevated modern Hebrew prose. Perhaps this combination of a fairly simple vocabulary and a semi-poetic rhythm, resulting in staccato intonation, is felt as a stylistic marker. In any case, the distance is small. This can also be seen in prayers composed in Israel for various occasions, which seem to be conceived in straightforward literary Hebrew.

The feature that most sets apart prayer from ordinary speech is intonation, a kind of *recitativo* with passages sung according to traditional melodies. It would be quite unthinkable for a prayer leader to recite the prayers in ordinary speech intonation. Likewise, all readings from the Bible are recited in a fixed *recitativo* melody, which is guided by the accents with which the Bible text is provided. "Learning," too, has its fixed intonation patterns. The intonational difference between liturgy and ordinary speech is probably most noticeable to the listener upon hearing a sermon in the synagogue. The intonation patterns of a sermon sound quite rough compared to the flowing melodies of the prayers and readings preceding it. Even within the sermon there is a clear opposition between "learning" passages in which Midrash, Talmud, or Bible are quoted and discussed and passages in which the speaker utters his opinions on moral or political matters. The "learning" material is recited in a modified form of the typical pattern, while the opinions are given in an intonation resembling an ordinary speech or lecture.

In summary: we witness in the case of Hebrew a process by which an originally distinct and autonomous language of prayer is now largely coalesced, at least in Israel, with common language.

NOTES

1. Traditionally, Jewish weddings are performed in private homes, restaurants, etc., or in the open air. The practice of holding weddings in synagogues is western and modern. Some of the Israeli synagogues have special courtyards for wedding ceremonies.

2. These are poems in praise of the Sabbath, dating from different periods. There is no standard collection, but various selections are printed in prayerbooks or in special booklets. Some enjoy wide popularity, but in fact everyone has his favorite items. It should be noted that Jewish prayerbooks often try to enhance their usefulness by including all kinds of additional materials used in religious activities; therefore the contents of different editions may differ widely.

3. The idea of Sabbath as bride and the Jewish people as bridegroom goes back to the Talmud. The Hebrew word *shabbath* is of feminine gender. The idea found its most beautiful expression in the hymn "Go forth, my friend, to meet the bride, let us welcome the Sabbath," sung on Friday evening services (Singer 1890: 111).

4. A tractate is a section dealing with a specific subject, e.g., a certain festival or an aspect of marital matters (wedding, divorce, levirate marriage, etc.) and the like. Tractates are classed into six "Orders": Agriculture, Festivals, Marital Affairs, Civil and Penal Law, Temple Service, Ritual Purity. (See Strack 1945: 29-64.) A complete English translation is available as Epstein 1935-52.

5. There is no objective criterion for this choice: it is a matter for the individual to decide whether he is able to follow the argument.

6. Mishnah, tractate Aboth 4, 3; in Danby 1933: 453, "a spade wherewith to dig." (Tractates are cited by folio and column number, as here: 4, 3.)

7. Orthodox girls in Israel sometimes make it a condition of marriage that the husband spend his day in "learning" and be maintained by his wife.

8. Diglossia—in one of its definitions—denotes a situation in which two distinct forms of language are employed by the same society according to established social custom for distinct purposes.

9. "Priests" descending from Aaron (Hebrew *kohen*, pl. *kohanim*) have today only one liturgical function—to recite the blessing of the congregation (Singer 1890: 238a), and one ritual function—to accept a small sum of money as "ransom" for a first-born son (Exodus 13: 13). They are honored in various small ways: for instance, being the first to be called up to read from the Pentateuch or having first right to summon the others to grace after the meal. The rabbi in traditional Judaism is a teacher and religious judge, and plays no liturgical role. Any one of the men present can lead the prayers. Salaried cantors and Pentateuch readers, if such are employed, are chosen for their voices and skill, but they have no authority. The role of the rabbi as prayer leader, especially in Conservative and Reform congregations, is a modern innovation.

10. The terminology is awkward: some forms of Aramaic are called "languages," others are referred to as "dialects," without any relation to linguistic difference or sociolinguistic independence. Moreover, the term "Jewish Aramaic" often is used to cover two entirely different idioms: Palestinian Jewish Aramaic, which belongs to the Western branch, and Babylonian (Jewish) Aramaic, which belongs to the Eastern branch and is closely connected with the Mandean "language." For details see E. Y. Kutscher 1971.

11. A cupboard-like structure on or near the east wall of the synagogue, in which the Pentateuch scrolls for public readings are kept. Its doors are opened at solemn moments in the service, and while it is open the congregation remains standing.

12. Traditionally, these are the two most learned old men, or men known to lead a saintly life.

13. According to Heinemann (1964: 163), the Kaddish is said in Aramaic, because at first it was meant to be recited at the conclusion of a Lesson, and originated at a time when Aramaic was spoken. This would provide another link between "learning" and liturgy. It should be noted, however, that the Aramaic of the Kaddish is the language of the Targum, not one of the spoken varieties.

14. The origin of this oft-quoted saying is a story in the Babylonian Talmud, tractate Shabbat, fol. 12b (Epstein, Shabbat L, p. 48), about a sage who blessed some sick people in Hebrew and some in Aramaic: "Did not Rab Judah say 'Let no one pray for his needs in Aramaic,' and did not Rabbi Johana say 'If a man prays for his needs in Aramaic, the ministering angels will not attend to his needs, for the ministering angels do not know (the word might also mean acknowledge) Aramaic'? Nay, the case of a sick person is different, because the Divine Presence dwells near a sick person." On this, the commentator Rashi (1040-1105) remarks: "And therefore there is no need for the ministering angels to carry the prayer to the Divine Presence." Since the meaning "to know" would imply that the angels had to understand the prayer in order to carry it to the Divine Presence, it seems to me that the meaning intended in the Talmud is "to acknowledge." Yet a gloss (*Tosafot*) slightly later than Rashi expresses amazement that the angels, who "know the thoughts in every man's heart, should not know Aramaic"; thus the interpretation "to know" was already dominant at the time.

15. The Hebrew script expresses (basically) only the consonants, and the vowels are indicated by signs placed above or below the letters, as is done in Arabic, Persian, etc., and in Indian scripts. There are twenty-two letters and fourteen vowels. The usual practice was for a child to learn each combination of a vowel and a consonant as a separate unit. In material printed for adults the vowels are normally not inserted. For the Jewish child this meant that once he got beyond Pentateuch and Prayerbook to the commentary of Rashi and to Mishnah and Talmud, there were no vowels, and pronunciation of the words, as well as their meaning, had to be learned orally from the teacher. In present-day Israel, Mishnah and some parts of the Talmud are available with the vowels for school teaching, though tradition-minded teachers disdain their use.

16. Mishnah, tractate Soṭah 3, 4. Danby 1933: 296 has "lechery" instead of "trifling," but this rendering is not supported by etymology.

17. Palestinian Talmud, tractate Pe'ah, fol. le. The heads of the Palestinian Jewish community, the Patriarchs, were in the 4th-5th Centuries specifically permitted by custom to teach their sons Greek because of their constant dealings with the Roman administration, who in the eastern part of the empire used Greek (Palestinian Talmud, tractate Abodah Zarah, fol. 41a).

18. Founded by Samson Raphael Hirsch (1808-1888), this movement sought to unite strict observance of Jewish religious customs with Western education and standards of behavior. Hirsch wrote German commentaries on some Biblical books and other works in which he expounded the Orthodox faith in terms adapted to 19th-Century thinking, partly by a daring use of etymology.

19. For details see Morag 1971. Aramaic has the same consonants and vowels as Hebrew (though these partly go back to different proto-Semitic sounds), and in almost all known pronunciations the letters and vowel signs of Aramaic texts are sounded the same way as in Hebrew.

20. These emphatics are sounded by Oriental Jews the same as in Arabic, i.e., they have a secondary articulation of raising the back of the tongue towards the soft palate, and thus acquire a sombre, u-like timbre. The Ashkenazim pronounce t as [t], q as [k], and $ṣ$ as [ts]. It is not clear whether in Biblical times these emphatics were sounded as in Arabic (velarized) or as in Ethiopic, where they are articulated with vocal cords pressed together and followed by an audible glottal plosive (i.e., as ejectives).

21. The Academy was established in 1890 under the name of "Language Committee" (Va'ad Ha-lashon) and given official status as Aqademiyah la-lashon ha-ivrit in 1953. Its decisions become law after having been countersigned by the Minister of Education and Culture. It has a maximum of forty-nine active members; members who have reached the age of seventy-five "are excluded from the count" so that others can be elected in their stead, but they continue to have voting rights at the meetings. The members are university teachers, writers, school teachers, and style editors. Its main activity is the establishment of terminology. For its working methods and problems in establishing other norms, cf. Rabin 1971.

22. The ^{c} is, however, not audible in certain positions. Some prayer books for oriental communities (e.g., Siddur Tefillat Yeshurun, Jerusalem 1949) show awareness of this fact by adding "let him sound the ^{c} properly" where its omission might result in theologically awkward meanings. (Israeli prayer books are marked on the spine "Ashkenaz," "Sepharad" for Hassidim, and "Sephardim" for oriental communities.) While the pharyngeals are consistently used by the regular radio announcers, other restitutions of phonetic items in the spelling, such as emphatics, consonant doubling, or the consistent sounding of historical e, are only sporadically enforced.

23. For a discussion, see Rabin 1972. The late E. J. Kutscher of Jerusalem made a close study of the Mishnaic vocabulary of Mendele and established that it derives from tractates which are most frequently "learned."

REFERENCES

Banitt, Menahem (ed.), 1972, *Le Glossaire de Bâle*. Jerusalem: Académie Nationale des Sciences et des Lettres d'Israël.

Danby, Herbert (trans.), 1933, *The Mishnah* (translated from the Hebrew). Oxford: Oxford University Press.

Déaut, R. le, 1966, *Introduction à la Littérature Targumique, Vol. I*. Rome: Institut Biblique Pontifical.

Epstein, Isidore (ed.), 1935-52, *The Soncino Talmud* (in translation). London: Soncino Press. [The volumes are not numbered, but bear the names of the tractates.]

Fleischer, Ezra, 1970, "Studies in the problems relating to the liturgical function of the types of early Piyyut." *Tarbiz* 40: 41-63. [In Hebrew, with English summary.]

Ginzberg, Louis, 1909-38, *Legends of the Jews*. Philadelphia: Jewish Publication Society.

Heinemann, Joseph, 1964, *Prayer in the Period of the Tannaim and Amoraim*. Jerusalem: Magnes Press. [In Hebrew.]

Kaddari [=Cadari], Menachem Zewi, 1956, *The Grammar of the Aramaic of the Zohar*. Jerusalem: Published by the author. [In Hebrew.]

Kutscher, Edward Yehezkel, 1971, "Aramaic." *Encyclopedia Judaica* [Jerusalem] 3:259-283.

Morag, Shelomoh, 1971, "Pronunciations of Hebrew." *Encyclopedia Judaica* 13: 1120-1145.

Poliak, Abraham N., 1945, *The Jews of Palestine at the War's End*. Merhavia: Sifriat Palim. [In Hebrew.]

Rabin, Chaim, 1968, "The translation process and the character of the Septuagint." *Textus* [Jerusalem] 6: 1-26.

———, 1971, "Spelling reform: Israel, 1968." In *Can Language be Planned?* ed. by Joan Rubin and Björn H. Jernudd. Honolulu: University of Hawaii Press, 95-121.

———, 1972, *Short History of the Hebrew Language*. Jerusalem: Jewish Agency.

Schirmann, Jefim, 1953, "Hebrew liturgical poetry and Christian hymnology." *Jewish Quarterly Review* 44: 123-161.

Scholem, Gershom G., 1946, *Major Trends in Jewish Mysticism*. 2nd ed. New York: Schocken Books.

Singer, S. (translator), 1890, *The Authorized Daily Prayer Book*. London: Eyre and Spottiswoode. (Annotated edition by Israel Abrahams, 1914.) [All editions have the same pagination.]

Strack, Hermann L., 1945, *Introduction to the Talmud and Midrash*. (Authorized translation of the 5th German ed.) Philadelphia: Jewish Publication Society.

Teitelbaum, Yoel, 1961, *Wa-yo'el Mosheh*. Brooklyn: Jerusalem Publishing and Book Store.

Zunz, Leopold, 1855, *Die synagogale Poesie des Mittelalters*. (Zweite Auflage von Aron Freimann, 1920.) Frankfurt am Main: J. Kauffmann.

11 The Use of Hebrew by Christians in Israel

Pinchas E. Lapide

The topic of "Hebraica Christiana" has been virtually ignored by scholars, both Jewish and Christian. For the former it has been by and large taboo—it smacked too much of apostasy; the latter seem to have considered it a mere adjunct to the "Mission to the Jews" rather than a topic for linguistic research.

Christians in Israel, who are mostly Arabs, have always been a small minority, though their number has doubled in the last twenty-five years, exceeding today a total of 100,000 souls, about three percent of the entire population. Three factors enhance their importance beyond their numerical dimension—both objectively and in their own eyes: all central shrines and sanctuaries of Christianity reside in their midst; the heads of all their churches reside in the Holy City, reunited Jerusalem; and a steady, ever-growing stream of Christian pilgrims from all five continents visits this cradle of monotheism, looking for inspiration, insights, or palpable evidence of their faith.

Owing to the ambition of many Christian churches to obtain their own congregational foothold in the Holy Land, there are today in Jerusalem alone thirty-one different Christian denominations—more than many other cities in the world. This ecclesiastical multiplicity, each of whose components jealously guards its own traditional privileges, liturgy, and dogmatic independence, can be divided into four major groups: Catholics, Orthodox, Monophysites, and Protestants.

Catholics, numbering some 55,000, are subdivided into Roman Catholics (24,000), Greek Catholics (23,000), about 3,000 Maronites, and a few hundred members of the Armenian, Syrian, and Chaldean Uniate Churches.

The main branch of Orthodoxy is the Greek Orthodox Church (some 40,000) headed by its autocephalous Patriarch of Jerusalem, who enjoys precedence among the spiritual leaders of all churches.

The third group, the Monophysites—Armenians, Copts, Syrian-Jacobites, and Ethiopians—originated in the 5th Century, owing to theological divergencies at the Council of Chalecedon. They excel in the antiquity of their links with the Holy Land and the Byzantine wealth of their liturgies, although they are few in numbers (3,500 in all).

Finally, there are some twenty Protestant churches and sects, including primarily the Anglicans, Lutherans, Baptists, Quakers, and Mennonites (with 2,500 adherents), whose presence dates back only to the missionary enterprises of the 19th Century. Untrammeled as they are by theological and possessive ties with specific holy places, they devote most of their energy to evangelization.

Attitudes towards Jews, Israel, and Hebrew

Common among these churches is considerable anti-Judaism—both in their theology on the "Jews" in abstraction and in their worldly attitude to contemporary Jews, as well as incipient reappraisals of Jewry and Judaism brought on by the events of 1948. We refer to the time when next to "Old Israel" (outdated Judaism) and "New Israel" (the Church) there emerged all of a sudden a third entity—Israel reborn, a Jewish state, which not only succeeded in regaining sovereignty in the land of its ancestors, but accorded immediate official status as the national language to Hebrew, which had only recently been revived and closely resembled the "lingua sacra" of Scripture.

Broadly speaking, there are three schools of thought in practically every one of the churches in Israel. There are those who still feel as the semi-official organ of the Vatican put it on the very day Israel regained statehood: "The Holy Land and its sacred places belong to Christendom, the true Israel"; or, as Pope Pius XII said, "Only Rome is the true Jerusalem" (quoted in Paluzzi 1943: 40). Then there are those who share the view of Monsignor Oesterreicher: "The State of Israel is the visible expression of the God-willed permanence of the Jewish people. (It is) . . . a banner of God's Fidelity" (1971: 37). Finally, there is the broad, indifferent middle, to whom time-honored tradition is the very soul of religion, with Israeli sovereignty being merely another change of secular décor within that immutable verity—the Holy Land.

These viewpoints are reflected in different attitudes to the Hebrew language—a stranger to none, since Hebraisms, such as Sabbath, Amen, Selah, Passah, Messiah, Hosannah, Hallelujah, and Rabbi abound in all Christian scriptures and liturgies.

While practically all Christians in Israel use Hebrew—or rather a sort of rudimentary "Basic Hebrew"—as a means of communication with Israeli authorities and Jewish friends, and while many are able to read the Psalms and Prophets in the original, only a few use it in their worship.

As far as could be ascertained in mid-1972 about one thousand Christians pray regularly at least once a week in Hebrew. The majority consists of (ex)Jewish immigrants, who see no contradiction between their creed and active Zionism, while a handful consider their messianic belief in Jesus the crowning part of their Judaism. Another small but articulate group refuse to be called Christian, as their belief in Jesus resembles that of the Ebionites, though no definite theology has yet emerged in their midst. The gentile minority comes from seventeen countries, belongs to seven churches, and consists primarily of priests, ministers, members of the monastic orders, and missionaries. Since 1968 their number is on the increase. With rare exceptions, Hebrew is for none of them the mother tongue, but rather the second, third, or fourth language learned in adulthood, and mastered—again with few exceptions—only by Israeli (ex)Jews, for whom it is also the prime medium of daily speech, as well as a status symbol of their successful acculturation and their newly gained nationality.

By and large all Hebraeophone Christians constitute a diglossic speech community of multilingual background. Their twofold attachment to Hebrew is aptly summed up by Father Marcel Dubois, the Superior of St. Isaiah House in Jerusalem and Lecturer at the Hebrew University: "There is nothing astonishing in the fact that Israel's Christians pray in their own language at the very scene of the central theme of their faith. If there is anything surprising, it is the fact that many do not know that Christian Israelis pray in Hebrew, that they celebrate the liturgy in the language of the country, which is also the language of the Bible. The language of present-day Israel is also that of the Biblical past" (1970: 18).

Steps toward Hebraization

Various Hebrew translations and adaptations of the New Testament and church texts are proliferating in Israel—for seven good reasons, which emerged from close to 200 recorded conversations with persons concerned.

1. There is a new kind of Christian Hebraeophilia, along the lines of what St. Jerome once defined as love for the "hebraica veritas," and subsequently backed up by his own Hebrew studies in Bethlehem. The thought behind St. Jerome's dictum was expressed a thousand years later by the Nuremberg Reformer, Andreas Osiander: "God did not want the books of the Jews to be burnt, for the sake of Christendom, so that by means of the Hebrew tongue the Christians could regain the proper understanding of their faith" (quoted in Eck 1541: 46).

The discovery of the Qumran Scrolls and other Hebrew manuscripts from the Bar Koghba era, the steady shift of stress in Biblical scholarship towards Semitics, which goes hand in hand with an endeavor to de-Hellenize the Christian kerygma in order to break through to Jesus' Jewish "Sitz-im-Leben"—all these factors, combined with a revival of Hebrew in our century, have given renewed impetus to an ever-growing number of Bible scholars, theologians, clergymen, and pious Christians at large, to go back to the cradle of their faith and to learn the first mother tongue of Scripture.

2. It is as if the mystique of "the Return"—the very soul of Zionism—had rubbed off on many doubt-ridden Christians. In a frivolous age of debunking and God-is-dead-movements, they hope to find in Israel's threefold return—to its land, its peoplehood, and its language—palpable proof that "The Bible is right after all."

Symptomatic for many of these back-to-the-sources pilgrims is the voice of Father J. Maigret, O.M.I., the initiator of "The Friends of Hebrew Language Studies," which has gained numerous adherents among Catholics in France, Belgium, Switzerland, and Israel: "All know that God has spoken in Hebrew. Now my pupils have experienced it for themselves . . . Hebrew is the most fruitful medium for Bible studies" (1968: 89). This insight, formulated in a score of different ways, has caused a steady stream of Christian students to join Hebrew courses in Jerusalem where, during the last ten years, three theological institutes have organized Upanim (Hebrew-language seminars) of their own. It has also made Hebrew fashionable for Christian theologians, displacing Latin and Greek to a great extent as a prestigious "language of higher communication." To season one's daily speech with Hebraisms seems nowadays the hallmark of being theologically "in." Thus, the English organ of the Baptists in Israel is called "Ha-yahad" (the Qumranic congregation's togetherness); a French Catholic quarterly in Jerusalem goes by the name "Šoreš" (root); church tradition is often referred to in debates as *halaka*; and ecumenical innovators are praised as *haluzim* (pioneers). Moreover, a Protestant settlement in Galilee, founded and inhabited by Christians from Germany, Holland, and the United States bears the Bible name "Ness-Amim" (a banner of the nations; see Isaiah 11: 10) while a Catholic peace village, founded in 1971 near Latrun, proudly calls itself "Nevé-Shalom" (the oasis of peace; see Isaiah 32: 18).

3. Progressive Christian Bible scholars are doing more than improving the traditional church attitude, which in the past has displayed attachment to the contents of the Old Testament, but little, if any, to its Hebrew text. Hebrew is now gaining new reverence also as the most likely idiom in which Jesus prayed and preached. R. L. Lindsey, referring to his work in translating Mark's gospel into Hebrew, speaks of "the frightening feeling of creating a new one" (1969: Introduction, p. 9). R. P. Jean Carmignac, the Catholic editor of the *Revue de Qumran,* speaks of all synoptic gospels when he writes: "Retranslating the gospels into Hebrew, reconstructing the original texts, we find ourselves listening to the actual voices of the eye-witnesses of Christ's activity" (1968-1969: 91).

4. An increasing number of church bodies in Israel and from abroad are holding Bible conferences, Israel-seminars and interfaith colloquies in the city of Jerusalem. To arrive at a true dialogue with Judaism in its world center a knowledge of Hebrew is indispensable. In the words of three participants in the Fifth World Congress of Judaic Studies, which took place in Jerusalem in 1969: "One has to get used to the fact that Hebrew is not limited any more to the role of lingua sacra; it has also become the *lingua franca* of Judaic scholars and international congresses on Judaic Studies" (Betz, et al. 1969: 6).

5. Hebrew has not only become the lingua franca of most Judaic scholars, teachers, and conventions, but also constitutes frequently the only medium of communication between non-Jews, including trainees from Black Africa, Asia, and Latin America, who meet in Israel. Thus it is no longer rare for ecumenical prayers, international symposia, and interfaith colloquies, to be conducted in Hebrew.

6. Intrinsic to the Christian creed remains the call to "teach all nations" (Matthew 28: 19) which apparently makes it incumbent upon a good number of eschatologically-minded Christians who perceive Christological implications in Israel's rebirth to intensify their "mission to the Jews." Among these people the use of Modern Hebrew seems to be growing in importance.

7. Finally, there is the hope of several members of the Union of Christian Churches in Israel that Hebrew might prove to be a catalyst of church unity in the land where the church was born as one single community and where the Biblical hope of "one single oikumene" was first formulated. This vision, which might begin to take shape as an inter-church conference, later to coalesce into an association of churches, was named "the Church of Israel" by the chairman of U.C.C.I. He ended his keynote address to the U.C.C.I. annual conference, in 1970 when the program was launched, with the words Theodore Herzl once applied to his utopia of a Jewish state, "If you believe, it will not remain a dream" (quoted in Lindsey 1970: 15).

The mass in Hebrew

Outstanding, though by no means unique in its vagaries, is the genesis of the Hebrew version of the Roman Catholic mass.

Early in 1955 Father Jean Leroy and two of his fellow clergymen joined an Israeli kibbutz where they spent their leisure hours in translating into semi-modern Hebrew the mass liturgy of the Syrian-Catholic Church, to which they had grown accustomed during their previous stay in Lebanon. This missal, like that of the Maronite and the so-called "Assyrian" Church, originally had been written in the Palestinian Church-Aramaic used by Galilean peasants of Jewish extraction, who, according to the late E. J. Kutscher, had been forcibly baptized in the 6th Century under the pressure of Justinian's persecutions (Kutscher 1968). Under nationalist pressure in the 19th Century the Arab clergy had translated the responsories of the congregation, the Credo, the Offertory, as well as a few other prayers into Arabic. These Arabic sections of the missal now were rendered into a mixture of modern and liturgical Hebrew.

In the winter of 1955 Leroy, who later also Hebraised his own name to Elihay, received permission from his Order in France to celebrate his Hebrew-Aramaic mass. This was in accordance with Rule Three of "The Little Brothers of Jesus," which enabled its monastic members since 1933 to pray in the national language of their respective countries of service.

Late in 1956 Elihay compiled an improved version of his bilingual mass, which, however, still contained a good number of linguistic Aramaisms and theological Judaisms in its Hebrew part in addition to several redundant overtranslations, such as Hebrew coinages for "Catholic," "Apostolic," and "Orthodox." The products of this Hebraic zeal are still comprehensible in the case of "Catholic" and "Apostolic," though neither will evoke in the Hebrew reader the emotions elicited by their counterparts in Christian readers in Europe. In the case of "Orthodox," however, the problem is both semantic and theological, since Judaism, and with it Hebrew, knows neither a theological body of obligatory dogmata nor the resultant concept of orthodoxy as the only correct belief.

In 1953 Father Bruno Hussar, a young Dominican monk of Jewish origin applied to Cardinal Tisserant, then Dean of the College of Cardinals and a Hebraist of no mean reputation, for permission to found a small conventicle in the heart of Jewish Jerusalem, which was to act as an "Anti-Torquemada"—bent on at least symbolic atonement for the sins committed against the Jewish people by the Grand Inquisitor Torquemada who, like Hussar, was a Dominican of Jewish extraction. He said: "A true Christian-Jewish dialogue can gain full credibility only in Israel. In order to start it properly, we must first of all say Yes to the Jewish state, integrate in Israel's society, and learn how to get to know the Jews as they really are." To this program, outlined in a memorandum which he submitted in the Vatican, Hussar added the practical conclusion: "To further these ends, we must learn, speak, and pray in Hebrew in Israel. Does our breviary not consist mainly of Hebrew Psalms? Why should we recite them in Latin, of all places, in Jerusalem?"

Cardinal Tisserant, who had learned Hebrew in Jerusalem from Eliezar Ben-Yehuda and later from Joseph Klausner, agreed with Hussar in principle but suggested that at first the Hebrew-Aramaic mass of Elihay be used. The latter was requested to submit a scientific treatise on the linguistic and theological practicability of a fully Hebraised mass liturgy. Meanwhile, Hussar was given permission to read the New Testament lections according to the Hebrew translation of Delitzsch (1888) and to revert in all Old Testament parts within the missal, such as the Trishagion, the Psalms, and the Benedicte, to the original Bible idiom. The rest of the text was read by Hussar and his congregation in Latin.

In February 1956, prior to their return to Israel, Hussar and Elihay celebrated their first improvised Hebrew mass—in the catacombs of Rome.

In January 1957 Elihay submitted his treatise proving the feasibility of an all-Hebrew mass liturgy, which Cardinal Tisserant thereupon recommended to Pope Pius XII. The main arguments for the Cardinal's theological approval rested upon Pope John VIII's permission granted in the year 879 to translate the Bible into Slavonic; on Psalm 150: 6 ("Let everything that has breath praise the Lord!"); and on Pius' own encyclical of 1943 "Divino Afflante Spiritu" in which the Pontiff appealed for Bible studies to concentrate on the original texts.

In February 1957 Elihay was requested telegraphically by the Holy See to suggest a Catholic priest to whom a special indult to pray in Hebrew would be granted. Elihay at once proposed Hussar who received the written indult within a few days.

The 18th of March 1957 was a great day for the two "Hebraisatores" as Monsignor Vergani, the Vicar General of the Latin Patriarch in Israel, called them. It was in his Haifa residence that six Catholic priests convened, in order to concelebrate for the first time on Israeli soil a full-fledged Hebrew mass. The experimental text was still uneven with numerous linguistic incongruities, but as subsequently more Hebraists of various faiths were co-opted to a loosely functioning Advisory Board, vocabulary, diction, and grammar gradually improved.

The corrected mass text, prepared for Easter 1958, finally obtained the imprimatur of the Latin Patriarch Alberto Gori—but only for the five priests, who had received meanwhile the Hebrew indult from the Vatican. He steadfastly refused to grant a general imprimatur or to sanction the transfer of Sunday mass to the Sabbath for the Hebrew celebrants, in spite of their repeated requests.

Two subsequent events lent impetus to the growing number of "Hebraisatores." The "Constitutio de sacra liturgia" approved by the Second Vatican Council in its second session and promulgated by Pope Paul VI on December 4, 1963, established in Article 36: "Since the use of the mother tongue, whether in the mass, the administration of the sacraments, or other parts of the liturgy, may frequently be of great advantage to the people, the limits of its employment may be extended."

That this "mother tongue" also applied to Hebrew seems to have been confirmed by the Pope personally, when a month later he expressed his gratitude to President Shazar for the state reception accorded him in Israel by means of a discourse which ended with the Biblical salutation: "Shalom, Shalom!" A few hours later the Pontiff listened attentively to a mixed choir of monks and nuns in the Dormition Abbey on Mount Zion, who sang for him the "Magnificat" and "Tu es gloria," the thanksgiving out of the fifteenth chapter of the Book of Judith. The Hebrew translation, the music, the orchestration, and the printing of these hymns were all the work of Israeli Catholics, as the Abbot of the Dormition promptly told the Pope, who acknowledged the fact with a smiling nod.

Although during the papal pilgrimage the "pre-historic" mass text (as it is now called) was still incomplete and had been distributed in the form of a modest mimeographed copybook, the first expertly printed "Ordinarium missae" later appeared in Hebrew, bearing the Nihil obstat of Father Samkowski and the Imprimatur of Monsignor Hanna Kaldany. (Lest it seem absurd that a Polish Jesuit and an Arab bishop pronounce judgment on the Hebraicity of the Catholic mass, it should be understood that both are well known Hebraists, like several other Christians in Israel.)

Among the many problems Christian translators are faced with one can cite words like "mass," "immaculate conception," and "oblation."

"Mass" was first translated, in deference to Pauline soteriology, as the "holy sacrifice," leading to amazement whenever Christians told their Jewish friends they had to leave early "in order to offer the sacrifice." The only image these words could conjure up was the annual slaughter of Paschal lambs on Mt. Gerizim by the Samaritan community in accordance with Exodus 12: 1-11. When Jews were blunt enough to point out this inevitable association, and some Catholics well-meaningly belabored the affinity by indicating the profound nexus between the Paschal lamb and the missal sacrifice, rumors soon spread that the mass was nothing but a ritual throwback to the bloody cult of Temple hecatombs. Only students of church-synagogue relations could savor the full irony of this turning-of-tables.

As a result, "mass" was retranslated into "the Lord's supper" (I Corinthians 11: 20) which shifts the emphasis into the older and more Jewish component of missal symbolism. The emotive fact that the Hebrew word used for "Lord" (*'adon*) today signifies primarily "Mister," while "supper" (*se^cuda*) is now any "meal," still bothers some translators but can hardly be circumvented.

Such inaccuracies may have been one of the reasons why the Latin Patriarch who, according to the Vatican Council's "Constitution on the sacred liturgy" was the competent ecclesiastical authority in all matters concerning vernacularization for Israel, Jordan, and Cyprus, refused to permit the public celebration of the Hebrew mass. Pressured from various quarters "to live up to the spirit of Pope John XXIII," he at last consented—provided at least ten Catholic priests could be found "idoneous" for the purpose. Since most of the applicants were Jewish Christians, it was considered significant that Patriarch Gori should have made the churchly celebration of mass contingent upon the very number laid down in Rabbinic Law as a quorum for communal prayer.

In February 1965, ten priests had obtained a Hebrew indult and Gori granted simultaneous permission for the mass to be celebrated in Arabic (in Jordan and Israel), in Greek (in Cyprus), and in Hebrew—as soon as the territorial bishops would approve the respective texts in the vernacular. The "Hebraisantes" were the first of the three language groups to obtain their episcopal imprimatur. High mass was first celebrated in Hebrew on March 7, 1965 in the diocesan Church of Haifa—with the exception of the canon, which was celebrated in Latin, at the request of four of the eleven priests who were as yet unfamiliar with the new Hebrew text.

Since August 11, 1968 the entire mass from the Introit to the final blessing is being celebrated there in Hebrew every week for an average congregation of some 150 Catholics. Roughly a third are Arabs, half a dozen are Jewish Christians, ten to fifteen are monks and nuns from various orders residing in the vicinity, and the rest are Catholic partners of mixed couples who have immigrated from Europe since 1948. The parish priest, Father Daniel, is a Jewish Carmelite of a Zionist family in Poland, who has obtained citizenship in accordance with the law of enfranchisement.

Father Daniel's mass is being read in Hebrew by his Arab parishioners and those Israel-born offspring of mixed marriages who opted for Christianity. For those whose Hebrew is still rudimentary, he has printed a transcription in Latin characters of the Hebrew mass text, spelled in accordance with a phonetic system which is a compromise between the rules of transliteration of the Hebrew Language Academy and Polish, Hungarian, and Czechoslovak orthography, the three main primary languages of the ex-Europeans in his congregation.

Like Catholics all over the world, those in Israel are now working at the reform of their "Ordo missae" in accordance with the new directives from Rome, which leave ample leeway not only for vernacularization but also for local initiative in textual variation—a flexibility which in the new experimental Hebrew mass has already resulted in several "Judaizations," every one of which might have brought its formulators to the stake a few centuries ago.

It is still premature to analyze these nascent trends, their philological precipitation, and the sociolinguistic impact they are having on Israeli Catholics of both Jewish and Gentile stock. Similar Hebraizations—both translations and free "Nachdichtung"—of liturgies, hymnals, catechisms, schoolbooks, and theological literature are being undertaken nowadays within the Greek Catholic Church, the Baptist Convention, the Churches of England and Scotland, the Lutheran Church, and in more than a dozen convents, conventicles, and congregations.

The consequences of Hebraization

Of the many psycholinguistic aspects involved in Christian Hebraeophilia, there is the ambivalent attitude of Christians toward Israel's national language, which has resulted in at least two differentiated language varieties: "High Hebrew" for worship and the domain of religion and a kind of basic "pidgin Hebrew" for secular usage. This diglossia which subdivides into media variants (written, read, and spoken Hebrew) is unequal in the case of Jewish Christians and of Gentile Christians, but these differences, though marked, have so far not been quantified.

Several factors have a perceptible impact on this phenomenon of diglossia. The translation of the New Testament into Hebrew often acts like a theological litmus paper, showing up linguistically what was originally Hebraic in thought and content and what was later Hellenistic accretion. It thus tends to make Jesus appear and sound a good deal more Jewish than his image in Christian tradition has allowed for.

Finally, the fact that Christian Arabs, owing to Semitic affinities, usually are quicker in mastering Hebrew than their foreign coreligionists, tends to lower its prestige in the eyes of many non-Israeli Christians and reduce it to the level of a Middle-Eastern vernacular. The resultant tendency is to differentiate— sociolinguistically, if not scientifically—between the "noble Bible tongue," which Christ prayed in, and common modern Hebrew.

How will spoken Hebrew affect the ethnic identity of Jewish Christians and Gentile Israeli Christians? What effect, if any, will it have on the "mission to the Jews? " Will it influence Bible translations and Bible interpretation? It is still too early to give cogent answers.

The recency of Christian Hebraeophilia, the microcosmic size of the speech community involved, and its easy accessibility for the purpose of scientific research—all these factors seem to make Christians in Israel, who worship in Hebrew, an ideal object of inquiry both for sociolinguists and psycholinguists.

REFERENCES

Betz, Otto, R. Mayer, and P. Schäfer, 1971, "Der fünfte Weltkongress für jüdische Studien in Jerusalem." In *Das Institutum Judaicum der Universität Tübingen, 1968-1970.* Tübingen, 12-14.

Carmignac, Jean, 1968-1969, "The Hebrew background of the synoptic Gospels." *Annual of the Swedish Theological Institute* [Jerusalem] 7: 64-93.

Dubois, Marcel, O. P., 1970, "Catholic life in Israel." *Christian News from Israel* 21 (2): 18-20. [Jerusalem: Ministry for Religious Affairs]

Eck, Johannes, 1541, *Ains Juden Büchleins Verlegung.* Ingolstadt, Germany.

Kutscher, Jehezel Edward, 1968, "'aramit." *Hebrew Encyclopedia.* Jerusalem.

Lapide, Pinchas E., 1973, *The Use of Hebrew in Christian Congregations.* Neukirchner-Vluyn, Germany: Neukirchner Verlag des Erziehungsvereins GmbH.

Lindsey, Robert, 1969, *A Hebrew Translation of the Gospel of Mark.* Jerusalem.

———, 1970, "The ecclesiological-ecumenical issue." *U.C.C.I. News* 1 (4): 13-15. [Jerusalem: United Christian Council in Jerusalem]

Maigret, Jean (Father), 1968, "God spoke in Hebrew." *Encounter Today* [Paris] 3 (2-3): 89-93.

Oesterreicher, John M. (Monsignor), 1971, *The Rediscovery of Judaism.* South Orange, New Jersey: Seton Hall University, Institute of Judaeo-Christian Studies.

Paluzzi, C. Galassi, 1943, *Roma onde Christo è Romano nella Parola di Pio XII.* Rome.

Index